AF437730

Table of Contents

GUIDE TO FILING A NON-PROVISIONAL
Utility Patent
IN THE U.S.

GUIDE TO FILING A NON-PROVISIONAL UTILITY PATENT IN THE U.S.

United States Patent and Trademark Office (USPTO) Official Website: https://www.uspto.gov/

Chapter 1: General Considerations

Introduction

Patents play a crucial role in the modern world, since the so-called industrial revolution which began in Great Britain in the second half of the 18th century and spread to other parts of the world during the 19th century, because through this strategy the invention, creation or new alternative that is being proposed, is safeguarded from being susceptible to copies or being used indiscriminately by hands that, in some way or another, may contravene the ultimate purpose of the same, in our case: to prevent, cure or treat diseases.

Justification

There are several key reasons for the use of patents:

1. Encouragement of Innovation.

Patents provide inventors and companies with exclusive rights to their inventions for a period of time (Generally, a patent lasts for 20 years from the date of application, after which the invention enters the public domain). This exclusive right encourages research and development by ensuring that innovators can recoup their investments and derive economic benefits from their inventions without the immediate fear of being copied or imitated by others.

To obtain a patent, the inventor must file an application with the patent office, describing his invention and demonstrating that it is novel, useful and non-obvious to experts in the field.

2. Intellectual Property Protection

Patents protect original ideas and technological advances by preventing others from making, using, selling or importing the invention without permission. This protection helps ensure that the rights of inventors are recognized and respected, fostering confidence in the innovation process.

3. Economic Boost

Patents contribute to economic growth by encouraging the creation of new companies and the expansion of existing ones (creation of new job opportunities). Companies can license their patents to other companies, generating additional revenue and creating opportunities for collaboration. In addition, patent protection can attract investment, as investors seek companies with valuable intellectual property assets.

4. Technological and Social Advancement

By protecting new inventions and technologies, patents promote scientific and technological advancement. Many of the technologies we use today, from innovative medicines to advanced electronic devices, have been driven by the patent system. This contributes to progress in crucial areas such as medicine, among others.

5. Disclosure of Knowledge

The patent system requires inventors to publish full details of their inventions. This public disclosure of technical information contributes to general knowledge and allows other researchers and developers to build on existing work, accelerating progress in various fields; hence, the scientific advances that have been achieved in the last century.

6. Fair Competition

Patents promote fair competition by establishing clear rules on intellectual property rights. This prevents companies, inventors or groups of inventors from unfairly benefiting from the inventions of others without adequate compensation and helps maintain a fair and competitive market environment.

7. International Protection

International treaties, such as the Paris Convention and the Patent Cooperation Treaty (PCT), allow inventors to obtain patent protection in multiple countries. This facilitates the international expansion of companies and access to global international markets.

Definition of patent

A patent is an exclusive right granted by a government to an inventor, allowing him to control the manufacture, use, sale and distribution of an invention for a specified time.

The importance of patenting a product lies in the legal protection it offers to the patent holder. By patenting an invention, the exclusive right to *manufacture, use and commercialize* is guaranteed, preventing competitors from copying the idea.

This encourages innovation by providing a period during which the inventor can enjoy the commercial benefits without direct competition. In addition, patents can increase the value of a company and serve as negotiable assets in commercial agreements or acquisitions.

In summary, patenting a product not only protects the invention from competition, but also provides significant economic and strategic benefits to the inventor or company holding the patent.

If someone infringes your patent, you can take legal actions. U.S. patents are effective only within the U.S. and its territories and possessions.

Types of patents:

These are the three types of patentes:

- Utility patents: for inventing a new or improved and useful process, machine, article of manufacture or composition of matter.

- Design patents: for inventing a new, original, and ornamental design for an article of manufacture

- Plant patents: for inventing or discovering and asexually reproducing any distinct and new variety of plant.

How long is a patent valid?

Utility patents and plant patents have a term of up to 20 years from the date on which the first non-provisional application for the patent was filed.

A design patent is granted for a term of 15 years from the date of grant. You must pay maintenance fees on a specified schedule after the utility patent is issued to keep it in force.

Under certain unusual conditions, patent terms may be extended or adjusted.

What is PTA and PTR

The Patent Term Adjustment (PTA) and Patent Term Restoration (PTR) are important mechanisms within the United States Patent and Trademark Office (USPTO) that affect the duration of patent protection. They aim to compensate for delays that occur either during the prosecution of a patent or due to regulatory review processes. Below is a detailed explanation of each:

Patent Term Adjustment (PTA)

PTA was introduced with the American Inventors Protection Act of 1999. Its purpose is to extend the term of a patent beyond the standard 20 years from the filing date of the application to compensate for delays caused by the USPTO during the patent examination process.

Types of Delays Compensated by PTA:

- **Type A Delays:** These occur when the USPTO fails to meet certain examination timelines. For example, if the USPTO does not issue an initial Office Action within 14 months of filing, respond to an applicant's reply within 4 months, or issue a patent within 4 months after the issue fee is paid.

- **Type B Delays:** These delays happen when the total pendency of the application exceeds three years. For instance, if a patent is granted more than three years after the application was filed, the patentee may be entitled to a PTA for the time beyond those three years, excluding any applicant-caused delays.

- **Type C Delays:** These are due to delays caused by interference, secrecy orders, or appeals. When these types of delays occur, the patent term may be adjusted accordingly.

Calculation and Reductions:

- The PTA is calculated by adding the days of USPTO-caused delay but is also subject to reductions for applicant-caused delays (e.g., late filings, extensions, or failure to promptly respond to USPTO communications).

- Any overlap between different types of delays is carefully considered, and adjustments are made to ensure there is no double-counting of delay periods.

Impact on Patent Rights:

- PTA can significantly extend the term of a patent, sometimes by several years, which can be crucial in industries where the value of patent protection is time-sensitive, such as pharmaceuticals or biotechnology.

- However, applicants need to be diligent in minimizing their own delays to maximize the PTA benefits.

Patent Term Restoration (PTR)

PTR is governed by the Hatch-Waxman Act (Drug Price Competition and Patent Term Restoration Act of 1984). Its primary purpose is to restore some of the patent term lost during the time a product undergoes regulatory review by agencies like the FDA before it can be commercially marketed.

Eligibility:

- PTR applies primarily to patents covering products that require regulatory approval, such as pharmaceuticals, medical devices, and food or color additives.

- The patent in question must cover a product that has been subject to a significant period of regulatory review before being allowed to enter the market.

Restoration Period:

- The period of PTR is calculated based on the time taken for regulatory approval, with half of the testing phase and the entire review phase being considered.

- The maximum period of restoration cannot exceed 5 years.

- Additionally, the total patent term, including the restoration period, cannot exceed 14 years from the date of FDA approval.

Application Process:

- The application for PTR must be submitted within 60 days of receiving regulatory approval.

- The USPTO, in consultation with the FDA (or other relevant regulatory agency), reviews the application to determine the eligible extension period.

Impact on Patent Rights:

- PTR is particularly critical for industries like pharmaceuticals, where extensive regulatory testing and approval processes can significantly eat into the effective patent life.

- It helps ensure that patent holders are able to recoup their investment in R&D by providing a longer period of market exclusivity.

Strategic Considerations

For patent applicants, understanding and effectively managing PTA and PTR can significantly enhance the value of their patent portfolio. Key strategies include:

- Proactive Prosecution: By responding promptly to USPTO communications and minimizing applicant-induced delays, one can maximize PTA benefits.

- Monitoring Regulatory Timelines: For patents eligible for PTR, it's important to closely monitor the regulatory approval process and prepare the necessary documentation to apply for PTR immediately upon approval.

Challenges and Controversies

Both PTA and PTR have been subject to legal challenges and interpretation issues over the years. For example:

- PTA: The interpretation of what constitutes a "delay" has led to several court cases, most notably involving how overlapping delays should be handled.

- PTR: Calculating the exact amount of term restoration has also been contested, especially in cases where the regulatory approval process is complex or involves multiple stages.

Provisional Application

This quick and inexpensive method of establishing a U.S. filing date for your invention can be claimed in a later-filed non-provisional application. A provisional application is automatically abandoned 12 months after its filing date and is not examined.

A provisional patent application includes:

- the application as a provisional application for patent;

- the name(s) of all inventors;

- inventor residence(s);

- title of the invention;

- name and registration number of attorney or agent and docket number (if applicable);

- correspondence address; and

- any U.S. Government agency that has a property interest in the application.

- A specification: A specification may include the following sections: –Background of the invention.– Summary of the invention .– Drawings describing the invention. – A detailed description of the invention.

- Fees

A provisional application will only receive a filing date if it includes a written description of the invention that meets all the requirements of 35 U.S.C. §112(a).

While you can get a filing date without submitting drawings, it's recommended to include any drawings necessary to understand the invention, as required by 35 U.S.C. 113. You cannot add essential drawings after the filing date because new material is not allowed. Additionally, 37 CFR 1.53(c) prohibits changes to provisional applications since they don't need to meet the full patent statute requirements.

To be complete, a provisional application must also include the filing fee as specified in 37 CFR 1.16(d).

If you decide to initially file a provisional application, you must file a corresponding non-provisional application during the 12-month period of the provisional application to benefit from the earlier provisional filing. Provisional applications have fewer requirements than non-provisional applications; for example, claims and an oath/declaration are not required.

Conversion from a provisional application to a non provisional application

37 CFR 1.53 (c3) A provisional application can be converted to a nonprovisional application and keep the original filing date of the provisional application. However, converting won't refund any fees paid for the provisional application or apply those fees to the nonprovisional application.

Converting a provisional application to a nonprovisional application will cause the patent term to start from the original filing date of the provisional application. This could shorten the overall patent term. Therefore, it's generally better for applicants to file a nonprovisional application that claims the benefit 35 U.S.C. 119(e) of the provisional application, instead of converting the provisional application directly.

To convert, you must submit a fee, an amendment with at least one claim (if the provisional application doesn't already include one), and pay the filing, search, and examination fees for the nonprovisional application. You must also pay a surcharge if the basic filing fee or the inventor's oath was not included in the original provisional application.

The request to convert must be filed before either: (i) The provisional application is abandoned, or (ii) Twelve months after the provisional application's filing date."

1. Direct Conversion of a Provisional Application to a Non-Provisional Application:

Patent Term: When you directly convert a provisional application into a non-provisional application, the patent term starts from the filing date of the original provisional application. This means that the 20-year patent term is measured from the provisional application's filing date. This can effectively shorten the patent's enforceable life because you lose up to one year of patent term compared to the alternative.

Fees: Conversion does not refund any fees paid for the provisional application, nor does it apply those fees to the non-provisional application. You will need to pay the standard fees for filing, search, and examination of the non-provisional application, along with any additional fees if certain documents (like the inventor's oath) were not included in the original provisional application.

Procedure: You must submit a request to convert, pay the associated fees, and ensure that the converted application includes at least one claim if it didn't already.

Filing a Non-Provisional Application Claiming the Benefit of a Provisional Application under 35 U.S.C. 119(e):

Patent Term: In this scenario, the patent term starts from the filing date of the non-provisional application, not the provisional application. This allows the applicant to maximize the full 20-year patent term from the non-provisional filing date, effectively giving you up to 21 years of protection if you file the non-provisional exactly 12 months after the provisional.

Example Scenario:

Provisional Application: Filed on January 1, 2023.

Non-Provisional Application: Filed on January 1, 2024, claiming the benefit of the provisional application.

In this case:

The patent term starts from January 1, 2024 (the non-provisional filing date), and will end 20 years later on January 1, 2044.

For prior art purposes, the invention is treated as if it were filed on January 1, 2023 (the provisional filing date).

This approach effectively gives the applicant up to 21 years of protection from the filing date of the provisional application if the non-provisional is filed exactly 12 months after the provisional.

Priority Date: The non-provisional application can claim the benefit of the filing date of the provisional application for any subject matter that was fully disclosed in the provisional. This means that while the patent term starts later, the non-provisional application is treated as having been filed on the date of the provisional for purposes of prior art.

Procedure: You simply file a new non-provisional application, citing the provisional application as a priority document under 35 U.S.C. 119(e). No formal conversion is required, and the provisional application remains unchanged.

Claiming Benefit under 35 U.S.C. 119(e): Maintains the full patent term, avoids the need for conversion, and allows you to claim priority from the provisional without affecting the patent's term length. This is generally the preferred approach for applicants looking to maximize the duration of their patent protection.

The direct conversion option exists primarily for flexibility and to accommodate certain unique situations where it might be advantageous or necessary. Although it is generally less beneficial compared to filing a non-provisional application that claims the benefit of a provisional under 35 U.S.C. 119(e), there are specific scenarios where direct conversion might be useful:

Administrative Simplicity: In some cases, an applicant might prefer the simplicity of directly converting a provisional application into a non-provisional application rather than preparing a new, separate non-provisional application. This might be the case if the applicant wants to maintain the original provisional application's structure with minimal changes.

Time Constraints: If the 12-month period for filing a non-provisional application claiming the benefit of the provisional is about to expire and the applicant is not prepared to file a complete new non-provisional application, direct conversion might be a quick solution to secure a non-provisional filing.

Cost Management: Although converting doesn't refund fees, some applicants might find it more straightforward to manage the transition from provisional to non-provisional through conversion rather than preparing and filing a completely new non-provisional application. This could happen in situations where the provisional application is very close to what the non-provisional would be, and the applicant prefers to avoid the costs and effort of preparing a new document.

Avoiding Abandonment: If an applicant realizes that a provisional application is about to be abandoned and is unable to prepare a non-provisional application in time, direct conversion might be a last resort to keep the application alive.

In summary, while direct conversion is generally less advantageous, it provides a legal mechanism for flexibility in managing patent filings, accommodating unusual circumstances, and offering a backup option when timing or resources are tight.

Under 35 U.S.C. § 154(a)(2), the term of a patent generally lasts 20 years from the date on which the non-provisional patent application was filed in the United States. However, when a non-provisional application claims the benefit of an earlier provisional application under 35 U.S.C. § 119(e), the 20-year term still begins from the filing date of the non-provisional application, not the provisional.

Non-provisional utility patent application

This can be granted as a patent if all patentability requirements are met. A non-provisional utility patent application includes:

- A specification (description and claims).
- Drawings (when necessary)
- An oath or declaration
- Filing, search and examination fees

All application documents must be in English, or an English translation will be required, along with a fee outlined in 37 CFR 1.17(i).

The filing date of the application, except for design patents or provisional applications, is the date on which the USPTO receives a specification (with or without at least one claim) and any drawings necessary to understand the subject matter of the application, or (in the case of a previously incomplete or defective application) the date on which the last required part is received by the filing date.

Filing a utility non-provisional patent in the United States involves preparing and submitting several key documents to the United States Patent and Trademark Office (USPTO). Here is a breakdown of the necessary documents:

Utility Patent Application Transmittal Form (Form PTO/AIA/15)

- This form is used to list the documents that are being submitted with the application. It helps the USPTO understand what is included in your application package. You must mark with a checkmark in the case in which it applies the following:
- **Specification**
- **Drawings**
- **Oath or Declaration (Form PTO/AIA/01)**
- **Application Data Sheet (ADS) (Form PTO/AIA/14)**
- **Filing, Search, and Examination Fees**
- **Information Disclosure Statement (IDS) (Form PTO/SB/08)**
- **Non-publication Request (optional) (Form PTO/SB/35)**
- **Power of Attorney (optional) (Form PTO/AIA/82A or 82B)**
- **Assignment (if applicable):** If the inventor assigns the invention to another party (such as a company), an assignment document should be recorded with the USPTO.
- **Micro Entity Certification (if applicable) (Form PTO/SB/15A or 15B):** If you qualify as a micro entity, you can file this form to reduce certain patent fees.
- **Request for Prioritized Examination (Track One) (optional):** If you want your application to be examined more quickly, you can request a prioritized examination for an additional fee.
- **Sequence Listing (if applicable):** If your invention

involves nucleotide and/or amino acid sequences, a sequence listing in a specific format is required.

- **Cover Sheet (for provisional application) (optional):** If you previously filed a provisional application, you should submit a cover sheet referencing the provisional application.
- **Request for Continued Examination (RCE) (if applicable):** If your application is initially rejected, you may need to file an RCE to continue prosecuting your application.

Publication of patent applications

Except in specific situations, such as when an applicant has requested non-publication, utility and plant patent applications are published before a patent is granted. Publication occurs after the expiration of a period of 18 months from the earliest effective filing date or priority date claimed by the application.

After publication, the application is no longer kept confidential by the USPTO, and anyone may request access to the complete application file history and view the application on the USPTO website.

Types of publications

Request Early Publication (Fee required at time of Request 37 CFR 1.219): Under 37 CFR 1.219, an applicant can submit a request to expedite publication, which reduces the 18-month timeframe to approximately 14 weeks after the completed application is filed. Any request for early publication must be accompanied by the publication fee set forth in § 1.18(d).

If the applicant does not submit a copy of the application in compliance with the USPTO patent electronic filing system requirements pursuant to § 1.215(c), the Office will publish the application as provided in § 1.215(a).

Request Not to Publish. 37 CFR § 1.213:

If the invention disclosed in an application has not been and will not be the subject of an application filed in another country, or under a multilateral international agreement, that requires publication of applications eighteen months after filing, the application will not be published under 35 U.S.C. 122(b) and § 1.211 provided:

(1) A request (nonpublication request) is submitted with the application upon filing;

(2) The request states in a conspicuous manner that the application is not to be published under 35 U.S.C. 122(b);

Step-by-step description of a patent:

24

What can be patented?

Legally, a utility patent can cover "any new and useful process, machine, manufacture, or composition of matter, or any new and useful improvement thereof." A design patent can cover "any new, original and ornamental design for an article of manufacture," and a plant patent can cover a "distinct and new plant variety, including cultivated varieties, mutants, hybrids, and newly found seedlings, other than plants propagated by tuber or plants found in an uncultivated state," invented or discovered and asexually reproduced.

Therefore, for a patent to issue, your invention must meet four conditions:

- **"Useful":** The invention must work and cannot be just a theory.

- **Clear description:** There must be a clear description of how to make and use the invention.

- **New or "novel":** It must be something that has not been done before.

- **"Non-obvious":** It must be an improvement that is not obvious over something already invented.

Patent law defines the limits of what can be patented. For example, laws of nature, physical phenomena and abstract ideas cannot be patented, nor just an idea or suggestion.

Other restrictions include patenting inventions exclusively related to nuclear material or atomic energy in an atomic weapon (see MPEP 2104.01). However, the subject matter that can be protected by patents is vast and varied.

Obtaining and maintaining a patent is a multi-step process. The USPTO (United States Patent and Trademark Office) has many resources to assist you throughout the preparation and filing of your application, the interaction with your examiner, the approval of your patent and its maintenance.

Foreign patents and treaties:

International patent law differs greatly from U.S. patent law; in fact, the differences are as numerous as they exist in other countries.

Since the rights granted by a U.S. patent extend only throughout the U.S. territory and have no effect in a foreign country, inventors seeking patent protection in other countries must apply for a patent in each of those countries or at regional patent offices, such as the European Patent Office (EPO).

Almost every country has its own patent laws, and those seeking a patent in a specific country must apply in that country according to its requirements. World Intellectual Property Organization treaties facilitate the filing of patent applications. The Patent Cooperation Treaty does so for utility patents in both the U.S. and many foreign countries. Similarly, the Hague System for the International Registration of Industrial Designs facilitates the filing of design patent applications and design registrations in the U.S. and in foreign countries.

The patent laws of many countries differ in several aspects from the U.S. patent law. In most foreign countries, publication of the invention prior to the filing date of the application will preclude entitlement to a patent. Some countries allow compulsory licenses to permit the use of the contents of a patent without the authorization of the patent holder, if certain conditions are met.

International agreements on patents and selected intellectual property protection provide an important basis for the global intellectual property system.

- Paris Convention for the Protection of Intellectual Property:

A patent-related treaty (adhered to by 176 countries at last count, including the United States) is known as the Paris Convention for the Protection of Industrial Property. It provides that each country guarantees to the citizens of the other countries the same patent and trademark rights that it grants to its own citizens.

The treaty also grants the right of priority with respect to patents, trademarks and industrial designs (design patents). This right means that, based on an initial application filed in one member country, you may (within a certain period of time) apply for protection in all other member countries. These subsequent applications will be considered as if they had been filed on the same day as the first application. Therefore, these subsequent applications will have priority over applications for the same invention that may have been filed by others during the same period of time.

In addition, these later applications, being based on the first application, will not be invalidated by intermediate actions. Examples of intermediate actions include publication or exploitation of the invention, sale of copies of the design or use of the trademark. The time period mentioned above, within which subsequent applications may be filed in the other countries, is 12 months for initial patent applications and six months for industrial designs and trademarks.

- Patent Cooperation Treaty:

The Patent Cooperation Treaty (PCT) is currently adhered to by more than 150 countries, including the United States. It facilitates the filing of patent applications for the same invention in member countries by providing, among other things, centralized filing procedures and a standardized application format.

Timely filing of an international application grants you an international filing date in each designated country. It also provides a search of the invention and a subsequent period during which national patent applications must be filed. Some patent attorneys specialize in obtaining patents in foreign countries.

The Patent Cooperation Treaty (PCT) is an international treaty that simplifies the process of filing patents in multiple countries. Administered by the World Intellectual Property Organization (WIPO), the PCT allows inventors to file a single "international" patent application, which is then recognized by over 150 PCT member countries, including the United States. The United States Patent and Trademark Office (USPTO) plays a critical role in the PCT process as both a Receiving Office and an International Searching Authority (ISA) and International Preliminary Examining Authority (IPEA). Below is a comprehensive overview of the PCT process at the USPTO, including terms, conditions, documents, fees, and more.

Key Stages in the PCT Process:

- **Filing an International Application**: This is the first step, where the applicant files a single PCT application. This application must be filed in one of the official languages of the PCT (English is commonly used in the USPTO).

- **International Search**: An International Searching Authority (ISA), such as the USPTO, conducts a search of prior art to assess the patentability of the invention. This results in an International Search Report (ISR) and a Written Opinion of the ISA.

- **International Publication**: After 18 months from the earliest priority date, the international application is published by WIPO, making the content of the application publicly accessible.

- **International Preliminary Examination (Optional)**: The applicant can request an International Preliminary Examination to further assess the patentability of the invention. This results in an International Preliminary Report on Patentability (IPRP).

- **National/Regional Phase Entry**: After the international phase, the applicant must enter the national or regional phase in each country where patent protection is sought. This involves filing the necessary documents and paying fees in each jurisdiction.

Key Terms and Conditions in PCT Filing at the USPTO

- **Receiving Office**: The USPTO acts as a Receiving Office for U.S. residents and nationals filing a PCT application. The Receiving Office is responsible for ensuring that the application meets formal requirements and forwarding it to the appropriate authorities.

- **International Searching Authority (ISA)**: The USPTO can serve as an ISA, conducting a prior art search and issuing an ISR and a Written Opinion. Other ISAs are also available, but the USPTO is commonly chosen by U.S. applicants.

- **International Preliminary Examining Authority (IPEA)**: The USPTO can also act as an IPEA, providing a more in-depth examination of the application upon request, which results in an IPRP.

- **Priority Date**: The filing date of a PCT application (or an earlier national application if priority is claimed) is considered the priority date, which is crucial for determining the novelty and prior art during the examination.

- **Filing Deadline**: A PCT application can be filed within 12 months of the earliest priority date (e.g., the filing date of a corresponding U.S. provisional or non-provisional application).

- **Language of Filing**: PCT applications filed at the USPTO are typically filed in English, although the PCT recognizes several official languages.

- **National Phase Deadline**: After the international phase, the applicant must enter the national phase in each country where patent protection is desired. This must be done within 30 or 31 months from the priority date, depending on the country.

Required Documents and Components

- **Request Form (PCT/RO/101)**: This form is used to submit the PCT application and includes the title of the invention, applicant and inventor information, priority claims, and designations of the countries in which patent protection is sought.

- **Description**: The description provides a detailed explanation of the invention, including how it works and the problem it solves. It must be sufficiently detailed to enable a person skilled in the art to replicate the invention.

- **Claims**: The claims define the scope of the patent protection being sought. They are the most critical part of the application and must be clear, concise, and supported by the description.

- **Abstract**: A brief summary of the invention, typically no more than 150 words, is required to give a general overview of the technical disclosure.

- **Drawings**: If the invention can be better understood through visual representation, drawings are required. These must comply with specific formatting requirements.

- **Priority Document**: If the PCT application claims priority from an earlier national or regional application, a certified copy of the priority document must be submitted, or a reference to an already filed application in the same office can be made.

● **International Search Report (ISR)**: Issued by the ISA, the ISR provides a list of prior art references that might affect the patentability of the invention.

● **Written Opinion of the ISA**: Accompanies the ISR and provides a preliminary, non-binding opinion on whether the claims appear to satisfy the patentability criteria of novelty, inventive step, and industrial applicability.

● **International Preliminary Examination Report (IPRP) (Optional)**: Provides a more detailed examination of the application, focusing on the patentability of the invention in light of the ISR and any amendments made by the applicant.

Fees Associated with PCT Filing at the USPTO

- **Basic Filing Fee**: The fee for filing a PCT application varies depending on the type of entity (large entity, small entity, or micro entity). The fee covers the processing of the application by the Receiving Office.

- **Search Fee**: The search fee is paid to the ISA for conducting the international search. The USPTO has a set fee for this service, which may vary if another ISA is chosen.

- **Transmittal Fee**: The transmittal fee covers the cost of transmitting the application to WIPO and other relevant authorities.

- **International Preliminary Examination Fee**: If the applicant requests an international preliminary examination, a fee is paid to the IPEA for this service.

- **National Phase Entry Fees**: When entering the national phase in different countries, separate fees must be paid in each jurisdiction. These fees can include filing fees, examination fees, and possibly translation costs.

- **Miscellaneous Fees**: Additional fees may apply for late submissions, corrections, or other services such as requesting certified copies of documents.

The International Search and Examination Process

International Search

• **Conducted by the ISA**: The ISA conducts a search to identify prior art that may be relevant to the patentability of the invention. The search is based on the claims as filed, along with the description and any drawings.

• **International Search Report (ISR)**: The ISR includes a list of documents considered relevant to the claims. It classifies the documents into categories, such as "X" (particularly relevant) or "Y" (relevant if combined with other documents).

• **Written Opinion of the ISA.**

International Preliminary Examination (Optional)

- **Requesting the Examination**: The applicant can request an international preliminary examination by filing a demand with the IPEA. This is optional but can be beneficial if the applicant wishes to refine the application before entering the national phase.

- **Amendments and Arguments**: During the preliminary examination, the applicant can amend the claims and present arguments to address issues raised in the ISR and the Written Opinion.

- **International Preliminary Report on Patentability (IPRP)**: The IPRP is the final output of the international preliminary examination and provides an assessment of the claims' patentability. While non-binding, it can influence the national phase examination in different countries.

National Phase Entry and Further Prosecution

- **Entering the National Phase**: After the international phase, the applicant must decide in which countries to seek patent protection. This involves filing the necessary documents and paying fees in each selected country or region.

- **National Phase Deadlines**: The deadline for entering the national phase is generally 30 months from the priority date (31 months in some jurisdictions).

- **National Patent Offices**: Once the application enters the national phase, it is subject to the national laws and regulations of each country. The national patent offices will examine the application based on their own criteria, which may include additional searches and examinations.

- **Translations**: In some countries, the application must be translated into the local language, which can add to the cost and complexity of the national phase entry.

Advantages and Strategic Considerations

• **Deferred National Phase Costs**: The PCT system allows applicants to defer the significant costs associated with national filings, including translation and attorney fees, for up to 30 or 31 months from the priority date.

• **Improved Patent Strategy**: The PCT system provides more time to evaluate the commercial potential of the invention and the relevance of different markets before committing to national filings.

• **International Search and Examination**: The ISR and Written Opinion provide valuable insights into the patentability of the invention before entering the national phase, allowing the applicant to make informed decisions and refine the application.

• **Global Recognition**: A PCT application is recognized by all PCT member countries, which simplifies the process of seeking patent protection internationally.

Challenges and Considerations

- **Complexity of National Laws**: While the PCT simplifies the initial filing process, the applicant must still navigate the specific requirements of each national patent office during the national phase.

- **Cost Considerations**: Although the PCT defers costs, the overall expense of pursuing patents in multiple countries can be substantial, especially when translation, attorney, and national filing fees are considered.

- **Timeliness**: The PCT process adds time to the overall patenting timeline. While this can be advantageous in terms of strategy, it may delay the grant of patents, which could be a concern in fast-moving industries.

- Hague Agreement:

The Hague Agreement is an international registration system that offers the possibility of protection for up to 100 industrial designs in designated member countries and intergovernmental organizations (known as Contracting Parties). It involves the submission of a single international application in one language, either directly to the International Bureau of the World Intellectual Property Organization (WIPO) or indirectly through your Contracting Party's office.

Patent Prosecution Highway (PPH)

The Patent Prosecution Highway (PPH) is an international initiative that enables faster patent examination processes by leveraging the work already done by a patent office in one country in another country's patent office. The United States has been an active participant in the PPH program, entering into agreements with multiple countries and regional patent offices around the world.

Key Points about PPH Agreements Involving the U.S.:

- **Purpose and Functionality**: The PPH agreements are designed to streamline and expedite the patent examination process. If an applicant has a patent application that has been allowed in one country (such as the U.S.), they can request fast-track examination of their corresponding application in another country, provided both countries are participants in a PPH agreement. This reduces duplication of effort and speeds up the time it takes to get a patent granted.

- **Global Participation**: The U.S. Patent and Trademark Office (USPTO) has signed PPH agreements with numerous countries, including Japan, Canada, the United Kingdom, and several others. These agreements form a network that facilitates quicker access to patent protection across multiple jurisdictions.

- **Benefits for Applicants**: By using the PPH, applicants can achieve faster patent grant times, which is particularly valuable for industries where time to market is critical. It also reduces costs by minimizing the need for repetitive examination procedures.

- **Harmonization of Standards**: While the PPH does not fully harmonize patent laws across different countries, it encourages convergence of examination practices. The examination conducted by one patent office can be used to accelerate the examination in another, assuming the claims are sufficiently similar.

• **Pilot Programs**: The PPH started as a series of pilot programs between various patent offices. Over time, as these programs proved successful, many have become permanent. The USPTO continues to expand its network of PPH agreements, reflecting the growing importance of global patent portfolios.

• **PPH MOTTAINAI**: The U.S. is also a participant in a specific type of PPH agreement known as PPH MOTTAINAI, which allows for more flexibility in the use of search and examination results. Under MOTTAINAI, applicants can request PPH based on the work of any participating office, not just the office of first filing, which broadens the utility of the PPH system.

Overview of the PPH Agreement Between the U.S. and Colombia:

• **Agreement Details**: The PPH agreement between the United States Patent and Trademark Office (USPTO) and the Superintendence of Industry and Commerce (SIC) of Colombia was established to allow patent applicants in both countries to benefit from an accelerated examination process. This agreement enables applicants who have received a favorable ruling on their patent claims in one of the countries to request fast-track examination of their corresponding claims in the other country.

• **Implementation and Scope**: The PPH agreement between the U.S. and Colombia applies to both national patent applications and PCT (Patent Cooperation Treaty) applications. Applicants can leverage the examination work already done by the patent office in one country to expedite the examination process in the other. This can significantly reduce the time to obtain patent rights in both jurisdictions.

• **Benefits to Applicants**:

○ **Accelerated Examination**: The primary benefit of the PPH program is the potential for a faster examination process. In Colombia, where patent examination times can be lengthy, this agreement allows for a more efficient route to obtaining patent protection.

○ **Reduced Costs**: By relying on the work done by the USPTO or SIC, applicants may reduce the costs associated with prosecuting patents in both countries, as there is less duplication of effort.

○ **Strategic Advantage**: For companies operating in both the U.S. and Colombia, the PPH agreement provides a strategic advantage by aligning patent protection efforts in these markets, which can be crucial for businesses in industries like pharmaceuticals, technology, and manufacturing.

● **Mutual Recognition of Work**: Under the PPH agreement, the SIC in Colombia and the USPTO recognize and utilize each other's examination results. This mutual recognition not only speeds up the process but also fosters greater consistency and predictability in patent prosecution between the two countries.

● **Promoting Innovation**: The PPH agreement is part of broader efforts by both countries to promote innovation and economic growth. By making it easier and faster to obtain patent protection, the agreement encourages inventors and businesses to invest in new technologies and bring them to market.

● **PPH MOTTAINAI**: Colombia also participates in the PPH MOTTAINAI program, which allows greater flexibility by enabling the use of examination results from any participating patent office, not just the office of first filing. This further broadens the utility of the PPH for applicants seeking protection in both the U.S. and Colombia.

In summary, the PPH agreement between the U.S. and Colombia is a valuable tool for patent applicants, offering the potential for faster, more efficient patent prosecution in both countries. It reflects the commitment of both nations to fostering innovation and protecting intellectual property rights.

Unitary Patent (EP)

The Unitary Patent (UP) system in the European Union (EU) represents a significant development in the landscape of intellectual property in Europe. It aims to simplify the process of obtaining patent protection across multiple European countries and has various implications for patent holders, including those in the United States.

Overview of the Unitary Patent (UP) System

- **What is the Unitary Patent?**

o The Unitary Patent is a single patent that provides protection across most EU member states through a single application process. Unlike the traditional European patent, which must be validated and maintained in each individual country, the Unitary Patent offers a streamlined route for obtaining and maintaining patent rights across multiple jurisdictions.

- **Centralized Process**:

o The Unitary Patent is granted by the European Patent Office (EPO), but once granted, it has unitary effect across all participating EU member states. This means that patent holders do not need to go through the separate processes of validation, translation, and renewal fees for each country, significantly reducing administrative burdens and costs.

- **Unified Patent Court (UPC)**:

o Alongside the UP, the Unified Patent Court (UPC) has been established to handle disputes related to Unitary Patents. The UPC provides a centralized forum for litigation, meaning that a single court decision can have effect across all participating states, rather than requiring litigation in multiple national courts.

Implications for U.S. Patent Holders

- **Simplified European Patent Protection**:

○ For U.S. companies and inventors seeking patent protection in Europe, the Unitary Patent offers a more efficient and cost-effective route to secure patent rights across multiple EU countries. Instead of managing a portfolio of national patents in Europe, U.S. applicants can now obtain a single patent with broad coverage.

- **Cost Efficiency**:

○ The cost of maintaining patent rights in Europe can be substantial due to the need for translations, validations, and the payment of separate renewal fees in each country. The UP significantly reduces these costs by offering a single renewal fee and eliminating the need for multiple validations and translations.

- **Strategic Considerations**:

○ U.S. companies may need to consider their European patent strategy in light of the UP system. The decision between opting for a Unitary Patent or traditional European patents in specific countries will depend on the company's business strategy, market presence, and the potential need for centralized vs. national litigation strategies.

- **Unified Patent Court (UPC) Considerations**:

o The UPC presents both opportunities and risks. On the one hand, it simplifies enforcement by providing a single forum for litigation. On the other hand, it introduces the possibility of pan-European injunctions and invalidations, which could have significant consequences for U.S. companies with valuable patent portfolios in Europe. U.S. patent holders must carefully consider the implications of UPC rulings, as a negative outcome could have widespread effects across the entire UP territory.

- **Potential Impact on Licensing**:

o The UP and UPC could also affect licensing strategies. With a UP, a single license agreement could cover all participating EU states, simplifying negotiations and enforcement. However, the centralized nature of the UPC also means that any disputes could impact the entirety of the licensed territory.

- **Opt-Out Option**:

o During a transitional period, U.S. patent holders can choose to "opt out" of the UPC system for their traditional European patents, keeping them under the jurisdiction of national courts. This allows companies to avoid the risks associated with centralized litigation in the UPC, at least temporarily.

Assistance for Inventors:

It is possible to obtain a patent on your own, but it is much easier with the help of us and qualified professionals. Make the most of the resources we offer (and those they provide).

The patent process is a complex set of laws, regulations, policies, and procedures. Therefore, the USPTO always recommends using a registered patent attorney or agent to assist in preparing your application. The USPTO also acknowledges that the cost of legal assistance can be prohibitive, especially for independent inventors and small businesses. The Pro Se Assistance Program helps you protect your valuable intellectual property.

The Inventors and Entrepreneurs Resources page covers most aspects of the patent process. It provides information on scams and how to avoid and report them.

Additionally, the Inventor Assistance Center (IAC) provides assistance and information about patents to the public. The IAC is staffed by former lead examiners and supervisory examiners who answer your questions to make the patent application process simpler and more efficient.

Pro Se Filing

Pro se filing at the United States Patent and Trademark Office (USPTO) refers to the process where an individual inventor or a small entity files and prosecutes a patent application without the assistance of a registered patent attorney or agent. This process is common among inventors who want to reduce the costs associated with obtaining a patent. However, it is a complex and highly technical process that requires a strong understanding of patent law, the patent application process, and the requirements set by the USPTO.

Key Aspects of Pro Se Filing at the USPTO

1. Eligibility and Considerations

- **Who Can File Pro Se?**

○ Any individual inventor or small entity (such as a small business) can file a patent application pro se. The USPTO provides resources to assist pro se applicants, but it strongly recommends seeking professional assistance due to the complexity of patent law.

- **Risks of Pro Se Filing**

○ Filing pro se can be risky because even minor errors in the application can lead to delays, rejections, or even the loss of patent rights. Common pitfalls include improper claim drafting, failure to meet statutory deadlines, and inadequate responses to USPTO communications.

2. Types of Patent Applications

● **Provisional Patent Application**

○ A provisional patent application allows an inventor to establish an early filing date without committing to a full patent application. It is less formal and requires fewer details than a non-provisional application, but it does not lead to a granted patent unless followed by a non-provisional application within 12 months.

● **Non-Provisional Patent Application**

○ A non-provisional application is the standard application that undergoes substantive examination by the USPTO. It requires a detailed description of the invention, claims that define the scope of the patent protection, and any necessary drawings.

● **Design Patent Application**

○ A design patent protects the ornamental design of an object rather than its functional aspects. The application process is similar to that of a utility patent but focuses on the visual aspects of the invention.

3. Key Documents and Components of a Patent Application

- Specification
- Claims
- Drawings
- Declaration or Oath

4. Filing Process

- **Electronic Filing**

o The USPTO encourages electronic filing through its EFS-Web system. This system allows for the submission of patent applications, fees, and other documents online.

- **Paper Filing**

o Paper filing is also an option but incurs additional fees. It is less common due to the convenience and cost-effectiveness of electronic filing.

- **Filing Fees**

o The USPTO charges various fees depending on the type of application and the entity size (large entity, small entity, or micro entity). Pro se filers who qualify as small or micro entities can benefit from reduced fees.

5. Examination Process

- **Initial Review**

○ After filing, the application is reviewed to ensure it meets the formal requirements. If deficiencies are found, the USPTO issues a Notice of Missing Parts, giving the applicant time to correct them.

- **Substantive Examination**

○ Once the application passes the initial review, it is assigned to an examiner who conducts a substantive examination, including a search for prior art and an evaluation of the claims' patentability.

- **Office Actions**

○ The examiner may issue an Office Action detailing any objections or rejections. The applicant must respond within a specified time frame (usually three months, extendable to six months with fees) to avoid abandonment of the application.

- **Interviews**

○ Pro se applicants can request interviews with the examiner to discuss the application, clarify issues, and potentially reach an agreement on claim amendments.

6. Appeal and Post-Allowance

● **Appealing a Rejection**

○ If the application is rejected and the applicant disagrees with the examiner's decision, they can appeal to the Patent Trial and Appeal Board (PTAB). The appeal process involves submitting a brief and possibly participating in an oral hearing.

● **Allowance and Issuance**

○ If the examiner allows the application, the applicant pays an issue fee, and the USPTO issues the patent. The patent grants the holder exclusive rights to the invention for 20 years from the filing date (15 years for design patents).

7. Maintenance and Post-Grant Considerations

- **Maintenance Fees**

○ Utility patents require the payment of maintenance fees at 3.5, 7.5, and 11.5 years after issuance to keep the patent in force. Failure to pay these fees results in the patent expiring.

- **Post-Grant Challenges**

○ Patents can be challenged post-grant through various mechanisms, including reexamination, inter partes review, and post-grant review. Pro se patentees must be prepared to defend their patents if such challenges arise.

8. Resources for Pro Se Applicants

● USPTO Pro Se Assistance Program

○ The USPTO offers a Pro Se Assistance Program that provides guidance and resources to pro se applicants, including workshops, a dedicated help line, and online resources.

● Pro Se Guide

○ The USPTO publishes a "Guide to Filing a Non-Provisional Patent Application" specifically for pro se applicants, offering step-by-step instructions on preparing and filing an application.

History and Functions of the USPTO

Rooted in the Constitution, the U.S. intellectual property system developed alongside a growing and changing nation. From the first patent law, signed by George Washington in 1790, to the current agency with over 13,000 employees, patents and trademarks have driven some of the greatest developments in U.S. history.

Most current USPTO employees examine patent and trademark applications, while others apply their technical and legal training to support the agency's mission. The agency receives over half a million patent applications annually. The USPTO headquarters is located in Alexandria, Virginia, with regional offices in Detroit, Dallas, Denver, and Silicon Valley (San Jose, California).

The Under Secretary of Commerce for Intellectual Property and Director of the USPTO (a single person holds both positions) leads the agency. The Director's Executive Committee includes Commissioners for both Patents and Trademarks and other leaders. As the head of the agency, the Director fulfills the following roles:

- Oversees all matters related to the granting and issuance of patents.

- Supervises all work of the USPTO.

- Establishes rules for the agency's activities and for the recognition of attorneys and agents (as approved by the Secretary of Commerce).

- Addresses legal questions.

- Performs other necessary administrative tasks.

The USPTO protects you, the inventor, by granting patents and administering patent law. Patent examiners review patent applications, and judges from the Patent Trial and Appeal Board review appeals from patent examiner decisions and also resolve disputes over issued patents. The USPTO publishes granted patents on the date of issuance and publishes most patent applications on or after 18 months from the filing date of your application.

Other functions include recording patent assignments, maintaining a research facility for public inspection of issued patents and related records, and providing physical and electronic copies of these records and other documents. It also educates the public about patent law. The USPTO does not have the authority to enforce patents.

Additionally, the USPTO grants patents that you can use to prevent others from making, using, selling, and importing your invention. It also registers trademarks and assists the President of the U.S., the Department of Commerce, and other government agencies in national and global intellectual property matters.

The USPTO helps protect intellectual property worldwide for inventors like you by working to include strong intellectual property provisions in all international agreements. It also promotes global respect for intellectual property and encourages U.S. trading partners to take intellectual property enforcement seriously.

Patent examiners review your application by assigning it to specialized units in broad and specific technical areas that best cover your invention. After reviewing your application, examiners either grant or deny the patent application. If an examiner denies your patent, you can appeal the decision to a special board. The Director of the USPTO can also review the decision.

Through the protection provided by patents, U.S. industry has flourished. People like you have invented new products, discovered new uses for old products, and created jobs. The economic strength of the U.S. depends on protecting your innovative ideas. The ongoing demand for patents demonstrates the inventive spirit of you and other inventors, whom the USPTO helps to promote.

Chapter 2

PROCESS TO FILE A NON-PROVISIONAL UTILITY PATENT

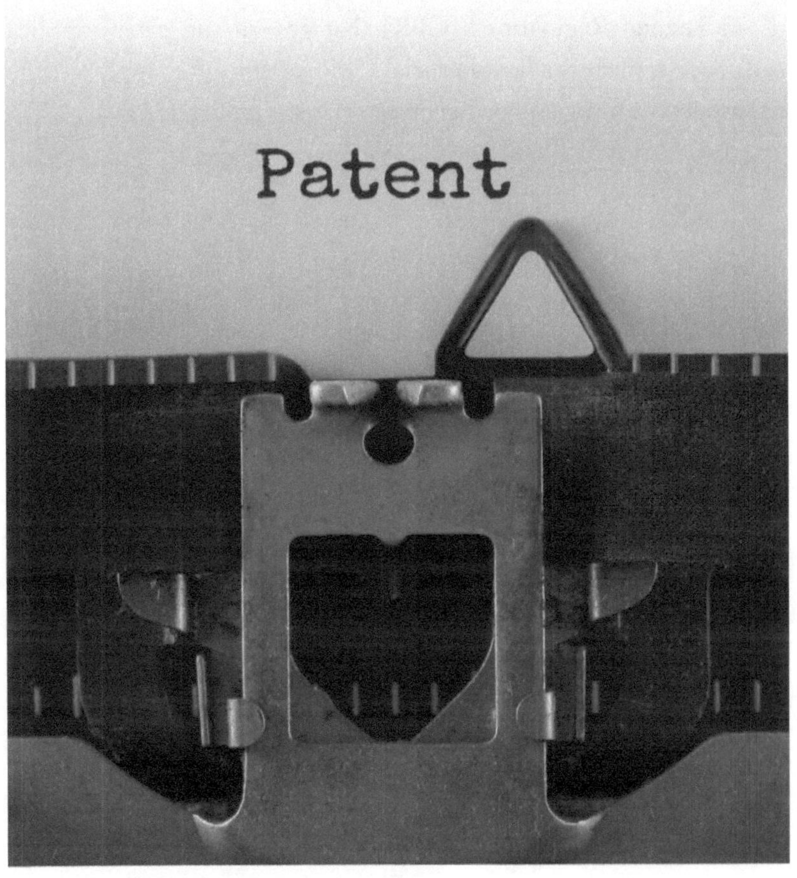

CHAPTER 2: PROCESS TO FILE A NON-PROVISIONAL UTILITY PATENT

When filing a non-provisional patent application with the USPTO, it is important to be familiar with various sections of the Code of Federal Regulations (CFR) that govern the patent application process. Here is a list of crucial CFR sections that apply to different aspects of filing and prosecuting a patent application:

37 CFR § 1.27 - Definition of small entities and establishing status as a small entity to permit payment of small entity fees

This section defines what qualifies as a "small entity" for the purposes of paying reduced patent fees to the USPTO. It outlines the criteria for determining small entity status, which includes individuals, small businesses, and certain nonprofit organizations. The section also specifies when an applicant must determine and declare their small entity status and when they must notify the USPTO if they no longer qualify for this status.

Fee discounts based on establishment of Small or Micro Entity Status

Most patent applicants pay regular undiscounted patent fees. However, fees for filing, searching, examining, issuing, appealing, and maintaining patent applications and patents are reduced by 60 percent for any small entity that qualifies for reduced fees under 37 CFR § 1.27(a), and are reduced by 80 percent for any micro entity that files a certification that the requirements under 37 CFR § 1.29(a) or (d) are met.

Small Entity Status: Before claiming small entity status and paying the reduced 60% fee, ensure you qualify under 37 CFR § 1.27(a). This status is typically appropriate if the inventors haven't assigned any rights to others and aren't obligated to do so. Filing electronically further reduces the fee. No special form is needed; just check the appropriate box on the transmittal form. but you should only pay small entity rates after ensuring that you qualify for the small entity status.

Micro Entity Status: Before claiming micro entity status and paying the 80% discounted fee, ensure you qualify under 37 CFR § 1.29(a) or (d). There are two USPTO micro entity certification forms, namely form PTO/SB/15A[1] for certifying micro entity status on the "gross income basis" under 37 CFR § 1.29(a), and form PTO/SB/15B[2] for certifying micro entity status on the "institution of higher education basis" under 37 CFR § 1.29(d).

Non-Electronic Filing Fee: As of November 15, 2011, filing a nonprovisional utility application by mail or hand-delivery incurs an extra $400 fee, reduced to $200 for small or micro entities. This fee can be avoided by filing via the Patent Center.

---

1. https://www.uspto.gov/sites/default/files/documents/sb0015a.pdf

2. https://www.uspto.gov/sites/default/files/documents/sb0015b.pdf

37 CFR § 1.32 - Power of attorney

An applicant may give a power of attorney to one or more patent practitioners or one or more joint inventors. A power of attorney to a joint inventor will be recognized even though the one to whom it is given is not a registered practitioner

You can appoint one or more of the joint inventors or registered patent practitioners linked to a specific Customer Number. Additionally, you may name up to ten registered patent practitioners by providing their names and registration numbers. The USPTO will only recognize up to ten practitioners per application or patent. If more than ten are named, a separate document must clarify which ten practitioners should be officially recognized by the USPTO. If these guidelines aren't followed, only the first ten practitioners listed will be recognized.

37 CFR § 1.33 - Correspondence respecting patent applications, patent reexamination proceedings, and other proceedings

When an attorney or agent is appointed to handle a patent application, all correspondence will be directed to them unless a different address is provided. If the attorney or agent uses a different address for correspondence, they must still maintain client confidentiality and remain responsible for responding to any notices from the Office. The Office will not send correspondence to both the applicant and their attorney or to two different representatives.

37 CFR § 1.43 Application for patent by a legal representative of a deceased or legally incapacitated inventor

If an inventor is deceased or legally incapacitated, their legal representative can apply for a patent on their behalf. If the inventor passes away after filing the application but before the patent is granted, the patent can be issued to the legal representative upon proper intervention. Refer to § 1.64 for information on how a legal representative can execute a substitute statement in place of an oath or declaration.

37 CFR § 1.45 - Application for patent by joint inventors

Joint inventors can apply for a patent together even if they did not work together at the same time, did not contribute equally, or did not contribute to every claim in the application. Each inventor must have contributed to at least one claim in a nonprovisional application, or to the content disclosed in a provisional application. Inventors do not need to sign the application separately; they just need to apply jointly and sign the required oath or declaration. If the inventorship changes, such as due to amendments to the claims, the application must be corrected according to 37 CFR 1.48. If a joint application includes multiple distinct inventions, it might need to be divided into separate applications, and the inventorship may need updating accordingly. A divisional application can retain the earlier filing date if necessary.

37 CFR § 1.46 - Application for patent by an assignee, obligated assignee, or a person who otherwise shows sufficient proprietary interest in the matter

If an application is filed by someone other than the inventor, it must include an application data sheet with the relevant information about the applicant. For an assignee or someone with an obligation to receive the assignment, documentary proof of ownership must be submitted by the time the issue fee is paid. For someone with significant proprietary interest, a petition must be filed showing their interest and appropriateness for making the application.

Any changes to the applicant's name or to the applicant itself must be updated through an application data sheet. The actual inventor or joint inventors must sign an oath or declaration, except under specific conditions. If a patent is granted, it will be issued to the real party in interest, and any changes in that party must be reported by the time the issue fee is paid. The Office may also publish a notice of the application in the Official Gazette.

37 CFR § 1.51 - General requisites of an application

Outlines the basic requirements that must be met for a patent application, including the necessity for a specification, claims, drawings (if necessary), an oath or declaration, and the prescribed fees.

37 CFR § 1.52 - Language, paper, writing, margins, compact disc specifications

Specifies the format and presentation requirements for the documents submitted to the USPTO, including language and physical specifications.

37 CFR § 1.53 - Application number, filing date, and completion of application

An application is assigned an application number and filing date upon receipt by the USPTO. The filing date is granted when the application includes a specification, at least one claim, and any necessary drawings. The rule also details the requirements for completing an application, including submitting the required fees, an oath or declaration, and other necessary documents. If these elements are missing, the application may be considered incomplete, potentially affecting the filing date or resulting in abandonment. This regulation also covers the procedures for converting provisional applications to non-provisional applications.

37 CFR § 1.55 - Claim for foreign priority

Under U.S. law (35 U.S.C. 119(b)), if an applicant wants to claim priority based on an earlier foreign application, they must meet certain formal requirements within a specified time. If these requirements aren't met, the priority claim is lost and can't be reclaimed. The deadline for filing a priority claim and submitting the necessary documents is before the patent is granted, but this deadline can be set earlier by the Director. Recent changes in the law have updated the procedures and deadlines for claiming foreign priority and submitting certified copies.

37 CFR § 1.57 - Incorporation by reference

This section explains that when you file a new application, you can reference a previously filed application to replace the need to submit a full specification and drawings right away. To do this, you must include a reference in the application data sheet, in English, that provides details about the previously filed application, such as its application number, filing date, and where it was originally filed. By doing this, the referenced application is treated as if it were the full specification and drawings for the new application, allowing the new application to receive a filing date.

37 CFR § 1.63 - Oath or declaration

Requires that each inventor named in a patent application submit an oath or declaration. This document affirms that the inventor believes they are the original or joint inventor of the claimed invention. The oath or declaration must also acknowledge that any intentional false statements made in it are punishable by law. Additionally, it must include the inventor's name, residence, and mailing address, and identify the application to which it relates. The oath or declaration must be submitted to the USPTO either before or with the application, or in a later filing under certain conditions.

37 CFR § 1.76 - Application data sheet (ADS)[1]

Discusses the content and use of the ADS, which provides bibliographic information about the application.

---

1. https://www.ecfr.gov/current/title-37/chapter-I/ subchapter-A/part-1/subpart-B/subject-group- ECFRfde9ad8bf027d31/section-1.76

37 CFR § 1.78 - Claiming benefit of earlier filing date and cross-references to other applications

Outlines the procedures for claiming the benefit of an earlier filing date and referencing other applications in the U.S. patent process. This regulation allows a new patent application to claim the filing date of an earlier application, effectively treating the new application as if it were filed on the same date as the earlier one, which can be advantageous for establishing priority over other filings or prior art.

To claim this benefit, the new application must be filed before the earlier application is patented, abandoned, or terminated. It must also contain or be amended to contain a specific reference to the earlier application. An amendment with this reference must be submitted within a time frame set by the Director of the U.S. Patent and Trademark Office (USPTO). If the reference is submitted late due to an unintentional delay, the Director may still accept it, though this may require a fee.

37 CFR § 1.97 - Filing of information disclosure statement (IDS)

Provides the rules for submitting an IDS to inform the USPTO of relevant prior art.

An Information Disclosure Statement[1] (also known as an IDS) is a document (IDS form PTO/SB/08a[2]) submitted to USPTO identifying the prior art[3] (e.g., patents, publications, non-patent literature) you're aware of. The purpose of the IDS is to satisfy your duty of candor and good faith[4] in dealing with the USPTO. Failure to submit the IDS may breach this duty and invalidate your patent. Be safe and submit the prior art via the IDS. *For more information about IDS, please refer to Page 72.*

---

1. https://www.uspto.gov/web/offices/pac/mpep/s609.html

2. https://www.uspto.gov/sites/default/files/patents/process/file/efs/guidance/updated_IDS.pdf

3. https://ocpatentlawyer.com/what-is-prior-art/

4. https://ocpatentlawyer.com/lesson/duty-search-disclose/

37 CFR § 1.10 Prioritized examination

Discusses the criteria and process for requesting and conducting a prioritized examination of a patent application.

37 CFR § 1.104 Nature of examination

Describes the examination process, including how the examiner will evaluate the claims, prior art, and other aspects of the application.

37 CFR § 1.111 Reply by applicant or patent owner to a non-final Office action

Covers the procedures for responding to an Office action issued by the USPTO examiner.

37 CFR § 1.114 Request for continued examination (RCE)

Provides the rules for filing a Request for Continued Examination, allowing an applicant to continue prosecution after the examiner has issued a final rejection.

In the U.S. patent prosecution process, a Request for Continued Examination (RCE) can be submitted to keep the examination of a patent application active after the United States Patent and Trademark Office (USPTO) has issued a final rejection. Here are key points about when to submit an RCE:

- **After Final Rejection**: An RCE is typically filed after receiving a final Office Action when the applicant still wishes to continue pursuing the claims but has been unable to resolve all the issues with the examiner. The RCE allows the applicant to submit new arguments, amendments, or evidence without abandoning the application.

- **Before Paying the Issue Fee**: If the applicant receives a Notice of Allowance but wants to introduce amendments or arguments related to the claims, an RCE may be filed instead of paying the issue fee to prevent the patent from issuing in its current form.

- **Within Statutory Time Limits**: The RCE must be filed within the statutory time frame for responding to the final rejection (usually 3 months, with the option to extend up to 6 months). If no action is taken within this period, the application may go abandoned.

- **To Avoid Abandonment**: If the applicant needs more time to make further arguments or amendments, the RCE is a tool to keep the examination open and avoid the case being closed by the USPTO.

In summary, an RCE should be submitted when the applicant wants to continue examination after a final rejection or if further action is needed before paying the issue fee.

37 CFR § 1.121 Manner of making amendments in application

Amending the Specification:

To delete, replace, or add paragraphs, provide clear instructions and show changes using underlining for new text and strike-through or double brackets for deleted text.

Entire sections can also be replaced, with changes shown in a similar way.

Previously deleted sections or paragraphs can only be reinstated by adding them back through a new amendment.

Amending Claims:

Amendments to claims must include the full text of the updated claims with changes marked (underlining for added text, strike-through for deletions).

A complete claim listing must be included, showing the status of each claim (e.g., original, amended, canceled).

Canceled claims should not show text, and reinstated claims must be added as new claims with a new number.

Amending Drawings:

Changes to drawings must be submitted on a replacement sheet, labeled "Replacement Sheet," showing all figures, even if only one was changed.

New figures should be on a "New Sheet." Any changes must be explained in detail.

No New Matter:

Amendments cannot introduce new information not originally disclosed.

Amendment Format:

Each section (e.g., claims, specification, drawings) of an amendment must begin on a separate sheet.

37 CFR 1.115 What is a preliminary amendments

A preliminary amendment is a change to a patent application that is submitted before the first Office action (the USPTO's initial review of the application). It must follow certain formatting rules, and it becomes part of the application if filed correctly and on time.

When It's Part of the Original Application:

If filed on the same day as the application (after September 21, 2004), the amendment is part of the original disclosure.

If filed later, it's not part of the original application.

How Preliminary Amendments Are Processed:

If a preliminary amendment can't be published due to format issues, the applicant will be asked to correct and submit it in a proper format.

If the amendment only modifies claims or adds references to earlier applications, special rules may apply to avoid unnecessary paperwork.

Timing Is Important:

Preliminary amendments must be submitted before the first Office action or they may not be considered.

The amendment should include an application number and filing date.

When an Applicant Can Amend:

Before the first Office action: Under rule 37 CFR 1.115, you can submit preliminary amendments before the Patent Office issues its first official communication (Office Action). These amendments are considered part of the original application if they are submitted on the filing date of the application.

After the first Office action: According to MPEP 714.02, you can modify the claims and specification in response to the first Office Action. You have a deadline specified by the examiner to submit your corrections or amendments.

After the second Office action: Following a second response from the Office, you can still submit amendments, although these will usually address specific objections from the examiner. In this case, changes can still be made, but they may be more limited depending on the stage of the process.

Before allowance: Under MPEP 714.12, you can continue modifying the claims and specification until you receive a Notice of Allowance. After receiving this notice, amendments are more restricted.

after the date of filing a notice of appeal pursuant to 37 CFR 41.31(a)[1], if the amendment meets the criteria of 37 CFR 41.33[2]; and

when and as specifically required by the examiner.

---

1.   https://www.uspto.gov/web/offices/pac/mpep/mpep-9020-appx-r.html#d0e356411

2.   https://www.uspto.gov/web/offices/pac/mpep/mpep-9020-appx-r.html#d0e356490

37 CFR § 1.136 Extensions of time

Describes the process and requirements for obtaining an extension of time to respond to USPTO actions.

- Extension for response within first month

  ○ Fee Code: 1251/2251/3251

  ○ 37 CFR §: 1.17(a)(1)

  ○ Fee: 220.00

  ○ Small entity fee: 88.00

- Extension for response within second month

  ○ Fee Code: 1252/2252/3252

  ○ 37 CFR §: 1.17(a)(2)

  ○ Fee: 640.00

  ○ Small entity fee: 256.00

- Extension for response within third month

  ○ Fee Code: 1253/2253/3253

  ○ 37 CFR §: 1.17(a)(3)

  ○ Fee: 1,480.00

  ○ Small entity fee: 592.00

- Extension for response within fourth month

  o Fee Code: 1254/2254/3254

  o 37 CFR §: 1.17(a)(4)

  o Fee: 2,320.00

  o Small entity fee: 928.00

- Extension for response within fifth month

  o Fee Code: 1255/2255/3255

  o 37 CFR §: 1.17(a)(5)

  o Fee: 3,160.00

  o Small entity fee: 1,264.00

When you can extend the reply time:

If you're required to reply within a shortened time frame, you can extend this up to five months, unless:

o You are told otherwise in an Office action.

o It involves specific actions like a reply brief, oral hearing request, or responses to decisions by the Patent Trial and Appeal Board.

How extensions work:

The date you file the petition and pay the fee determines the extension period. You must submit your reply before the extended period ends to avoid abandonment. You can't go beyond the maximum time allowed by law.

Future extensions:

You can authorize the USPTO to automatically apply any required fees and treat future replies as requests for an extension if needed. Paying the required fee can also be treated as a request for an extension.

Extensions when automatic options are not available:

If you can't use the automatic extension option, you can still request an extension for cause, but you must submit the request by the reply due date and pay the petition fee. Extensions cannot go beyond the statutory limit.

No extensions after a "Notice of Allowability":

Once you receive a "Notice of Allowability," the deadlines for submitting the inventor's oath, formal drawings, or making a deposit are not extendable.

37 CFR § 1.137 Revival of abandoned application, terminated reexamination prosecution, or lapsed patent

Provides the rules for petitioning to revive an abandoned application.

37 CFR § 1.213 - Nonpublication request

If an invention has not been and will not be filed in another country or under an international agreement that requires publication 18 months after filing, the application can remain unpublished. To do this, a nonpublication request must be submitted with the application. The request must clearly state that the application should not be published, include a certification confirming that the invention won't be filed elsewhere requiring 18-month publication, and be signed according to the required rules.

37 CFR § 1.215 Patent Application Publication

Outlines the process for publishing a patent application. When an application is published under 35 U.S.C. 122(b), a patent application publication is created based on the original application, including the specification, drawings, application data sheet, and any amendments made before the publication process begins. The publication date is noted, and technical preparations for publication generally start four months before the projected date. The publication will include the name of the assignee or a person with sufficient proprietary interest if that information is provided in the application data sheet and submitted in time. Providing this information in the datasheet does not replace the requirement to officially record an assignment. The applicant can choose to have the publication based on an updated version of the application if it is submitted electronically within a specific timeframe, which is either within one month of the first Office communication or fourteen months from the earliest filing date. If the submitted copy doesn't meet electronic requirements, the Office will publish the original application. However, if the publication process hasn't started, the Office may use the late-filed updated copy instead.

37 CFR § 1.64. Substitute statement in lieu of an oath or declaration

Allows using a "substitute statement" instead of an oath or declaration in a patent application if the inventor is deceased, legally incapacitated, unwilling to sign, or cannot be reached. The substitute statement must identify the inventor, the person making the statement, and the reason for using it. It should also include each inventor's legal name and contact details. The person making the statement must understand the application and their duty to disclose relevant information. False statements can lead to fines or imprisonment. A missing inventor or their legal representative can later join the application with a standard oath or declaration, but this does not affect any powers of attorney.

37 CFR § 1.98 - Content of information disclosure statement.

Outlines the requirements for an information disclosure statement (IDS) in the context of patent applications. An IDS is a document submitted by a patent applicant to the United States Patent and Trademark Office (USPTO) that discloses all information known to the applicant to be material to the patentability of the invention.

37 CFR § 3.73(c) - Establishing right of assignee to take action.

If an assignee who is not the original applicant wants to take action in a patent matter, they must prove their ownership of the patent. This can be done by submitting a signed statement identifying the assignee, along with documentary evidence showing the chain of title from the original owner to the assignee, or by referencing where this evidence is already recorded in the Office's records. If the assignee has only partial ownership, the Office may require statements from all owners to confirm that the entire right, title, and interest are accounted for. If there are conflicting claims from multiple assignees, the Director will decide which assignee, if any, can control the application process.

37 CFR § 11.9 - Limited recognition in patent matters

Only U.S. citizens or permanent residents can be fully registered to practice patent law before the USPTO. However, the USPTO may grant limited recognition to nonimmigrant aliens who are authorized to work or train with a specific employer in patent matters. If you have limited recognition, you must clearly state that you have limited recognition status when presenting yourself to the public, and you cannot claim to be fully registered to practice patent law before the USPTO. If you don't follow this rule, your limited recognition could be revoked. You can apply for full registration if you become a U.S. permanent resident or citizen.

When filing a non-provisional patent application with the USPTO, it is important to be familiar with various sections of the U.S.C. (United States Code), which is the official compilation of the general and permanent federal laws of the United States. Here there are some important U.S.C:

35 U.S.C. 111(c) - Prior Filed Application.

Under certain conditions set by the Director, an applicant can file a new application by referencing a previously filed application (instead of submitting a full specification and drawings right away). To do this, the applicant must mention the application number and where it was originally filed.

However, the applicant must eventually submit a copy of the specification and drawings from the original application within a specific timeframe. If they fail to do so, the new application will be considered abandoned, as if it were never filed.

35 U.S.C. 117 - Death or incapacity of inventor

If an inventor dies or becomes legally incapacitated before a patent application is filed or before the patent is granted, a legal representative (like an executor of the estate or a guardian) can apply for the patent on behalf of the inventor. If the inventor dies after filing the application but before the patent is granted, the patent can still be issued to the legal representative.

35 U.S.C. 119(e) - Benefit of earlier filing date; right of priority

Is about claiming the benefit of an earlier filing date from a provisional patent application. If you first file a provisional application, and then later file a regular (non-provisional) patent application within a year, you can use the earlier filing date of the provisional application for your regular application. This can help you secure an earlier priority date, which is important for establishing the novelty of your invention.

35 U.S.C. 120. Benefit of earlier filing date in the United States.

Allows a patent application to claim the benefit of the filing date of an earlier application filed in the U.S. (or in certain international applications) if the invention is disclosed in the same way as required by law (except for the "best mode" requirement). This means that the new application can be treated as if it was filed on the same date as the earlier one, which can be important for establishing priority over other filings. Applies to non-provisional applications, particularly continuation, divisional, and CIP applications.

A non-provisional patent application is the formal application submitted to the patent office that, if granted, leads to the issuance of a patent. It's a comprehensive document that includes a full description of the invention, claims that define the scope of the patent protection, drawings (if applicable), and other required forms. Non-provisional applications are typically the next step after filing a provisional patent application, though a non-provisional can also be filed without a preceding provisional.

Within the realm of non-provisional applications, there are specialized types, including continuation, divisional, and continuation-in-part (CIP) applications. Here's a detailed explanation of each:

Continuation Application

A continuation application is a type of non-provisional application filed to pursue additional claims based on the same disclosure as a previously filed non-provisional application (the "parent" application). Key points include:

- **Purpose:** A continuation is typically filed when the applicant wants to seek protection for additional aspects of the invention that were disclosed in the parent application but were not claimed or were claimed but not allowed during prosecution.

- **Claims:** The continuation application must be directed to the same invention as disclosed in the parent application, but it can include new or amended claims.

- **Filing Date:** It must be filed while the parent application is still pending.

- **Benefit:** The continuation application benefits from the filing date of the parent application, meaning it is treated as if it were filed on the same date as the parent.

Divisional Application

A divisional application is a type of non-provisional application filed when a patent examiner issues a "restriction requirement," forcing the applicant to choose between different inventions or distinct groups of claims within the same application. Key points include:

- **Purpose:** A divisional application allows the applicant to pursue protection for an invention or group of claims that were separated out from the original application due to the examiner's determination that multiple distinct inventions were present.

- **Claims:** The divisional application includes claims directed to the distinct invention that was not pursued in the original application due to the restriction requirement.

- **Filing Date:** Like a continuation, it must be filed while the original application is still pending and benefits from the filing date of the parent application.

Continuation-in-Part (CIP) Application

A CIP application is a non-provisional application that allows the applicant to add new subject matter to the original disclosure. It can include both new material and the content disclosed in the original application. Key points include:

- **Purpose:** A CIP is used when the applicant wants to introduce new information, such as improvements or modifications to the original invention, while still maintaining the original application's benefit.

- **Claims:** The CIP can include claims directed to the original disclosure and claims based on the newly added material.

- **Filing Date:** Claims that are fully supported by the original disclosure benefit from the original filing date, while claims based on new matter receive the filing date of the CIP application.

- **Complexity:** A CIP introduces complexity because it involves determining which claims are entitled to the original filing date and which are only entitled to the later CIP filing date. This distinction can affect the validity of the patent if intervening prior art arises.

35 U.S.C. 122(b).

This statement explains that if an applicant, at the time of filing, certifies that the invention has not been and will not be the subject of an application filed in another country or under any international agreement that requires publication 18 months after filing, then the application will not be published according to the standard 18-month rule. Essentially, this allows the applicant to keep the application from being published if it meets specific criteria.

Forms

There is a wide variety of forms available. Each form, along with its instructions, often references another form using a simplified code that starts with the acronym "CFR", which stands for "Code of Federal Regulations".

Here is a list of some common USPTO forms used for filing a patent application, along with the corresponding Code of Federal Regulations (CFR) references:

1. PTO/AIA/15 - Utility Patent Application Transmittal
2. PTO/AIA/14 (01-22) - Application Data Sheet (ADS) - CFR Reference: 37 CFR 1.76
3. PTO/AIA/80 (07-17) POWER OF ATTORNEY TO PROSECUTE APPLICATIONS BEFORE THE USPTO CFR Reference: 37 CFR 1.32
4. SB/08A - Declaration for Utility or Design Patent Application (35 U.S.C. 115(a)) - CFR Reference: 37 CFR 1.63
5. PATENT/PATENT APPLICATION ASSIGNMENT
6. SB/06 - Fee Transmittal - CFR Reference: 37 CFR 1.16 and 37 CFR 1.17
7. SB/05 - Information Disclosure Statement (IDS) by Applicant - CFR Reference: 37 CFR 1.97 and 37 CFR 1.98
8. SB/15 - Certificate of Mailing or Transmission - CFR Reference: 37 CFR 1.8

Utility Patent Application Transmittal

A Utility Patent Application Transmittal Form (Form PTO/AIA/15) or a transmittal letter should accompany every non provisional patent application under 37 CFR 1.52(b). It clearly identifies the items being submitted, such as the specification, drawings, declaration, and information disclosure statement. This form specifies the first named inventor, the type of application, the title of the invention, the contents of the submission, and any additional enclosures. For all correspondence following the initial filing, Form PTO/SB/21 should be used.

Header of the form

Attorney docket number: Reference text of up to 25 alphanumeric characters that is used to identify a patent application.

First inventor: Among the list of inventors.

Title: Of the invention

Express Mail Label Number: Tracking number provided by the United States Postal Service (USPS) when an application or other documents are sent to the USPTO using the Express Mail service

Application elements

Check all the boxes that apply

Fee transmittal form: A Fee Transmittal Form is used to submit payment for various fees related to patent applications, such as filing, search, and examination fees.

Applicant claims small entity status. See 37 CFR 1.27: This status allows applicants, such as individuals, small businesses, or non-profits, to pay reduced patent fees.

Applicant certifies micro entity status. See 37 CFR 1.29: This status provides further fee reductions for applicants meeting specific income or academic requirements, and requires submission of Form PTO/SB/15A or B to certify eligibility.

Specifications: Include number of pages taking into consideration that both the claims and abstract must start on a new page (See MPEP § 608.01(a) for information on the preferred arrangement).

Drawing(s) (with total sheets):

Oath or Declaration (with total sheets):

Substitute statements (See 37 CFR 1.64) to replace traditional oaths or declarations in patent filings.

Assignments (See 37 CFR 1.63(e)) to also serve as oaths or declarations, confirming required statements.

Option a. Newly executed (original or copy): This refers to submitting a fresh, newly signed oath or declaration. The document can be either the original signed by the inventor(s) or a copy of the original. This is typically required when the application is being filed for the first time, or if there have been changes that necessitate a new declaration.

Option b. A copy from a prior application (37 CFR 1.63(d)): This option applies when the current application is a continuation or divisional application of a previously filed application. Instead of requiring the inventor(s) to sign a new oath or declaration, you can submit a copy of the oath or declaration from the prior application. This is allowed under 37 CFR 1.63(d), which permits the reuse of a previously executed declaration as long as the previous application is properly referenced and the new application meets the requirements of a continuation or divisional filing.

Application Data Sheet (ADS): This form (PTO/AIA/14 or equivalent) provides bibliographic data about the patent application, such as the applicant's details, invention title, and priority claims. It's governed by 37 CFR 1.76.

CD-ROM or CD-R in duplicate, large table, or Computer Program (Appendix): This field is for submitting digital content, such as large tables or computer programs, on CD-ROMs or CD-Rs.

Two copies must be provided, especially if the content is too large for the application itself.

Nucleotide and/or Amino Acid Sequence Submission: If your application includes nucleotide or amino acid sequences, this section applies. It requires:

Computer Readable Form (CRF): The sequence data must be submitted in a machine-readable format.

Specification Sequence Listing: This can be submitted on:

- i. CD-ROM or CD-R (2 copies): The sequence listing must be provided in two digital copies.

- ii. Paper: Alternatively, the sequence listing can be submitted in paper form.

Statements verifying identity of above copies: The applicant must provide a statement ensuring that the sequence data on the submitted CD-ROMs, CD-Rs, or paper copies are accurate and match each other exactly

Accompanying application papers

Assignment Papers (cover sheet & document(s)): Refers to the documentation submitted to the USPTO that officially transfers the ownership of a patent or patent application from the original inventor(s) to another party, known as the assignee . The "cover sheet" is a form that summarizes the assignment details (only required for provisional applications), while the "document(s)" include the actual legal paperwork that effectuates the transfer (the notarized patent application assignment). The "Name of Assignee" specifies the individual or entity receiving the rights to the patent.

Statement under 37 CFR 3.73(c): Is required when an assignee, who is not the original applicant, seeks to take action on the application. This is necessary when the assignee wants to be recognized as the applicant, meaning they are taking over the rights of the original inventor(s) and wish to be listed as the applicant. The 3.73(c) statement establishes their ownership and right to prosecute the application. Additionally, if the assignee needs to make decisions or submissions related to the application, such as filings, amendments, or formal requests with the USPTO on behalf of the original applicant, they must file this statement to show their authority. At any time the assignee takes over the prosecution of a patent, they must establish their ownership via a 3.73(c) statement. This statement should accompany any paper where the assignee is requesting or taking action, or it can be submitted beforehand to establish the assignee's rights.

Power of attorney: Allows an applicant to authorize a patent attorney or agent to act on their behalf in patent matters, including filing documents and handling communications with the USPTO.

English Translation Document (if applicable): Refers to a document that provides the English translation of a non-English patent application or related documents. This translation is necessary when the original documents are in a language other than English and are being submitted to a patent office, such as the USPTO, where English is the required language for filings.

Information Disclosure Statement (IDS): Is a form (PTO/SB/08 or PTO-1449) that allows applicants to disclose prior art or other materials that may affect the patentability of their invention. Filing an IDS helps ensure that the USPTO has all relevant information when examining the application.

Copies of citations attached: Checking this box confirms that you've attached copies of the references you're disclosing to the USPTO.

Preliminary Amendment: This field is used when the applicant is submitting changes or corrections to the patent application before it has been examined.

Return Receipt Postcard (MPEP § 503): This field refers to a postcard sent by the applicant with the filing, which the USPTO will return as proof of receipt. The postcard should be itemized to match the contents submitted.

Certified Copy of Priority Document(s): This is used when claiming priority to an earlier foreign patent application. A certified copy of the original foreign application must be provided.

Nonpublication Request Under 35 U.S.C. 122(b)(2)(B)(i): This field is for requesting that the patent application not be published. The applicant must include form PTO/SB/35 or an equivalent form.

Other: This field is for any additional items or documents being submitted that don't fall under the specific categories listed (like certificate of mailing).

Correspondence Address

This field is used to specify where the USPTO should send all communications regarding the patent application. You can either:

- Provide a Customer Number associated with a pre-registered address on file with the USPTO (Customer Numbers are typically used by attorneys and law firms).

- Fill in the specific correspondence address below if it's different from the one linked to the Customer Number.

Registration No. (Attorney/Agent): Refers to the unique identification number assigned to a patent attorney or agent by the USPTO.

Application Data Sheet (ADS)

The application data sheet (ADS) is a form that includes information such as inventor details, applicant details, correspondence address, the application, domestic benefits (the rights or advantages that an applicant can claim in their home country based on a prior application filed in that same country), foreign priority (the right of a patent applicant to claim the filing date of a prior application in another country), and assignee information. This form can also be used to request that the application not be published and must be signed by the applicant. It is mandatory when inventors have assigned their rights to a company (assignee) and that company is filing the application. It is also required when the applicant wishes to claim the benefit of a prior application, whether provisional or nonprovisional, or the priority of a prior foreign or international application.

Foreign priority: Under U.S. law (35 U.S.C. 119(b)), if an applicant wants to claim priority based on an earlier foreign application, they must meet certain formal requirements within a specified time. If these requirements aren't met, the priority claim is lost and can't be reclaimed. The deadline for filing a priority claim and submitting the necessary documents is before the patent is granted, but this deadline can be set earlier by the Director. Recent changes in the law have updated the procedures and deadlines for claiming foreign priority and submitting certified copies.

Domestic benefit: Refers to the ability to claim the filing date of an earlier patent application within the same country (or patent jurisdiction) when filing a new, related application. In the U.S., for example, an applicant can claim the benefit of an earlier filing date from a provisional application, a parent application, or a prior nonprovisional application when filing a new application, such as a continuation, continuation-in-part, or divisional application. This allows the new application to be treated as if it were filed on the same date as the earlier application, which can be crucial for establishing priority over other competing applications or prior art.

Header

Data entered in the Application Information section will populate the header information.

Secrecy Order Checkbox

Under 37 CFR 5.2, if an invention is deemed a national security concern, the Commissioner for Patents can impose a secrecy order, keeping the invention confidential. Applicants must inform the Office of any related cases under secrecy. Documents for applications under a Secrecy Order cannot be filed electronically.

Inventor Information

Inventor: Contributes to the conception of an invention.

Prefix: Optional (Mr, Mrs, etc)

Given Name: Enter the first or given name of the inventor.

Middle name: Optional

Family Name: Enter the last or family name of the inventor.

Suffix: Optional (Jr, Sr, II, etc)

Residence information: Select the radio button that describes the inventor's residence (US Residency, Non US Residency and Active US Military Service).

City: REQUIRED if the inventor is a U.S. resident.

State / Province: REQUIRED if the inventor is a U.S. resident. See State/Province List for choices.

Active US Military Service: REQUIRED if the inventor is in the active U.S. military service.

Country of Residence: If the inventor resides in the US, it will automatically default to "US." This field is required, and a complete list of country codes and abbreviations is available in the Country Code Table.

Address 1 and 2: The first and second line of the inventor's mailing address.

City: Enter the city of the inventor's mailing address.

State / Province: For mailing address in the US. See State/Province List for choices.

Postal Code: 5 - 9 digit postal code of the inventor's mailing address. For foreign countries is optional.

Country: Enter the country of the inventor's mailing address. See Country Code Table for complete listing, along with abbreviation.

Additional Inventors: Joint inventors must apply for a patent together, and each inventor must submit the necessary oath or declaration. No individual inventor, or fewer than all inventors, can apply for a patent on an invention they created together, unless specific exceptions apply under 37 CFR 1.43, 1.45, and 1.46. If there are multiple inventors, additional inventor information must be included in the application.

Remove: Choose this button to remove an inventor from this section.

Add Button: Additional inventor information Blocks may be generated.

Correspondence Information (For further information see 37 CFR 1.33(a))

An Address is being provided for the correspondence Information of this application: Check this box if you want correspondence for this application sent to an address that isn't linked to a specific Customer Number. If you don't provide a correspondence address, the Office might use the mailing address of the first listed inventor (if available, see §§ 1.76(b)(1) and 1.63(b)(2)) as the default correspondence address.

Customer Number: Provide the Customer Number linked to the address where application correspondence should be sent. This number, assigned by the Office, streamlines address updates, appointing a practitioner, or setting the fee address for a patent. Customer Numbers are typically used by attorneys and law firms.

Provide a customer address: If a Customer Number is not provided, the correspondence address must be entered manually.

Name – 1 and 2: Enter the name for the correspondence address.

Address -1 and 2: Enter the first and second line of the correspondence address.

State / Province: REQUIRED for a correspondence address that is in the U.S.

Country: See Country Code Table for complete listing, along with abbreviation.

Postal Code: 5 - 9 digit postal code of the inventor's mailing address. For foreign countries is optional.

Phone and fax number: Telephone/fax number for the correspondence address.

Email address: e-mail address for the correspondence address.

Add email: Select the Add Email button to add an email address. You may enter up to 3.

Remove email: Select the Remove Email button to remove the email address associated with the button.

Application Information

Title of the invention: The title of the invention can be up to 500 characters long and must be concise and specific. It can include standard keyboard characters as well as special characters like f, ™, ©, and various accented letters.

Attorney Docket Number: This field is optional. It may be used to enter an internal reference number (limited to 25 characters) associated with this submission.

Small Entity Status Claimed: An independent inventor, a small business concern, or a nonprofit organization eligible for reduced patent fees.

Application Type: May be either provisional or non-provisional.

Subject Matter: An application may be either a utility application, a design application, or a plant application.

Total number of drawing sheets: Indicate the specified sheets with drawings.

Suggested figure for publication: If the applicant has a particular figure that best represents the invention and would like it to be highlighted in the published patent document, they can indicate this figure in the ADS. If no figure is suggested, the USPTO may choose one based on their guidelines, or no figure may be included on the cover page at all.

Filing by reference: Refers to a process where an applicant files a patent application without providing the full specification, claims, and drawings at the time of filing. Instead, the applicant refers to a previously filed application (either a U.S. or foreign application) as the basis for the new filing. This method is used when the applicant wants to secure a filing date but isn't ready to submit the complete application details. The description and any drawings of the present application are replaced by those of the reference given in that field of a previously filed application.

This section should only be completed if you are filing an application by reference under specific rules (35 U.S.C. 111(c) and 37 CFR 1.57(a)).

Publication Information

Request Early Publication: Select if the application should be published as soon as possible.

Request Not to Publish: Check this box if a request for non-publication under 35 U.S.C. 122(b) and 37 CFR 1.213 is being made.

Representative Information: Representative information should be provided for all practitioners having a power of attorney in the application.

Customer Number Selection: Check this box if you want to assign a Customer Number for patent practitioners associated with this application.

Customer Number Entry: If Customer Number is selected enter the Customer Number associated with patent practitioner information for this application.

U.S. Patent Practitioner: Check this box if you want to input a US Patent Practitioner name.

Registration number: Enter the USPTO registration number of the patent practitioner.

Add Additional Representatives: If a patent practitioner is chosen, enter their name and registration details, then click the Add button. Repeat this for each practitioner, with a maximum of 10 allowed.

Limited Recognition: Check this box if you want to input a name under Limited Recognition (37 CFR 11.9) (refers to a special status granted by the USPTO to individuals who are not fully registered patent practitioners but are authorized to practice before the USPTO in specific circumstances).

Domestic Benefit/National Stage Information:

You need to state if you are claiming benefits under specific U.S. laws (35 U.S.C. 119(e), 120, 121, 365(c), or 386(c)) or entering the National Stage from a PCT application.

When claiming benefits from previous applications, list them starting with the most recent and go backward in order. If you have multiple chains of applications, handle each chain separately in the same manner. This ensures that the claims are recognized and processed correctly by the Office's systems.

Prior Application status: When referring to a previous application, it could be either patented, pending, abandoned or expired.

Application Number: For new applications, this field should be blank. Click the "Add" button to enter any application numbers.

Continuity Type: To specify the relationship between patent applications, choose from one of the seven options in the drop-down menu:

Continuation of – A new application for the same invention as a prior nonprovisional application, filed before the original application is abandoned or patented. (MPEP 201.07)

Division of – A new application for a distinct invention, separated from a pending application and only including subject matter disclosed in the original application. (MPEP 201.06)

Continuation-in-part of – An application filed while an earlier nonprovisional application is still active, which includes some content from the earlier application and adds new matter. (MPEP 201.08).

371 of international – A U.S. patent application that has entered the national stage from an international application under the Patent Cooperation Treaty (PCT). (MPEP 1893).

Substitution of – A new application that is a duplicate of an earlier application abandoned before the new one was filed. It does not maintain continuity with the earlier application. (MPEP 201.02)

Reissue of – An application for a new patent to replace an existing unexpired patent that is defective due to an error. (MPEP 201.05).

Claims benefit of provisional – An application claiming the benefit of a provisional application, which establishes a priority date under the Paris Convention.

Prior application number: Enter the application number of the related application that your application is claiming benefit from. If the prior application is an international design application for the U.S., you can provide either the U.S. application number or the international registration number.

Filing Date or 371(c) Date: Choose the filing date or 371(c) date of the prior related application from the drop-down menu, which opens a calendar. The date should be selected from the calendar and must follow the format YYYY-MM-DD.

Add/Remove Domestic Priority Data: Add/delete the information to the continuity information list by selecting the Add button.

Foreign Priority Information

This section enables the applicant to claim foreign priority. Including this information in the Application Data Sheet fulfills the priority claim requirement under 35 U.S.C. 119(b) and 37 CFR 1.55.

Application Number: Enter the Foreign Document Number of the related foreign-filed application in the Application Number field. Use the PCT number format: PCT/aaYY/xxxxx or PCT/aaYYYY/xxxxx, where "aa" is the valid foreign receiving office/country code, "YY" or "YYYY" is the year, and "xxxxx" is the five-digit number.

Country: Enter the country where the application was filed and the abbreviation.

Filing Date: Enter the foreign filing date in the Date field. The date should be in the format YYYY-MM-DD.

Access Code: The access code number is a unique identifier used to securely access a patent application that has been registered in the WIPO DAS (World Intellectual Property Organization Digital

Access Service). WIPO DAS is an electronic system allowing patent offices and applicants to securely share and exchange priority documents and other important information.

When a patent application is registered in WIPO DAS, the applicant is given an access code. This code is essential for retrieving the application and related documents from the WIPO DAS system. By entering this access code, other patent offices or authorized parties can verify the priority claim and access the relevant documents without needing physical copies. This streamlines the process of managing international patent applications and reduces the need for duplicate submissions of documents across multiple jurisdictions.

Add/Remove: Add/delete additional information to the Foreign Priority Information list by selecting the Add button.

Statement under 37 CFR 1.55 or 1.78 for AIA (First Inventor to File) Transition Applications

You need to check this option in your Application Data Sheet (ADS) if your patent application meets both of the following conditions:

Claims Priority or Benefit to an Earlier Application: Your current application claims priority to, or benefits from, an earlier application that was filed before March 16, 2013. This could include a provisional application, a nonprovisional application, or a foreign application.

Contains a Claim with an Effective Filing Date on or After March 16, 2013: Your current application contains (or has ever contained) a claim to an invention that has an effective filing date on or after March 16, 2013. This could happen if you added new subject matter to the current application that was not disclosed in the earlier application, leading to a new effective filing date for those claims.

If both of these conditions apply, you must check this option because your application will be examined under the "first inventor to file" provisions of the America Invents Act (AIA).

Authorization or Opt-Out of Authorization to Permit Access by a foreign intellectual property office(s) to an application-as-filed via Priority Document Exchange or to Search Results from the instant application

When you properly sign and file the Application Data Sheet (ADS) with your application, you are giving permission for certain foreign intellectual property (IP) offices to access your application and related information.

Access to Application: If you do not opt out by checking the appropriate box, you authorize the USPTO to share your application and its data with the European Patent Office (EPO), Japan Patent Office (JPO), Korean Intellectual Property Office (KIPO), State Intellectual Property Office of China (SIPO), World Intellectual Property Organization (WIPO), and other foreign IP offices participating in document exchange agreements. This includes your filed application, any applications it claims priority from, and the date of this authorization.

Search Results: If you do not opt out, you also allow the USPTO to share search results from your application with the EPO if a European patent application claiming priority from your application is filed.

If you do not want to provide this authorization, you must check the opt-out boxes (A or B) in subsection 2 of the ADS. Note that once your application is published or publicly available, the USPTO may still provide access in accordance with the rules.

Applicant information

If the applicant is the inventor (or the remaining joint inventor(s) under 37 CFR 1.45), you do not need to fill out this section. This section should only be completed with the name and address of the legal representative who is the applicant under 37 CFR 1.43, or the name and address of the assignee, the person to whom the inventor is obligated to assign the invention, or the person who otherwise has sufficient proprietary interest in the invention who is applying under 37 CFR 1.46. If the applicant is someone under 37 CFR 1.46 (such as an assignee or person with sufficient proprietary interest) along with one or more joint inventors, then the joint inventor(s) who are also applicants should be listed in this section.

Assignee: An assignee is a person or entity to whom the inventor has transferred (assigned) their rights in the invention. The assignee becomes the owner of the patent rights and can apply for the patent in their own name.

Legal Representative under 35 U.S.C. 117: This refers to a person authorized to act on behalf of an inventor who is deceased, legally incapacitated, or otherwise unable to file the application. The legal representative can file the patent application on behalf of the inventor.

Joint Inventor: A joint inventor is one of multiple inventors who contributed to the creation of the invention. In cases where the patent application is filed by more than one inventor, each joint inventor has a share in the invention and can be listed as an applicant.

Person to whom the inventor is obligated to assign: This applies when the inventor is legally or contractually required to transfer their rights to another party, such as an employer. The assignee can then apply for the patent.

Person who shows sufficient proprietary interest: This applies to someone with a significant financial or proprietary stake in the invention, even without a formal assignment. They must demonstrate their substantial interest to qualify as the applicant.

If applicant is the legal representative, indicate the authority to file the patent application, the inventor is: This field is used when the applicant filing the patent application is not the inventor themselves but rather a legal representative. Here, you need to indicate the legal basis or authority under which the legal representative is filing the patent application on behalf of the inventor. This could involve situations where the inventor has passed away or is incapacitated.

If the Applicant is an Organization check here: Check this box if the applicant is an organization.

Organization Name: Enter the name of the organization

Name and address fields: Fill them just the way you did in the equivalent fields in the above sections (inventor and correspondence information).

Assignee Information including Non-Applicant Assignee Information:

Fill out this section to include assignee information, including non-applicant assignee details, on the patent application publication as per 37 CFR 1.215(b). If the assignee is already listed as the applicant in the "Applicant Information" section, they will automatically appear as the applicant in the publication. However, if you want the assignee to be identified as both the applicant and assignee on the publication, you should also complete this section.

If the assignee or non-applicant assignee is an Organization: Check this box if the assignee or non-applicant assignee is an organization.

Organization Name: Enter the name of the organization

Name and address fields: Fill them just the way you did in the equivalent fields in the other sections (inventor and correspondence information).

Signature

This form must be signed according to 37 CFR 1.33(b). However, if the Application Data Sheet is submitted with the initial filing and neither box A nor B is checked in subsection 2 of the "Authorization or Opt-Out of Authorization to Permit Access" section, the form must also be signed under 37 CFR 1.14(c).

If one or more of the applicants is a juristic entity (e.g., corporation or association), a patent practitioner must sign the Application Data Sheet. If the applicant consists of two or more joint inventors, the form must be signed by either a patent practitioner, all joint inventors who are the applicant, or one or more joint inventor-applicants with power of attorney (e.g., see USPTO Form PTO/AIA/81) on behalf of all joint inventor-applicants. For more details, refer to the signature requirements and certifications outlined in 37 CFR 1.4(d).

Signature: This signature is an electronic legal signature. The individual must provide a signature in the format /###/, where ### represents any combination of letters, numbers, spaces, or punctuation (excluding / or ?). It cannot consist solely of spaces or punctuation. For example: "/John Doe/". For more details, refer to 37 CFR 1.4(d)(3).

Date: The date format should be in the form YYYY-MM-DD.

First Name, Last Name: Type or write the filer's name.

Registration number: Please enter a Registration Number if you are a patent practitioner.

Power of attorney to prosecute applications before the USPTO

Under 37 CFR 1.32, a power of attorney for a patent application must designate one or more registered patent practitioners, joint inventors, or practitioners associated with a Customer Number. A power of attorney cannot name more than ten patent practitioners unless it includes a separate document specifying which ten practitioners are to be recognized. Powers of attorney naming firms or more than ten practitioners without the required additional document will not be accepted. If an unregistered individual is named, the power of attorney will be considered ineffective, and the filing receipt will be sent to the applicant instead. For validity, the appointed attorney or agent must be registered with the U.S. Patent and Trademark Office.

Whenever you use this Power of Attorney (POA) form for a patent application, you must also file a copy of the form along with a statement under 37 CFR 3.73(c) (such as Form PTO/AIA/96 or a similar form). The statement should be completed by one of the practitioners named in the POA and must clearly identify the specific patent application to which the POA applies. This ensures proper documentation and processing of the POA for that application.

I hereby revoke all previous powers of attorney given in the application identified in the attached statement under 37 CFR 3.73(c).

This statement means that the individual is formally canceling or nullifying all previously granted powers of attorney related to a specific patent application, as referenced in the attached document. Under 37 CFR 3.73(c), this revocation is done following patent office regulations to ensure that only the new power of attorney or representative is recognized going forward. Essentially, it updates the record to reflect that all earlier appointments of representatives for that patent application are no longer valid.

I hereby appoint: This field is where you indicate the representative(s) you are designating to act on your behalf.

Practitioners associated with Customer Number: If you have a Customer Number (a unique identifier assigned to you or your organization by the U.S. Patent and Trademark Office), you can appoint all patent practitioners associated with this number.

Practitioner(s) named below (if more than ten patent practitioners are to be named, then a customer number must be used): If you choose to name specific practitioners individually and there are more than ten, you must also provide a Customer Number. This ensures the Office can properly recognize and manage the list of practitioners. For fewer than ten practitioners, you can list their names and registration numbers directly without needing a Customer Number.

Please change the correspondence address for the application identified in the attached statement under 37 CFR 3.73(c) to:

The address associated with Customer Number: Use this option to automatically update the address to the one already linked with a specific Customer Number you have on file.

Firm or individual name, Address, City, State, Zip, Country, Telephone, email: Use this option to manually enter a new address and contact details if you want to provide a different address than the one associated with your Customer Number.

Assignee name and address: Enter the name and contact details of the current patent holder.

SIGNATURE of Assignee of Record

the authorized representative of the patent assignee signs to confirm their authority to act on behalf of the assignee. This field includes:

Signature: The actual signature of the authorized person.
Date: The date on which the signature was made.
Name: The printed name of the person who signed.
Telephone: A contact number for the signer.
Title: The job title or position of the person who signed.

Declaration for Utility or Design Patent Application

Each inventor must make an oath or declaration stating that the application was submitted or authorized by him or her, that he or she believes to be the original inventor or one of the original joint inventors of the claimed invention in the application, and that he or she acknowledges that any willful false statement made in the declaration is punishable under 18 U.S.C. 1001, with a fine, imprisonment for less than five years, or both.

For continuing applications that claim benefits under specific U.S. Code sections, a new oath or declaration is not required if one was previously filed and a copy is submitted with the continuing application. Inventorship for the continuing application is based on the datasheet or the earlier-filed application's oath or declaration.

An assignment can serve as an oath or declaration if it includes all required information and is recorded as specified.

Requirements for Oath or Declaration: The inventor, or each joint inventor, must provide an oath or declaration for the patent application. This must:

- Identify the inventor or joint inventor by their legal name.

- Specify the application to which the declaration pertains.

- State that the signer believes themselves to be the original inventor or a joint inventor of the claimed invention.

- Confirm that the application was made or authorized by the signer.

Title of Invention:

field refers to the descriptive name given to the invention being claimed in the patent application.

As the below-named inventor, I hereby declare that:

For an Attached Application: If the declaration is directly related to the application attached to the document.

For a Specific Application Number: If the declaration is intended for a specific U.S. application or PCT international application, fill in the blanks with the relevant details: insert the application number and insert filing date.

Statements:

- The above-identified application was made or authorized to be made by me.

- I believe that I am the original inventor or an original joint inventor of a claimed invention in the application.

- I hereby acknowledge that any willful false statement made in this declaration is punishable under 18 U.S.C. 1001 by fine or imprisonment of not more than five (5) years, or both.

LEGAL NAME OF INVENTOR

Inventor: Write the full legal name of the inventor as it appears in official documents.

Date (Optional): You may include the date on which the declaration is being signed. This is optional, but if included, it should be the date on which the inventor signs the document.

Note:

An application data sheet (PTO/SB/14 or equivalent), including naming the entire inventive entity, must accompany this form or must have been previously filed. Use an additional PTO/AIA/01 form for each additional inventor.

Assignment Document

This document effectively transfers all rights to the invention from the Assignor to the Assignee, ensuring that the Assignee has full legal control over the invention and any future patents associated with it.

Right, Title, and Interest: The Assignor is transferring their entire right, title, and interest in the invention to the Assignee, both in the United States and worldwide. This includes the right to file any related patent applications, such as provisional, non-provisional, divisional, continuation, continuation-in-part, or reissue applications.

Consideration: This indicates that the Assignor acknowledges receiving good and valuable consideration (i.e., compensation) for the transfer of rights, although the specific amount is not mentioned in the document.

Legal Obligations: The Assignor agrees to assist the Assignee with any legal actions necessary to obtain, sustain, reissue, or enforce the patent for the invention, without further compensation and at no expense to the Assignor.

Warranties: The Assignor guarantees that they have not granted any rights to others that conflict with the rights granted to the Assignee in this agreement.

Authorization to Issue Patents: The Assignor authorizes and requests the Commissioner of Patents and Trademarks in the United States and all foreign countries to issue any patent granted for the invention to the Assignee.

Notarization in the U.S: The notarization of documents for the assignment can be conveniently conducted online within the United States. This process allows for the notarization to be carried out in front of a camera, facilitating the secure and efficient electronic transmission of the consent related to the assignment document.

This modern approach ensures that all legal requirements are met while providing the flexibility of remote notarization.

Assignor: This is the individual or entity transferring their rights to the invention. The document identifies the Assignor and their location (choose as location the place where the document will be notarized).

Assignee: This is the individual or entity receiving the rights to the invention. The document identifies the Assignee and their location.

Invention: This section describes the invention being assigned. It acknowledges that a patent application has been or will be filed for this invention.

IN WITNESS WHEREOF, Assignor has executed this Assignment on the date first below written and as set forth below:

Date: The date on which the Assignment Agreement is signed by the Assignor. This is the effective date of the transfer of rights.

By: This line is where the signature of the person executing the assignment (the Assignor) is placed. It indicates that the individual is formally agreeing to the terms outlined in the document. It has to be signed in front of the notary.

Name: The full name of the person signing the document. This helps to identify the individual who is executing the assignment.

Title: The job title or position of the person signing the document. This is important if the individual is signing on behalf of a company or organization, as it indicates their authority to make the assignment.

Notary Details

This section pertains to notarization, which is the process of certifying a document's authenticity and the identity of the signatory. This is filled in the notary

State/Commonwealth of County of: These fields indicate the location where the notarization took place. "State" or

"Commonwealth" refers to the U.S. state or commonwealth where the notary is commissioned, and "County" refers to the specific county within that state or commonwealth.

This instrument was signed and sworn before me on this day of _____________, 20____ by _______________________________.: This line is for recording the date the document was signed and notarized. The blank spaces should be filled with the actual date and the name of the person who signed the document in front of the notary.

Notary Signature: The notary public's signature is required to validate the notarization.

Notary Printed Name: The full printed name of the notary public. This helps to clearly identify the notary who performed the certification.

Notary Public for the State/Commonwealth of: The state or commonwealth where the notary is authorized to perform notarizations. This confirms the notary's jurisdiction.

My Commission expires on: The expiration date of the notary public's commission. This indicates how long the notary's authority to perform notarizations is valid.

Notary seal may be placed below this fields

Fee Transmittal:

Header

Application Number: It helps identify the specific patent application to which the IDS is related. If you know this number, you should enter it here (herewith).

Filing Date: This refers to the date on which the patent application was officially submitted to the USPTO. The filing date is critical because it can affect the priority of the patent rights (herewith).

First Named Inventor: This field is for the name of the first inventor listed on the patent application. The first named inventor is often used as a reference point for the application.

Art Unit: The Art Unit is a division within the USPTO that handles specific types of patent applications based on their subject matter. Each Art Unit specializes in certain areas of technology (To be determined).

Examiner Name: This is the name of the USPTO patent examiner assigned to review your application. If you know the name of the examiner, you should include it in this field.

Attorney Docket Number: This is an internal reference number used by the attorney or law firm handling the patent application. It helps them track and manage the case internally.

Applicant asserts small entity status. See 37 CFR 1.27: Small entities are eligible for reduced patent fees.

Applicant certifies micro entity status. See 37 CFR 1.29: Micro entities are entitled to even further reduced fees than small entities. The form PTO/SB/15A or 15B, or an equivalent certification, must be submitted to confirm this status.

TOTAL AMOUNT OF PAYMENT: This field is where the applicant enters the total dollar amount of the fees being paid. If applicable, the total should reflect any reductions based on the applicant's small or micro entity status.

Method of Payment

This section allows the applicant to indicate the method they are using to pay the patent fees. The applicant can select one or more of the following payment options: Check,

credit card (note the warning below about not including credit card information directly on this form), money order,

or other (if using another payment method specify it in the space provided).

Deposit Account: This is a pre-paid account that applicants, attorneys, and other entities can establish. If the applicant has a deposit account with the USPTO, they can choose to pay fees using that account. The applicant should fill in the following:

- Deposit Account Number: Enter the number of the deposit account to be charged.

- Deposit Account Name: Enter the name associated with the deposit account.

For the above-identified deposit account, the Director is hereby authorized to: This section is used to authorize the USPTO to perform specific actions related to the deposit account:

- Charge fee(s) indicated below: Select this if the applicant authorizes the USPTO to charge the fees listed on the form to the deposit account.

- Charge fee(s) indicated below, except for the filing fee: Select this if the applicant authorizes charging all listed fees to the deposit account, except the filing fee.

• Charge any additional fee(s) or underpayment of fee(s): Select this if the applicant authorizes the USPTO to charge any additional fees or any underpayment to the deposit account.

• Credit any overpayment of fee(s): Select this if the applicant authorizes the USPTO to credit any overpayment to the deposit account.

WARNING: Credit card details should be provided on a separate, secure form (PTO-2038).

FEE CALCULATION

A section of the fee transmittal form used to determine the total amount due for filing, search, and examination fees for a patent application.

BASIC FILING, SEARCH, AND EXAMINATION FEES:

These are the primary fees associated with filing a patent application. They are categorized by the type of application (Utility, Design, Plant, Reissue (to correct an error in an already granted patent), provisional (a temporary application that establishes an early filing date)) and the applicant's status (undiscounted, small entity, micro entity). For more information see the Patent fees section.

The fees vary based on the applicant's status:

• U ($): Undiscounted fee for large entities.
• S ($): Small entity fee, typically half the undiscounted fee.
• M ($): Micro entity fee, typically one-quarter of the undiscounted fee.

Filing Fees: The cost to submit the patent application.

Search Fees: Fees for the USPTO to perform a search to identify prior art relevant to the patentability of the invention. The fee varies based on entity status.

Examination Fees: Fees for the USPTO to examine the patent application. Again, this fee varies based on entity status.

Fees Paid ($): This column is where the applicant enters the total amount paid for each type of fee (Filing, Search, Examination) for the selected application type.

Note: The $128 small entity filing fee for a utility application is further reduced to $64 for a small entity applicant who files the application via Patent Center or EFS-Web.

EXCESS CLAIM FEES: Deals with additional fees that apply when a patent application exceeds the standard number of claims included in the basic filing fee.

This section outlines the types of extra claims for which additional fees are charged:

- **Each claim over 20**: This fee applies to each claim in the application beyond the 20th claim.

- **Each independent claim over 3**: This fee applies to each independent claim beyond the 3rd independent claim.

- **Multiple dependent claims**: This fee applies to claims that depend on more than one other claim, which are more complex and thus incur additional costs.

Total Claims: List the total number of claims included in your application.

Extra Claims: Subtract 20 (the maximum allowed under the basic filing fee) from the "Total Claims" to calculate the highest number of extra claims (HP).

Extra Claims Fee ($): Use the fee corresponding to your entity status (40, 192, or 344) for each extra claim beyond the first 20.

Fee Paid ($): Multiply the HP by the "Extra Claims Fee ($)" to determine the total "Fee Paid."

Indep. Claims

List the total number of independent claims included in your application.

HP (Highest Number of Extra Independent Claims)

Subtract 3 (the maximum allowed under the basic filing fee) from the "Indep. Claims" to calculate the highest number of extra independent claims (HP).

Extra Claims Fee ($)

Use the fee corresponding to your entity status (100, 480, or 860) for each extra independent claim beyond the first 3.

Fee Paid ($)

Multiply the HP by the "Extra Claims Fee ($)" to determine the total "Fee Paid."

Multiple Dependent Claims

Indicates whether your application includes multiple dependent claims.

Fee ($)

Enter the fee associated with multiple dependent claims based on your entity status.

Fee Paid ($)

Enter the total amount paid for multiple dependent claims. If no multiple dependent claims are included in your application, this amount would be $0.

APPLICATION SIZE FEE

If the specification and drawings exceed 100 sheets of paper (excluding electronically filed sequence or computer listings under 37 CFR 1.52(e)), an application size fee of $420 is required for each additional 50 sheets or portion thereof. This fee is reduced to

$168 for small entities and $84 for micro entities. Refer to 35 U.S.C. 41(a)(1)(G) and 37 CFR 1.16(s) for details.

Total Sheets This field represents the total number of sheets of specification and drawings in the application.

Extra Sheets Subtract 100 from the total number of sheets. The result represents the number of extra sheets beyond the 100-sheet threshold.

Number of Each Additional 50 or Fraction Thereof Divide the number of extra sheets by 50. If the result is not a whole number, round it up to the next whole number. This value represents the number of additional 50-sheet increments or portions thereof.

Fee ($) Enter the applicable fee per additional 50 sheets or fraction thereof.

Fee Paid ($) Multiply the number of additional 50-sheet increments by the fee per increment to calculate the total fee paid.

OTHER FEE(S)

Non-English Specification: If the specification is not in English, a translation fee must be paid. The fee is $140 for undiscounted entities, $56 for small entities, and $28 for micro entities.

Non-Electronic Filing Fee (Under 37 CFR 1.16(t) for a Utility Application): If a utility application is filed in a non-electronic format, this fee applies.

Other (e.g., Late Filing Surcharge): This field is for any additional fees that may apply, such as a surcharge for late filing. You should specify the reason for the fee (e.g., "late filing surcharge") and the corresponding amount.

SUBMITTED BY

Signature: The person (typically the attorney or agent) who is submitting the form must sign here to validate the submission.

Registration No. (Attorney/Agent): This is the registration number of the attorney or agent who is representing the applicant.

Telephone: The telephone number where the person submitting the form can be contacted.

Name (Print/Type): The full name of the person signing the form, printed or typed. This identifies who is taking responsibility for the submission.

Date: The date on which the form is signed. This is important for tracking and ensuring that the submission is timely.

Information disclosure statement (IDS):

The Information Disclosure Statement (IDS) is a document required by the USPTO that obliges the inventor/applicant/ attorney to disclose all known information before filing the application, including results of similar patents and non-patent publications. This information will help the examiner refine their search of the prior art and assess the novelty and non obviousness of the invention. Failure to disclose this information in an IDS may result in sanctions, and the parties involved could be treated as if they had defrauded the USPTO.

37 CFR § 1.98 outlines the requirements for submitting an Information Disclosure Statement (IDS) to the United States Patent and Trademark Office (USPTO). The regulation is structured into several subsections, each detailing specific aspects of the IDS submission process.

Subsection (a): This section specifies what must be included in an IDS:

1. List of Documents: The IDS must include a list of all patents, publications, applications, or other relevant information. U.S. patents and U.S. patent application publications should be listed separately from other documents. Each page of this list must include the application number, a column for the examiner's initials, and a heading clearly indicating that it is an IDS.

2. Copies of Documents: The applicant must provide legible copies of foreign patents, publications, portions of unpublished U.S. applications, and any other relevant information that caused these documents to be listed. U.S. patents and published U.S. patent applications are exempt from this requirement unless the USPTO specifically requests them.

3. Non-English Documents: For any document not in English, the applicant must provide a concise explanation of its relevance and, if available, an English translation. The explanation can be separate or incorporated into the application.

Subsection (b): This section details how documents in the IDS must be identified:

1. U.S. Patents: These must be identified by the inventor, patent number, and issue date.

2. U.S. Patent Application Publications: These should be identified by the applicant, publication number, and publication date.

3. U.S. Applications: These must be identified by the inventor, application number, and filing date.

4. Foreign Patents and Applications: These should be identified by the issuing country or patent office, document number, and publication date.

5. Publications: These must be identified by the publisher, author, title, relevant pages, and date and place of publication.

Subsection (c): If multiple documents in the IDS are substantively cumulative, meaning they provide the same information, the applicant can submit only one of these documents, along with a statement indicating that the others are cumulative.

Subsection (d): A copy of any document listed in an IDS must be provided even if it was previously submitted in an earlier related application. However, this requirement can be waived if the earlier application is properly referenced in the new IDS and the earlier IDS complied with the regulations.

These requirements are intended to ensure that the patent examiner has all relevant information necessary to perform a thorough examination of the patent application.

Header

"use as many sheets as necessary": if the list of documents (e.g., patents, publications, applications) that you need to disclose is too long to fit on a single page, you should continue listing them on additional sheets. There is no limit to the number of pages you can use; you should include all relevant information necessary for the patent examiner's review.

Here's an explanation of each field under "Complete if Known" in the Information Disclosure Statement (IDS) form:

Application Number: It helps identify the specific patent application to which the IDS is related. If you know this number, you should enter it here (herewith).

Filing Date: This refers to the date on which the patent application was officially submitted to the USPTO. The filing date is critical because it can affect the priority of the patent rights (herewith).

First Named Inventor: This field is for the name of the first inventor listed on the patent application. The first named inventor is often used as a reference point for the application.

Art Unit: The Art Unit is a division within the USPTO that handles specific types of patent applications based on their subject matter. Each Art Unit specializes in certain areas of technology (To be determined).

Examiner Name: This is the name of the USPTO patent examiner assigned to review your application. If you know the name of the examiner, you should include it in this field.

Attorney Docket Number: This is an internal reference number used by the attorney or law firm handling the patent application. It helps them track and manage the case internally.

U.S. PATENTS and U.S.PATENT APPLICATION PUBLICATIONS: The fields apply to both

Examiner Initial: A space for the examiner to initial, indicating they have reviewed the cited document.

Cite No: A sequential number assigned to each cited reference.

Patent Number: The unique number assigned to the U.S. patent.

Kind Code: A code indicating the type of document (e.g., A for published application, B for granted patent).

Issue Date: The date on which the patent was officially granted.

Name of Patentee or Applicant of cited Document: The name of the person or entity to whom the patent was granted or who applied for it.

Pages, Columns, Lines where Relevant Passages or Relevant Figures Appear: Specific locations within the patent document where relevant information can be found.

FOREIGN PATENT DOCUMENTS:

Examiner Initial: A space for the examiner to initial, indicating they have reviewed the cited document.

Cite No: A sequential number assigned to each cited reference.

Foreign Document Number: The unique number assigned to the foreign patent document.

Country Code: A two-letter code representing the country or regional office that issued the patent document (e.g., US for the United States, EP for the European Patent Office).

Kind Code: A code indicating the type of document (similar to U.S. patents, e.g., A for application, B for granted patent).

Publication Date: The date on which the foreign patent document was published.

Name of Patentee or Applicant of cited Document: The name of the person or entity to whom the patent was granted or who applied for it.

Pages, Columns, Lines where Relevant Passages or Relevant Figures Appear: Specific locations within the foreign patent document where relevant information can be found.

T5: Indicates if the document is a translation or if it was originally in a language other than English. Use "T" if there is a translation provided and leave it blank if the document is in english or mark "N" if no translation is provided.

Non-patent literature documents

Examiner Initials: Provide the initials of the examiner who will review this document.

Cite No: Assign a citation number for the document, used for reference in the list.

Include name of the author: Write the name of the author in CAPITAL LETTERS.

Title of the article: Enter the title of the article if applicable.

Title of the item: Specify the type of publication such as book, magazine, journal, serial, symposium, catalog, etc.

Date: Include the publication date of the document.

Pages(s): Indicate the specific pages of the document that are relevant.

Volume-Issue Number(s): Provide the volume and issue numbers if applicable.

Publisher: Name the publisher of the document.

City and/or Country where published: State the city and country where the document was published.

T5: Same as in the above section.

EXAMINER SIGNATURE

Examiner Signature: This field is where the patent examiner signs to acknowledge receipt and review of the IDS. The signature confirms that the examiner has seen the listed references and information.

Date Considered: This field is for entering the date when the examiner reviewed the IDS. It provides a record of when the information was considered in the examination process.

Certificate of Mailing or Transmission under 37 CFR 1.8

Correspondence required to be filed within a specific time frame at the USPTO is considered timely if it is mailed or transmitted before the deadline. The correspondence must be properly addressed and sent through first class mail via the U.S. Postal Service, by facsimile to the USPTO, or through the Office's electronic filing system (EFS-Web). Each piece of correspondence must include a certificate stating the date of mailing or transmission.

The procedure described does not apply to certain filings, such as national patent applications, papers for Patent Trial and Appeal Board cases, international applications, and other specific submissions like declarations of abandonment, redacted applications, and third-party submissions. If the USPTO does not receive the correspondence after a reasonable time, the sender must inform the USPTO promptly, resend the correspondence with the original certificate, and include a statement attesting to the original timely filing. Additional evidence, such as a facsimile transmission report or an electronic filing system receipt, may be required to support the statement.

This process ensures that correspondence is considered timely filed, even if it is lost or not received by the USPTO.

I hereby certify that this correspondence is being:

Deposited with the United States Postal Service (USPS): This field certifies that the correspondence has been mailed using first-class mail through the USPS.

Date: The sender must enter the date on which the correspondence is being mailed.

Facsimile Transmitted to the USPTO: This field certifies that the correspondence has been sent via fax to the USPTO.

Transmitted by the USPTO Patent Electronic Filing System: This field certifies that the correspondence has been sent through the USPTO's electronic filing system, which is a secure online platform for filing patent documents.

Signature

The signature on this form can be provided by either the applicant (inventor) or their attorney/agent. The purpose of the signature is to certify the method of mailing or transmission of the correspondence to the USPTO.

The date field next to the signature should reflect the day the form is signed and the correspondence is either mailed, transmitted by facsimile, or submitted via the USPTO's electronic filing system.

Note: Each paper must have its own certificate of mailing or transmission, or this certificate must identify each submitted paper.

Chapter 3

HOW TO PREPARE YOUR APPLICATION DOCUMENTS

CHAPTER 3: HOW TO PREPARE YOUR APPLICATION DOCUMENTS

35 U.S.C Section 111 (a) - Application

The application must be written or authorized to be made by the inventor(s). This application must include:

Contents:

35 U.S.C. Section 112 - Specification

The specification must include a written description of the invention and the method and process for making and using it, in terms that are sufficiently complete, clear, concise, and exact to enable anyone skilled in the relevant field, or in the closest related field, to make and use the invention. Additionally, it must disclose the best mode contemplated by the inventor(s) for carrying out the invention. The specification should conclude with one or more claims that particularly point out and claim what the inventor(s) regard as the invention.

The new formatting requires the use of paragraph numbers in brackets ([0001], [0002], etc.) as opposed to line numbers.

The following guidelines illustrate the preferred layout for the specification of a utility application. These guidelines are suggested for the applicant's use.

Arrangement of the Specification

As provided in 37 CFR 1.77(b), the specification of a utility application should include the following sections in order. Each of the lettered items should appear in upper case, without underlining or bold type, as a section heading. If no text follows the section heading, the phrase "Not Applicable" should follow the section heading:

(a) TITLE OF THE INVENTION.

(b) CROSS-REFERENCE TO RELATED APPLICATIONS.

(g) BACKGROUND OF THE INVENTION.

(1) Field of Invention.

(2) Description of Related Art including information disclosed under 37 CFR 1.97[1] and 1.98[2].

(h) BRIEF SUMMARY OF THE INVENTION.

(i) BRIEF DESCRIPTION OF THE SEVERAL VIEWS OF THE DRAWING(S).

(j) DETAILED DESCRIPTION OF THE INVENTION.

(k) CLAIM OR CLAIMS (commencing on a separate sheet).

(l) ABSTRACT OF THE DISCLOSURE (commencing on a separate sheet).

(m) SEQUENCE LISTING. (See MPEP § 2422.03[3] and 37 CFR 1.821[4]-1.825[5]). A "Sequence Listing" is required on paper if the application discloses a nucleotide or amino acid sequence as defined in 37 CFR 1.821(a)[6] and if the required "Sequence Listing" is not submitted as an electronic document either on read-only optical disc or as a text file via the patent electronic system.

Content of Specification

(a) TITLE OF THE INVENTION: See 37 CFR 1.72(a)[7] and MPEP § 606[8]. The title of the invention should be placed at the top of the first page of the specification unless the title is provided in an

---

1. https://www.uspto.gov/web/offices/pac/mpep/mpep-9020-appx-r.html#d0e321609

2. https://www.uspto.gov/web/offices/pac/mpep/mpep-9020-appx-r.html#d0e321738

3. https://www.uspto.gov/web/offices/pac/mpep/s2422.html#d0e245191

4. https://www.uspto.gov/web/offices/pac/mpep/mpep-9020-appx-r.html#d0e333653

5. https://www.uspto.gov/web/offices/pac/mpep/mpep-9020-appx-r.html#d0e334511

6. https://www.uspto.gov/web/offices/pac/mpep/mpep-9020-appx-r.html#d0e333661

7. https://www.uspto.gov/web/offices/pac/mpep/mpep-9020-appx-r.html#d0e320224

8. https://www.uspto.gov/web/offices/pac/mpep/s606.html#d0e41684

application data sheet. The title of the invention should be brief but technically accurate and descriptive, preferably from two to seven words. It may not contain more than 500 characters.

(b) CROSS-REFERENCES TO RELATED APPLICATIONS: See 37 CFR 1.78[9] and MPEP § 211[10]

(g) BACKGROUND OF THE INVENTION: See MPEP § 608.01(c)[11]. The specification should set forth the Background of the Invention in two parts:

(1) Field of the Invention: A statement of the field of art to which the invention pertains. This statement may include a paraphrasing of the applicable U.S. patent classification definitions of the subject matter of the claimed invention. This item may also be titled "Technical Field."

(2) Description of the Related Art including information disclosed under 37 CFR 1.97 and 37 CFR 1.98: A description of the related art known to the applicant and including, if applicable, references to specific related art and problems involved in the prior art which are solved by the applicant's invention. This item may also be titled "Background Art."

The USPTO recommends breaking down the "Background of the Invention" into two parts: (1) Field of the Invention, which briefly describes the field related to the invention, and (2) Description of the Related Art, which discusses the state of the prior art known to the applicant, including references to specific prior works.

However, identifying and discussing specific prior art can be risky. Once something is admitted as prior art, it becomes part of the prior art. Since the 2007 KSR v. Teleflex decision, it's become

---

9.   https://www.uspto.gov/web/offices/pac/mpep/
      mpep-9020-appx-r.html#aia_d0e320662

10.   https://www.uspto.gov/web/offices/pac/mpep/s211.html#ch200_d1ff71_1bd25_18b

11.   https://www.uspto.gov/web/offices/pac/mpep/s608.html#d0e44561

easier for patent examiners to reject claims as obvious. As a result, "Backgrounds" have become very short. Only in rare cases, where there is a strong reason, should the Background be anything other than brief and vague. Inventors and those new to patent law should aim to keep it concise and non-specific.

(h) BRIEF SUMMARY OF THE INVENTION: See MPEP § 608.01(d)[12]. A brief summary or general statement of the invention as set forth in 37 CFR 1.73[13]. The summary is separate and distinct from the abstract and is directed toward the invention rather than the disclosure as a whole. The summary may point out the advantages of the invention or how it solves problems previously existent in the prior art (and preferably indicated in the Background of the Invention). In chemical cases, it should point out in general terms the utility of the invention. If possible, the nature and gist of the invention or the inventive concept should be set forth. Objects of the invention should be treated briefly and only to the extent that they contribute to an understanding of the invention.

(i) BRIEF DESCRIPTION OF THE SEVERAL VIEWS OF THE DRAWING(S): See MPEP § 608.01(f)[14]. A reference to and brief description of the drawing(s) as set forth in 37 CFR 1.74[15].

(j) DETAILED DESCRIPTION OF THE INVENTION: See MPEP § 608.01(g)[16]. A description of the preferred embodiment(s) of the invention as required in 37 CFR 1.71[17]. The description should be as short and specific as is necessary to describe the invention adequately and accurately. Where elements or groups of elements, compounds, and processes, which are conventional and

---

12.   https://www.uspto.gov/web/offices/pac/mpep/s608.html#d0e44589

13.   https://www.uspto.gov/web/offices/pac/mpep/mpep-9020-appx-r.html#d0e320249

14.   https://www.uspto.gov/web/offices/pac/mpep/s608.html#d0e44626

15.   https://www.uspto.gov/web/offices/pac/mpep/mpep-9020-appx-r.html#d0e320259

16.   https://www.uspto.gov/web/offices/pac/mpep/s608.html#d0e44731

17.   https://www.uspto.gov/web/offices/pac/mpep/mpep-9020-appx-r.html#d0e320131

generally widely known in the field of the invention described, and their exact nature or type is not necessary for an understanding and use of the invention by a person skilled in the art, they should not be described in detail. However, where particularly complicated subject matter is involved or where the elements, compounds, or processes may not be commonly or widely known in the field, the specification should refer to another patent or readily available publication which adequately describes the subject matter.

(k) CLAIM OR CLAIMS: See 37 CFR 1.75[18] and MPEP § 608.01(m)[19]. The claim or claims must commence on a separate sheet or electronic page (37 CFR 1.52(b)(3)[20]). Where a claim sets forth a plurality of elements or steps, each element or step of the claim should be separated by a line indentation. There may be plural indentations to further segregate sub combinations or related steps. See 37 CFR 1.75 [21]and MPEP 608.01(i)[22]-(p)[23].

When drafting the set of claims, it is important to ensure that the total number does not exceed 20 claims, with a maximum of 3 independent claims. Additionally, care should be taken to avoid multiple dependencies within the claims. This approach streamlines the examination process and aligns with best practices for clear and efficient patent prosecution, minimizing potential complications during the examination phase.

(l) ABSTRACT OF THE DISCLOSURE: See 37 CFR 1.72[24](b) and MPEP § 608.01(b)[25]. The abstract is a brief narrative

---

18.   https://www.uspto.gov/web/offices/pac/mpep/mpep-9020-appx-r.html#d0e320269

19.   https://www.uspto.gov/web/offices/pac/mpep/s608.html#d0e45061

20.   https://www.uspto.gov/web/offices/pac/mpep/mpep-9020-appx-r.html#d0e318439

21.   https://www.uspto.gov/web/offices/pac/mpep/mpep-9020-appx-r.html#d0e320269

22.   https://www.uspto.gov/web/offices/pac/mpep/s608.html#d0e44872

23.   https://www.uspto.gov/web/offices/pac/mpep/s608.html#d0e46258

24.   https://www.uspto.gov/web/offices/pac/mpep/mpep-9020-appx-r.html#d0e320224

25.   https://www.uspto.gov/web/offices/pac/mpep/s608.html#d0e44136

of the disclosure as a whole, as concise as the disclosure permits, in a single paragraph preferably not exceeding 150 words, commencing on a separate sheet following the claims. In an international application which has entered the national stage (37 CFR 1.491(b)[26]), the applicant need not submit an abstract commencing on a separate sheet if an abstract was published with the international application under PCT Article 21[27]. The abstract that appears on the cover page of the pamphlet published by the International Bureau (IB) of the World Intellectual Property Organization (WIPO) is the abstract that will be used by the USPTO. See MPEP § 1893.03(e)[28].

Form: Claims should be drafted based on the technical features necessary to define the product/method, and each claim determines and defines the legal scope of protection for the invention. The USPTO requires the applicant to 'claim' and describe the 'object' of the invention. From the claims, the USPTO can determine whether the invention is patentable.

A claim may be drafted in an independent form or, if applicable, in a dependent or multiple dependent form.

In general, the USPTO allows two types of patent claims: independent and dependent. An independent claim is one that, as written, includes all the limitations necessary to fully define the invention. All patent applications must have at least one independent claim. Conversely, a dependent claim refers to a previous claim in the application.

Independent Claims: An independent claim is a claim that defines the invention fully on its own. It contains all the necessary

---

26. https://www.uspto.gov/web/offices/pac/mpep/
mpep-9020-appx-r.html#aia_d0e329149

27. https://www.uspto.gov/web/offices/pac/mpep/mpep-9025-appx-t.html#d0e363622

28. https://www.uspto.gov/web/offices/pac/mpep/s1893.html#d0e192440

limitations to describe the invention without referencing any other claim.

Dependent Claims: A dependent claim must refer to a previously established claim and then specify an additional limitation of the claimed subject matter. A dependent claim incorporates by reference all the limitations of the claim it refers to. This is useful to provide a range of coverage.

Multiple Dependent Claims: A multiple dependent claim must refer, only alternatively, to more than one previously established claim and then specify an additional limitation of the claimed subject matter. A multiple dependent claim cannot serve as the basis for any other multiple dependent claim. It is interpreted to incorporate by reference all the limitations of the particular claims to which it refers.

Example of Independent Method Claims:

"1. *A method of making a ball, comprising: forming an inner sphere by forming an outer shell with a fluid mass center; forming a plurality of core parts; arranging and joining the core parts around the inner sphere to form an assembled core; molding a cover around the assembled core*"

Example of Dependent Method Claims:

" 2. *The method of claim 1, further comprising molding nonplanar mating surfaces on the core parts, wherein the core parts comprises meshing the mating surfaces.*"

Example of multiple dependent claim:

"3. *The method described in either Claim 1 or Claim 2, with an added step that the outer shell is made from a thermoplastic material.*"

Types of claims – invention categories

Product - A claim that is directed to elements that can be:

Active (Device/Apparatus/Machine)

Non-active (Composition of Matter or Article of Manufacture)

Combination thereof

Method (Process) - A claim that describes/ defines a series of acts or steps for performing a desired function or accomplishing an intended result

How to write a claim

Preamble: Every claim needs a preamble, which is the introductory phrase of a claim. The general rule is that the preamble of a claim does not limit the scope of the claim, but it should avoid functional language. For example:

Draft: "A shovel..."

Instead of: "A shovel for digging..."

Transitional Phrase: Every claim needs a transitional phrase. The most common transitions are: "comprising," "consisting essentially of," and "consisting of." Determine whether the claim is "open," "closed," or "partially open." In other words, assess the extent to which a claim is limited solely to those elements recited in the body of the claim.

Transitional Phrases

1. "Comprising"

- Meaning: Open-ended; includes the listed elements but allows for additional, unlisted elements.

- Example: A claim describing a safety razor blade unit "comprising" certain blades can include more blades than listed.

2. "Consisting of"

- Meaning: Closed; only includes the specified elements and excludes any others.

- Example: A claim stating a kit "consisting of" certain chemicals is not infringed by a kit with additional items unrelated to the chemicals.

3. "Consisting essentially of"

- Meaning: Limits to the specified elements plus those that do not materially affect the key characteristics of the invention.

- Example: A composition "consisting essentially of" specific components allows for the inclusion of additional components as long as they don't change the fundamental properties of the composition.

4. Other Phrases

- "Having": Typically open-ended, allowing for additional elements unless specified otherwise.

- "Composed of": Interpreted based on context; can be either closed or open-ended depending on the case.

*"Claim: A widget **comprising a** housing, **a** circuit board, and **a** display screen, wherein the housing encloses the circuit board and the display screen."*

A lack of clarity may arise when a claim refers to "said object," "an object," or "the object," when the claim does not contain any or a limitation of an object, and when it is unclear to which element the limitation refers.

Example of a claim according to the general standard:

"The invention of claim 1 further comprising D, which is [insert connection/relation] "

"The method of claim 1, wherein forming the inner sphere comprises freezing a sphere of a fluid"

A claimed invention must be novel, non-obvious, and useful; moreover, it should not be too broad (it may lack value) nor too specific (it may not be patentable).

Example of an overly broad claim

"*Claim 1. A vehicle comprising: a frame body; a first and second front wheel and a first and second back wheel aligned and spaced from the first and second front wheel, each wheel rotatably connected to the frame body; a seat connected to the frame body; and a removable top portion made of cloth connected to the frame body.*"

Example of an overly specific claim

"*Claim 1. A vehicle comprising: a motor; a yellow frame body including a plurality of hinged doors; a first and second front wheel and a first and second back wheel and aligned and spaced from the first and second front wheel, each wheel rotatably connected to the frame body and made of rubber; a seat connected to the frame body; a plurality of glass windows connected to the frame body; two red lights connected to the frame body; two metal bumpers connected to the frame body; and a removable top portion made of cloth.*"

Current Regulations on Drafting Claims

2173 - Claims must particularly point out and distinctly claim the invention

Optimizing patent quality by providing clear notice to the public of the boundaries of the inventive subject matter protected by a patent grant fosters innovation and competitiveness. The Office recognizes that issuing patents with clear and definite claim language is a key component to enhancing the quality of patents and raising confidence in the patent process.

The primary purpose of this requirement of definiteness of claim language is to ensure that the scope of the claims is clear so the public is informed of the boundaries of what constitutes infringement of the patent. A secondary purpose is to provide a clear measure of what the inventor or a joint inventor regards as the invention so that it can be determined whether the claimed invention meets all the criteria for patentability and whether the specification meets the criteria of 35 U.S.C. 112

It is of utmost importance that patents issue with definite claims that clearly and precisely inform persons skilled in the art of the boundaries of protected subject matter. Therefore, claims that do not meet this standard must be rejected under 35 U.S.C. 112(b)

The claim language must be "definite" to comply with35 U.S.C. 112. Conversely, a claim that does not comply with this requirement, is considered "indefinite."

Defined: A claim is "defined" if it is clear about what is covered and the boundaries of the invention.

Indefinite: A claim is "indefinite" if it is not clear, meaning that it is not well understood what is being claimed.

2173.05 (g) Functional Language

A claim term is functional when it recites a feature "by what it does rather than by what it is" (e.g., as evidenced by its specific structure or specific ingredients). There is nothing inherently wrong with defining some part of an invention in functional terms. Functional language does not, in and of itself, render a claim improper.

In fact, 35 U.S.C. 112(f)[1] and pre-AIA 35 U.S.C. 112[2], sixth paragraph, expressly authorize a form of functional claiming (means- (or step-) plus- function claim limitations discussed in MPEP § 2181[3] *et seq.*). Functional language may also be employed to limit the claims without using the means-plus-function format.

A functional limitation must be evaluated and considered, just like any other limitation of the claim, for what it fairly conveys to a person of ordinary skill in the pertinent art in the context in which it is used. A functional limitation is often used in association with an element, ingredient, or step of a process to define a particular capability or purpose that is served by the recited element, ingredient or step

2173.05 (d) Exemplary claims

Description of examples or preferences is properly set forth in the specification rather than the claims. If stated in the claims, examples and preferences may lead to confusion over the intended scope of a claim. In those instances where it is not clear whether the claimed narrower range is a limitation, a rejection under 35 U.S.C. 112(b)[4], second paragraph should be made. The examiner should analyze whether the metes and bounds of the claim are clearly set

---

1.   https://www.uspto.gov/web/offices/pac/mpep/

mpep-9015-appx-l.html#al_d1d85b_2ae7b_ec

2.   https://www.uspto.gov/web/offices/pac/mpep/mpep-9015-appx-l.html#d0e302824

3.   https://www.uspto.gov/web/offices/pac/mpep/s2181.html#d0e219279

4.   https://www.uspto.gov/web/offices/pac/mpep/

mpep-9015-appx-l.html#al_d1d85b_2ae65_215

forth. Note that the mere use of the phrase "such as" or "for example" in a claim does not by itself render the claim indefinite.

Examples of claim language which have been held to be indefinite because the intended scope of the claim was unclear are:

(A) "R is halogen, for example, chlorine";

(B) "material such as rock wool or asbestos"

(C) "lighter hydrocarbons, such, for example, as the vapors or gas produced"

Example A: "R is a halogen, for example, chlorine" – Here, the use of "for example" does not clearly define whether the halogen must be chlorine or any other halogen.

Example B: "material such as rock wool or asbestos" – The term "such as" does not clarify whether it refers only to these specific materials or if other similar materials are also included.

Example C: "lighter hydrocarbons, such as the vapors or gas produced" – It is unclear which specific hydrocarbons are covered.

2173.05 - Breadth is not indefiniteness

Breadth of a claim is not to be equated with indefiniteness. ("Breadth is not indefiniteness."). A broad claim is not indefinite merely because it encompasses a wide scope of subject matter provided the scope is clearly defined. But a claim is indefinite when the boundaries of the protected subject matter are not clearly delineated and the scope is unclear. For example, a genus claim that covers multiple species is broad, but is not indefinite because of its breadth, which is otherwise clear. But a genus claim that could be interpreted in such a way that it is not clear which species are covered would be indefinite (e.g., because there is more than one reasonable interpretation of what species are included in the claim).

2173.05 (a) New Terminology

The meaning of every term used in a claim should be apparent from the prior art or from the specification and drawings at the time the application is filed. Claim language may not be "ambiguous, vague, incoherent, opaque, or otherwise unclear in describing and defining the claimed invention."

. Applicants need not confine themselves to the terminology used in the prior art, but are required to make clear and precise the terms that are used to define the invention whereby the metes and bounds of the claimed invention can be ascertained. During patent examination, the pending claims must be given the broadest reasonable interpretation consistent with the specification.

Courts have recognized that it is not only permissible, but often desirable, to use new terms that are frequently more precise in describing and defining the new invention. *In reFisher,* 427 F.2d 833, 166 USPQ 18 (CCPA 1970). Although it is difficult to compare the claimed invention with the prior art when new terms are used that do not appear in the prior art, this does not make the new terms indefinite.

New terms are often used when a new technology is in its infancy or is rapidly evolving. The requirements for clarity and precision must be balanced with the limitations of the language and the science. If the claims, read in light of the specification, reasonably apprise those skilled in the art both of the utilization and scope of the invention, and if the language is as precise as the subject matter permits, the statute (35 U.S.C. 112(b)[5] or pre-AIA 35 U.S.C. 112[6], second paragraph) demands no more.

2173.05 (b) Relative Terminology

Terms like "about," "substantially," or "approximately" in a patent claim aren't automatically unclear or "indefinite." These terms are fine if someone skilled in the field can understand what they mean by looking at the rest of the patent.

---

5. https://www.uspto.gov/web/offices/pac/mpep/
mpep-9015-appx-l.html#al_d1d85b_2ae65_215

6. https://www.uspto.gov/web/offices/pac/mpep/mpep-9015-appx-l.html#d0e302824

For example, if a claim says "the material should be heated to a temperature *about* 200 degrees," it's not indefinite if the patent explains that "about 200 degrees" means anywhere between 195 and 205 degrees. Even though it's not an exact number, the explanation gives enough guidance to understand what "about" means in this context.

During prosecution, an applicant may also overcome an indefiniteness rejection by providing evidence that the meaning of the term of degree can be ascertained by one of ordinary skill in the art when reading the disclosure. For example, in *Enzo Biochem,* the applicant submitted a declaration under 37 CFR 1.132[7] showing examples that met the claim limitation and examples that did not

Reference to an object that is variable may render a claim indefinite

Imagine you have a patent claim that says:

"The device includes a handle attached to the object."

If it's not clear what "the object" is or how exactly the handle is attached to it, the claim could be considered indefinite. This is because the examiner wouldn't be able to determine the exact relationship between the handle and the object. For instance, if "the object" could be a box, a rod, or any other shape, and "attached" could mean glued, screwed, or something else, the claim isn't specific enough. Without clarity on what "the object" is or how the attachment is done, the claim could have multiple interpretations, making it indefinite.

Approximations

About": The term "about" can be definite if the patent explains its context. For example, in one case, "exceeding about 10% per second" was clear because it could be measured with a stopwatch. However, in another case, "at least about" was unclear because the range wasn't specified, making the claim indefinite.

---

7.   https://www.uspto.gov/web/offices/pac/mpep/mpep-9020-appx-r.html#d0e323552

"Essentially": The term "essentially" was considered definite when it described a material "essentially free of alkali metal" because the patent provided enough detail to distinguish between minor impurities and key ingredients.

"Similar": The term "similar" was found indefinite when used in claims like "for high-pressure cleaning units or similar apparatus" because it wasn't clear what "similar" meant, making it unclear what the patent covered.

"Substantially": The term "substantially" is broad but can be definite if the patent provides guidelines. For instance, "substantially equal illumination patterns" was clear because someone skilled in the field would understand what "substantially equal" meant.

"Type": Adding "type" to a term can make it indefinite. For example, "ZSM-5-type aluminosilicate zeolites" was unclear because it wasn't clear what "type" referred to, making it hard to determine the exact scope of the claim.

Subjective Terms in Patent Claims

When a patent claim uses a subjective term (like "aesthetically pleasing"), it must have an objective standard or guideline in the specification to define that term. If the claim relies on personal judgment without clear guidance, it may be considered indefinite.

For example, in the case of *Datamize*, the claim described a computer interface with an "aesthetically pleasing look and feel." This term was found to be indefinite because what is "aesthetically pleasing" could vary from person to person, and the patent didn't provide a clear standard to define it.

To avoid indefiniteness, applicants can remove the subjective term or provide evidence that someone skilled in the field would understand the term based on the patent's description. However, just giving examples isn't always enough to make the term definite.

2173.05 (c) Numerical Ranges and Amount Limitation

I. NARROW AND BROADER RANGES IN THE SAME CLAIM

Use of a narrow numerical range that falls within a broader range in the same claim may render the claim indefinite when the boundaries of the claim are not discernible. Description of examples and preferences is properly set forth in the specification rather than in a single claim. A narrower range or preferred embodiment may also be set forth in another independent claim or in a dependent claim. If stated in a single claim, examples and preferences lead to confusion over the intended scope of the claim. In those instances where it is not clear whether the claimed narrower range is a limitation, a rejection under 35 U.S.C. 112(b[1], second paragraph should be made. The Examiner should analyze whether the metes and bounds of the claim are clearly set forth. Examples of claim language which have been held to be indefinite are (A) "a temperature of between 45 and 78 degrees Celsius, preferably between 50 and 60 degrees Celsius"; and (B) "a predetermined quantity, for example, the maximum capacity."

While a single claim that includes both a broad and a narrower range may be indefinite, it is not improper under 35 U.S.C. 112(b)[2], second paragraph, to present a dependent claim that sets forth a narrower range for an element than the range set forth in the claim from which it depends. For example, if claim 1 reads "A circuit ... wherein the resistance is 70-150 ohms." and claim 2 reads "The

---

1.   https://www.uspto.gov/web/offices/pac/mpep/

mpep-9015-appx-l.html#al_d1d85b_2ae65_215

2.   https://www.uspto.gov/web/offices/pac/mpep/

mpep-9015-appx-l.html#al_d1d85b_2ae65_215

circuit of claim 1 wherein the resistance is 70-100 ohms.", then claim 2 should not be rejected as indefinite.

II. OPEN-ENDED NUMERICAL RANGES

Open-ended numerical ranges should be carefully analyzed for definiteness. For example, when an independent claim recites a composition comprising "at least 20% sodium" and a dependent claim sets forth specific amounts of non sodium ingredients which add up to 100%, apparently to the exclusion of sodium, an ambiguity is created with regard to the "at least" limitation (unless the percentages of the non sodium ingredients are based on the weight of the non sodium ingredients). On the other hand, the court held that a composition claimed to have a theoretical content greater than 100% (i.e., 20-80% of A, 20-80% of B and 1-25% of C) was not indefinite simply because the claims may be read in theory to include compositions that are impossible in fact to formulate. It was observed that subject matter which cannot exist in fact can neither anticipate nor infringe a claim. *In reKroekel,* 504 F.2d 1143, 183 USPQ 610 (CCPA 1974).

2173.05 (f) Reference to limitation in another claim

A claim which makes reference to a preceding claim to define a limitation is an acceptable claim construction which should not necessarily be rejected as improper. For example, claims which read: "The product produced by the method of claim 1." or "A method of producing ethanol comprising contacting amylose with the culture of claim 1 under the following conditions ....." are not indefinite

2173.05 (e) Antecedent Basis

Antecedent basis refers to the requirement that all words in a claim must be explained in the specification so that the words can be clearly understood. Otherwise, the claim will be rejected or invalidated for being indefinite.For example, if you use the word "valve" in the claim, the detailed description must explain whether that is a liquid valve or a heart valve if it cannot be determined from the context of the claim or the detailed description.

The lack of clarity could arise where a claim refers to "said lever" or "the lever," where the claim contains no earlier recitation or limitation of a lever and where it would be unclear as to what element the limitation was making reference. Similarly, if two different levers are recited earlier in the claim, the recitation of "said lever" in the same or subsequent claim would be unclear where it is uncertain which of the two levers was intended.

Obviously, however, the failure to provide explicit antecedent basis for terms does not always render a claim indefinite. If the scope of a claim would be reasonably ascertainable by those skilled in the art, then the claim is not indefinite.

2173.05 (m) - Prolix

Claims are rejected as prolix when they contain long recitations that the metes and bounds of the claimed subject matter cannot be determined.

2173.05 (n) - Multiplicity

Where, in view of the nature and scope of applicant's invention, applicant presents an unreasonable number of claims which are repetitious and multiplied, the net result of which is to confuse rather than to clarify, a rejection on undue multiplicity based on 35 U.S.C. 112(b)[1]

---

1. https://www.uspto.gov/web/offices/pac/mpep/

mpep-9015-appx-l.html#al_d1d85b_2ae65_215

2173.05 (q) - "Use" Claims

"Use" claims that do not purport to claim a process, machine, manufacture, or composition of matter fail to comply with 35 U.S.C. 101[1]. For example, a claim which read: "a process for using monoclonal antibodies of claim 4 to isolate and purify human fibroblast interferon" was held to be indefinite because it merely recites a use without any active, positive steps delimiting how this use is actually practiced.

---

1. https://www.uspto.gov/web/offices/pac/mpep/mpep-9015-appx-l.html#d0e302376

2173.05 (r) - Omnibus Claims

Some applications are filed with an omnibus claim which reads as follows: A device substantially as shown and described. This claim should be rejected. because it is indefinite in that it fails to point out what is included or excluded by the claim language.

2173,05 (s) - Reference to figures and tables

Where possible, claims are to be complete in themselves. Incorporation by reference to a specific figure or table "is permitted only in exceptional circumstances where there is no practical way to define the invention in words and where it is more concise to incorporate by reference than duplicating a drawing or table into the claim. Incorporation by reference is a necessity doctrine, not for applicant's convenience."

2173.05 (t) - Chemical Formula

Claims to chemical compounds and compositions containing chemical compounds often use formulas that depict the chemical structure of the compound. These structures should not be considered indefinite nor speculative in the absence of evidence that the assigned formula is in error.

2143.03 - All claims limitations must be considered.

The writing of the claims and the limitations plays a crucial role as to understand to what extent your invention/method would be covered on what can or cannot do a company/person (infringement). Dependent claims can add additional structure that is not in the independent claim.

All words in a claim must be considered in judging the patentability of that claim against the prior art."

Examiners must consider all claim limitations when determining patentability of an invention over the prior art. The subject matter of a properly constructed claim is defined by the terms that limit the scope of the claim when given their broadest reasonable interpretation.

For example:

Claim 2: The car of claim 1, further comprising a rain guard attached to said roof *(additional structure)*

Since claim 2 comes from claim 1, it makes it even more limiting (protected) claim. It further limits or narrows the scope and it is useful to provide a range of coverage.

2111-Claim Interpretation; Broadest Reasonable Interpretation

During patent examination, the pending claims must be "given their broadest reasonable interpretation consistent with the specification. Because applicant has the opportunity to amend the claims during prosecution, giving a claim its broadest reasonable interpretation will reduce the possibility that the claim, once issued, will be interpreted more broadly than is justified.

The Patent and Trademark Office ("PTO") determines the scope of claims in patent applications not solely on the basis of the claim language, but upon giving claims their broadest reasonable construction "in light of the specification as it would be interpreted by one of ordinary skill in the art."

Imagine you have a patent application for a new type of "door lock" and the claims in the application are written as follows:

Claim 1: A door lock comprising a "mechanical locking mechanism."

Specification: The specification describes the door lock in detail, explaining that it uses gears and levers to lock the door. It also describes that this locking mechanism can be used in residential or commercial settings.

Interpretation Process:

1. Broadest Reasonable Interpretation:

○ The term "mechanical locking mechanism" in Claim 1 should be interpreted broadly. This means that the term should be understood in its widest sense, covering various types of mechanical systems that could lock a door, not just the specific types described in the specification.

2. Consistency with the Specification:

○ Even though the interpretation is broad, it must still be consistent with what is described in the specification. The term should not cover locking mechanisms that are purely electronic if the specification only describes mechanical systems.

CONCLUSION.—The specification shall conclude with one or more claims particularly pointing out and distinctly claiming the subject matter which the inventor or a joint inventor regards as the invention.

(B) a drawing as prescribed by section 113; [1]and

Most patent applications contain drawings. The applicant must submit a drawing when necessary for the understanding of the subject matter sought to be patented. The drawings must show each feature of the invention as specified in the claims. This means that every important feature of your invention must be shown in your patent drawings.

Someone reading the patent and viewing the drawings must understand how your invention works in order to manufacture and develop your invention. Where the nature of the subject matter permits its illustration by drawings and the applicant has not submitted them, the Director may require their submission within a period of less than two months from the date of dispatch of a notice to that effect.

Just as drawings may be submitted when filing the application, there is also the possibility of adding photographs. Photographs are generally not allowed in utility or design patent applications, but the USPTO will accept photographs in these types of patents or color drawings if they are the only feasible means of illustrating the claimed subject matter.

By a micro entity (§ 1.29): $28.00

By a small entity (§ 1.27(a)): 56.00

By other than a small or micro entity: 140.00

§ 1.84—for accepting color drawings or photographs.

§ 1.91—for entry of a model or exhibit.

§ 1.102(d)—to make an application special.

§ 1.138(c)—to expressly abandon an application to avoid publication.

§ 1.313—to withdraw an application from issue.

§ 1.314—to defer issuance of a patent.

---

1.   https://www.uspto.gov/web/offices/pac/mpep/
mpep-9015-appx-l.html#d0e302850

<u>General specifications on image requirements:</u>

Identification of Drawings: Each drawing must include the following information in the top margin: the title of the invention, the name of the inventor, and the application or file number (if assigned). If no application number is available, leave that part out.

If you submit new drawings after the application's filing date, label them as "Replacement Sheet" or "New Sheet." If the examiner requests a marked copy of any amended drawing figure, include annotations showing the changes. This marked copy must be clearly labeled as "Annotated Sheet" and should be submitted with the amendment or remarks explaining the changes made.

Graphic forms in drawings: Chemical or mathematical formulas, tables and waveforms are considered drawings. Each chemical or mathematical formula should be labeled as a separate figure, using parentheses where necessary, to show that the information is properly integrated. Each group of waveforms should be presented as a single figure, using a common vertical axis with time extending along the horizontal axis. Each individual waveform should be identified with a separate letter next to the vertical axis.

Views: The drawing must contain as many views as necessary to show the invention. The views may be sectional, front, side, top, internal components, exploded, process steps, before & after or perspective views. Detail views of portions of elements, on a larger scale if necessary, may also be used. All views of the drawing must be grouped together and arranged on the sheet(s) without wasting space, preferably in an upright position, clearly separated from one another, and must not be included in the sheets containing the specifications, claims, or abstract. Views must not be connected by projection lines and must not contain center lines. Waveforms of electrical signals may be connected by dashed lines to show the relative timing of the waveforms.

Perspective View: Starting with a perspective view of the invention as figure 1 quickly provides the reader of your patent application with a quick general understanding of your invention.

A perspective view provides a three dimensional representation of the invention from an angle to showing depth. In contrast an orthogonal view, with provides a two-dimensional representation of a side of the invention.

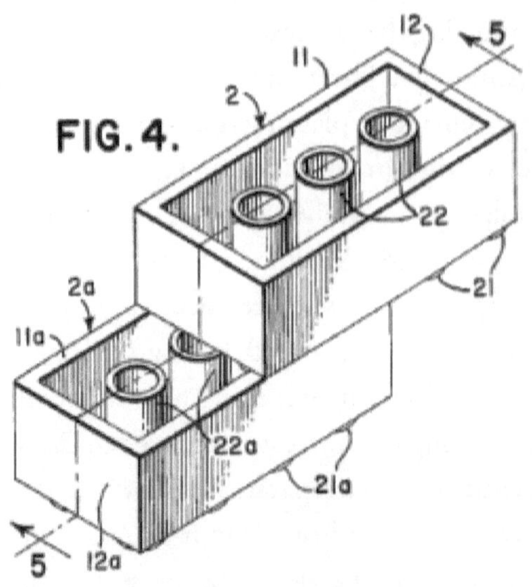

Perspective View Figure.
Source:https://www.waltmire.com/2016/02/19/patent-drawings-introduction/

Sectional Views: A sectional view can reveal hidden internal components or intricate details that are not visible in external views.

Indicate the cutting plane on the view with a broken line, labeled with numerals and arrows showing sight direction. Use hatching with regularly spaced lines at about 45° to show cut sections. Hatching should not obscure reference characters. Different materials should have different hatching patterns.

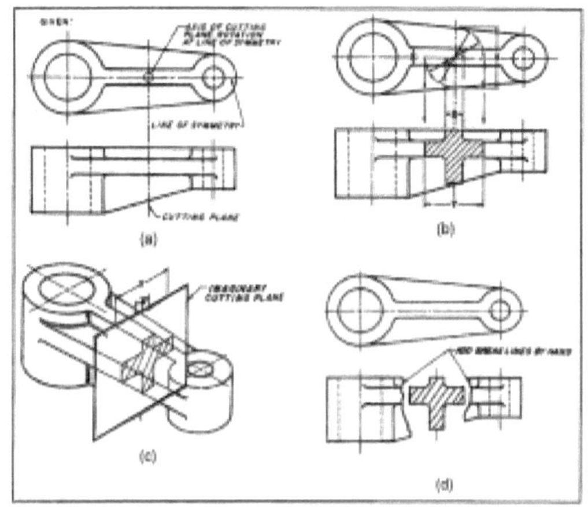

Figure 6.9: Revolved section
Source: Goetsch, Nelson & Chalk, Technical drawing: Fundamental, CAD & Design

Sectional View Figure.
Source: https://wan7097.blogspot.com/2016/09/sectional-view-type-of-sectional-view.html

Exploded Views: Exploded views showing the assembly order with parts separated by brackets are allowed.

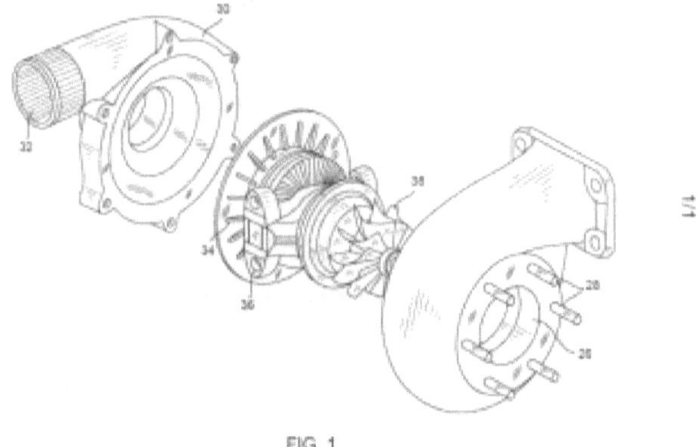

FIG. 1

Exploded View Figure.
Source: https://boldip.com/blog/
patent-drawings/#:~:text=Patent%20drawings%20are%20graphic[2]

For example, an exploded view can be invaluable in showing the relationships between different parts (usually mechanical) of the invention, how they are assembled, and how they work together to achieve the intended function.

Front, Side and Top View: These views are taken from only one perspective at a time, and provide details of the invention that might not be seen from the one isometric view.

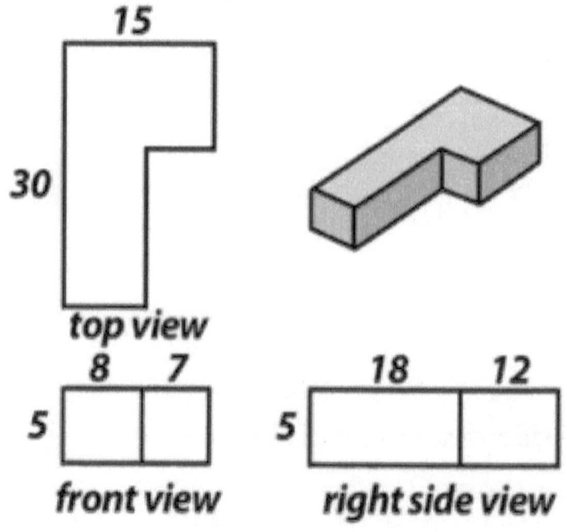

Front, Side and Top View Figure.
Source:https://boldip.com/blog/
patent-drawings/#:~:text=Patent%20drawings%20are%20graphic[3]

2. *https://boldip.com/blog/*
   patent-drawings/#_853ae90f0351324bd73ea615e6487517__4c761f170e016836ff84498202b99827__853ae90
   f0351324bd73ea615e6487517_text_43ec3e5dee6e706af7766fffea512721_Patent_0bcef9c45bd8a48eda1b26eb0
   c61c869_20drawings_0bcef9c45bd8a48eda1b26eb0c61c869_20are_0bcef9c45bd8a48eda1b26eb0c61c869_20gr
   aphic

3. *https://boldip.com/blog/*
   patent-drawings/#_853ae90f0351324bd73ea615e6487517__4c761f170e016836ff84498202b99827__853ae90
   f0351324bd73ea615e6487517_text_43ec3e5dee6e706af7766fffea512721_Patent_0bcef9c45bd8a48eda1b26eb0
   c61c869_20drawings_0bcef9c45bd8a48eda1b26eb0c61c869_20are_0bcef9c45bd8a48eda1b26eb0c61c869_20gr
   aphic

Flowcharts and Schematics: These are very useful for computer-implemented applications, where the claim is usually a method claim or process (with steps). And a flowchart shows very well the relationships between various steps in time/sequence.

There are standard symbols used in various flowcharting processes, the USPTO will not require specific project management standards – all they require is consistency across similar blocks so they can be easily understood by the examiner (and by people in the industry/skill).

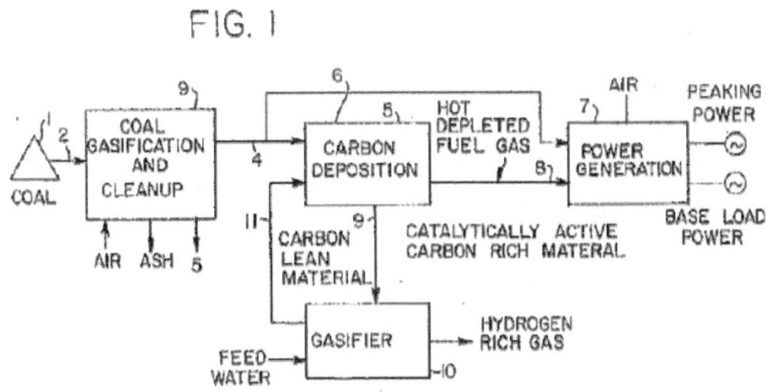

Flowchart Figure.
Source: https://boldip.com/blog/
patent-drawings/#:~:text=Patent%20drawings%20are%20graphic[4]

Alternate Position: Show moved positions with a broken line on the same view if there's enough space; otherwise, use a separate view.

Partial Views: Large machines or devices can be broken into partial views on one or more sheets. Each partial view must align

---

4. *https://boldip.com/blog/*
patent-drawings/#_853ae90f0351324bd73ea615e6487517__4c761f170e016836ff84498202b99827__853ae90
f0351324bd73ea615e6487517_text_43ec3e5dee6e706af7766fffea512721_Patent_0bcef9c45bd8a48eda1b26eb0
c61c869_20drawings_0bcef9c45bd8a48eda1b26eb0c61c869_20are_0bcef9c45bd8a48eda1b26eb0c61c869_20gr
aphic

edge-to-edge with others, with no overlapping parts. Include a smaller-scale overall view showing the arrangement of partial views. Enlarged portions should be labeled as separate views.

1. **Single Complete View:** When multiple sheets together form a complete view, they must be arranged so the full figure can be assembled without hiding parts.
2. **Long Views:** For very long views, divide them into sections on a single sheet with clear relationships between parts.

Character of lines, numbers, and letters: All drawings must be made by a process which will give them satisfactory reproduction characteristics. Every line, number, and letter must be black (except for color drawings), well-defined. The weight of all lines and letters must be heavy enough to permit adequate reproduction. This requirement applies to all lines however fine, to shading, and to lines representing cut surfaces in sectional views. Lines and strokes of different thicknesses may be used in the same drawing where different thicknesses have a different meaning.

Shading: The use of shading in views is encouraged if it aids in understanding the invention and if it does not reduce legibility. Shading is used to indicate the surface or shape of spherical, cylindrical, and conical elements of an object. Flat parts may also be lightly shaded. Such shading is preferred in the case of parts shown in perspective, but not for cross sections. Spaced lines for shading are preferred. These lines must be thin, as few in number as practicable, and they must contrast with the rest of the drawings. As a substitute for shading, heavy lines on the shade side of objects can be used except where they superimpose on each other or obscure reference characters. Light should come from the upper left corner at an angle of 45°. Surface delineations should preferably be shown by proper shading. Solid black shading areas are not permitted, except when used to represent bar graphs or color.

Symbols: Graphical drawing symbols may be used for conventional elements when appropriate. The elements for which such symbols and labeled representations are used must be adequately identified in the specification. Known devices should be illustrated by symbols which have a universally recognized conventional meaning and are generally accepted in the art. Other symbols which are not universally recognized may be used, subject to approval by the Office, if they are not likely to be confused with existing conventional symbols, and if they are readily identifiable.

Legends: Suitable descriptive legends may be used subject to approval by the Office or may be required by the examiner where necessary for understanding of the drawing. They should contain as few words as possible.

Numbers, letters, and reference characters.

Reference characters (numerals are preferred), sheet numbers, and view numbers must be plain and legible, and must not be used in association with brackets or inverted commas, or enclosed within outlines. They must be oriented in the same direction as the view so as to avoid having to rotate the sheet. Reference characters should be arranged to follow the profile of the object depicted.

The English alphabet must be used for letters, except where another alphabet is customarily used, such as the Greek alphabet to indicate angles, wavelengths, and mathematical formulas.

Numbers, letters, and reference characters must measure at least .32 cm. (1/8 inch) in height. They should not be placed in the drawing so as to interfere with its comprehension. Therefore, they should not cross or mingle with the lines. They should not be placed upon hatched or shaded surfaces. When necessary, such as indicating a surface or cross section, a reference character may be underlined and a blank space may be left in the hatching or shading where the character occurs so that it appears distinct. Patent drawings that include reference numbers help the reader understand how to use your invention to meet the necessary requirement to apply for a patent.

The same part of an invention appearing in more than one view of the drawing must always be designated by the same reference character, and the same reference character must never be used to designate different parts.

Reference characters not mentioned in the description shall not appear in the drawings. Reference characters mentioned in the description must appear in the drawings.

Lead lines: Lead lines are those lines between the reference characters and the details referred to. Such lines may be straight or curved and should be as short as possible. They must originate in the immediate proximity of the reference character and extend to the feature indicated. Lead lines must not cross each other. Lead lines are required for each reference character except for those which indicate the surface or cross section on which they are placed. Such a reference character must be underlined to make it clear that a lead line has not been left out by mistake. Lead lines must be executed in the same way as lines in the drawing.

Arrows: Arrows may be used at the ends of the lines, provided that their meaning is clear, as follows:

(1) On a lead line, a freestanding arrow to indicate the entire section towards which it points;

(2) On a lead line, an arrow touching a line to indicate the surface shown by the line looking along the direction of the arrow; or

(3) To show the direction of movement.

Numbering of sheets of drawings: The sheets of drawings should be numbered in consecutive Arabic numerals, starting with 1, within the sight as defined in this guide. These numbers, if present, must be placed in the middle of the top of the sheet, but not in the margin. The numbers can be placed on the right-hand side if the drawing extends too close to the middle of the top edge of the usable surface. The drawing sheet numbering must be clear and larger than the numbers used as reference characters to avoid confusion. The number of each sheet should be shown by two Arabic numerals placed on either side of an oblique line, with the first being the sheet number, and the second being the total number of sheets of drawings, with no other marking.

Numbering of views:

(1) The different views must be numbered in consecutive Arabic numerals, starting with 1, independent of the numbering of the sheets and, if possible, in the order in which they appear on the drawing sheet(s). Partial views intended to form one complete view, on one or several sheets, must be identified by the same number followed by a capital letter. View numbers must be preceded by the abbreviation "FIG." Where only a single view is used in an application to illustrate the claimed invention, it must not be numbered and the abbreviation "FIG." must not appear.

(2) Numbers and letters identifying the views must be simple and clear and must not be used in association with brackets, circles, or inverted commas. The view numbers must be larger than the numbers used for reference characters.

Security markings: Authorized security markings may be placed on the drawings provided they are outside the sight, preferably centered in the top margin.

Holes: No holes should be made by the applicant in the drawing sheets.

To present drawings:

There are two categories for the development of utility and design patent applications. They are the following:

Black ink: Black and white drawings are normally required. India ink, or its equivalent that secures solid black lines, must be used for drawings.

Color: Color drawings are permitted in design applications. Where a design application contains color drawings, the application must include the number of sets of color drawings required by:

-One (1) set of color drawings if submitted via the USPTO patent electronic filing system or three (3) sets of color drawings if not submitted via the USPTO patent electronic filing system.

-An amendment to the specification to insert (unless the specification contains or has been previously amended to contain) the following language as the first paragraph of the brief description of the drawings.

The patent or application file contains at least one drawing executed in color. Copies of this patent or patent application publication with color drawing(s) will be provided by the Office upon request and payment of the necessary fee.

On rare occasions, color drawings may be necessary as the only practical medium by which to disclose the subject matter sought to be patented in a utility patent application. The color drawings must be of sufficient quality such that all details in the drawings are reproducible in black and white in the printed patent. Color drawings are not permitted in international applications (PCT Rule 11.13). The Office will accept color drawings in utility patent applications only after granting a petition filed explaining why the color drawings are necessary. If the Office does not grant the petition, the Office will object to the color drawings as being improper and require the Applicant either to cancel the drawings or to provide substitute black and white drawings.

The patent or application file contains at least one drawing executed in color. Copies of this patent or patent application publication with color drawing(s) will be provided by the Office upon request and payment of the necessary fee.

Where there are drawings, you must include a listing of all figures by number (e.g., Figure 1A) and with corresponding statements explaining what each figure depicts. Each element in the drawings should be mentioned in the description.

To present photographs:

A patent application must comply with the following specifications:

Black and white: Photographs, including photocopies of photographs, are not ordinarily permitted in utility and design patent applications. The Office will accept photographs in utility and design patent applications, however, if photographs are the only practicable medium for illustrating the claimed invention. If the subject matter of the application admits of illustration by a drawing, the examiner may require a drawing in place of the photograph. The photographs must be of sufficient quality so that all details in the photographs are reproducible in the printed patent. Again, if the request is not granted, the Office will object to the color photographs as inadequate and require the applicant to cancel the photographs or provide substitute black and white drawings.

Color photographs: Color photographs will be accepted in utility and design patent applications if the conditions for accepting color drawings and black and white photographs have been satisfied.

The photographs and color drawings submitted in utility or design patent applications must be of sufficient quality such that all details in the photographs and drawings are reproducible in black and white in the printed patent.

The USPTO will accept color drawings or photographs in utility applications only after granting a petition explaining why the color drawings or photographs are necessary. Additionally, because color drawings are not permitted in international applications (PCT), color drawings and color photographs filed in a national stage application will be treated as an amendment and will be objected to if they introduce new matter.

Color drawings and photographs (black and white or color) may be submitted in applications for registration of an international design under section 401 of the Administrative Instructions for the Application of the Hague Agreement. The USPTO may object to the drawings and photographs and require corrections or deletions if they do not comply with 37 CFR 1.84 or PCT Rule 11.13.

In the case of continuation utility patent applications where a request for color drawings or photographs has been accepted, the applicant must renew the request even if a similar request was filed in the original utility application. When the patent is issued, a set of color drawings or photographs will be attached to the Letter Patent. Although copies of the patent are printed in black and white, upon special request and payment of a fee, the Office will provide copies of the patent with color drawings or photographs.

Graphic Symbols in Patent Drawings (37 CFR 1.84(n)):

- **Accepted Use:** Graphic symbols and labeled representations can be used for conventional elements in patent drawings, but their use is subject to USPTO approval. The USPTO will review each case to ensure that symbols are clear and appropriate.

- **Reference Organizations**: ANSI (American National Standards Institute) and ISO (International Organization for Standardization) publish standards, including those related to graphic symbols. Symbols from these standards are generally accepted in patent drawings, but the USPTO does not "approve" any collection of symbols as a whole; each symbol's clarity and use are evaluated on a case-by-case basis.

- **Avoid Specific or Confusing Symbols**: Symbols that are overly specific or have unclear meanings should be avoided. If unclear symbols are used, they should be labeled for clarification.

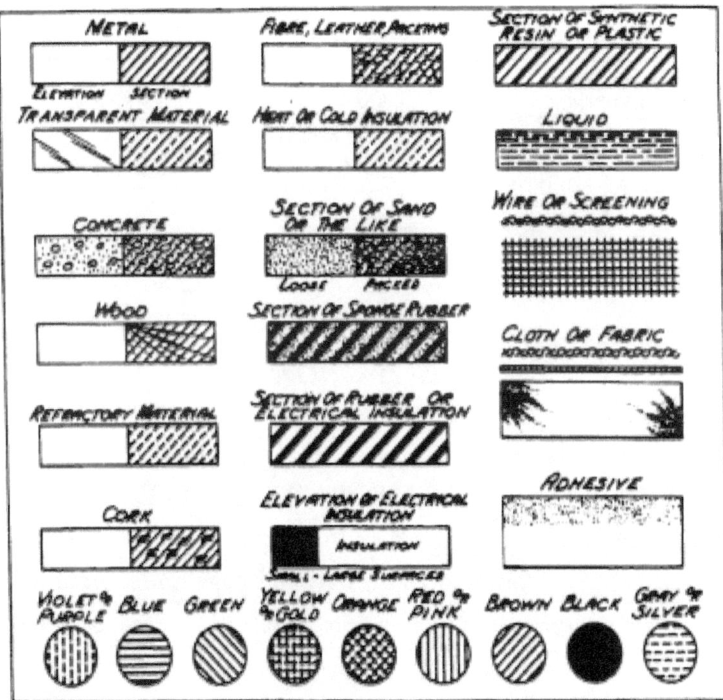

Graphic Symbols Figure.

Source: https://www.bitlaw.com/source/mpep/608-02.html

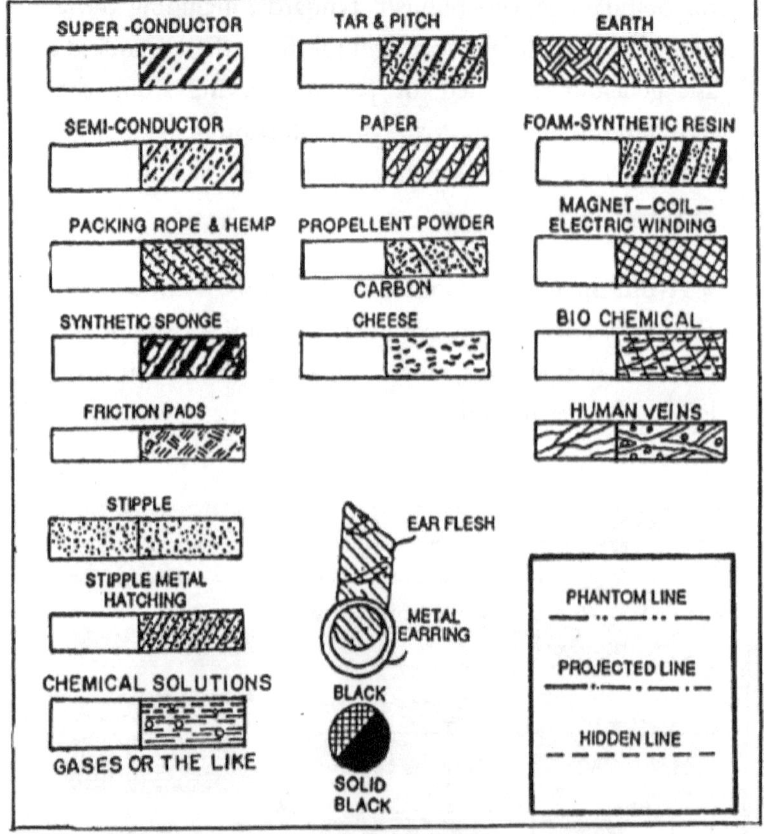

Graphic Symbols Figure.

Source: https://www.bitlaw.com/source/mpep/608-02.html

(C) An oath or declaration as prescribed by section 115[5].

NAMING THE INVENTOR; INVENTOR'S OATH OR DECLARATION.—An application for patent that is filed under section 111(a)[6] or commences the national stage under section 371[7]

5. https://www.uspto.gov/web/offices/pac/mpep/mpep-9015-appx-l.html#d0e302875912

6.   https://www.uspto.gov/web/offices/pac/mpep/

mpep-9015-appx-l.html#pltd0e302678aia

7.   https://www.uspto.gov/web/offices/pac/mpep/mpep-9015-appx-l.html#d0e307164

shall include, or be amended to include, the name of the inventor for any invention claimed in the application

An oath or declaration under this subsection must contain statements that:

- The application was made or authorized to be made by the declarant.

- The declarant believes that he or she is the original inventor or an original joint inventor of the invention claimed in the application.

Additional Requirements:

The Director of the Patent Office may specify additional information related to the inventor and the invention that must be included in the oath or declaration.

Substitute Statement:

General Provisions: Instead of executing an oath or declaration, the applicant may provide a substitute statement under the circumstances described in paragraph (2) and any additional circumstances that the Director may specify by regulation.

Permitted Circumstances: A substitute statement is permitted for an individual who:

- (A) Cannot file the oath or declaration because:

  - (i) The individual is deceased;

  - (ii) The individual is legally incapacitated; or

  - (iii) The individual cannot be found or contacted after a diligent effort.

- (B) Is under an obligation to assign the invention but has refused to make the required oath or declaration.

Contents: The substitute statement must:

- (A) Identify the person to whom the statement applies;

- (B) Set forth the circumstances justifying the filing of the substitute statement in place of the oath or declaration; and

- (C) Include any additional information required by the Director.

TIME FOR FILING.—The applicant for patent shall provide each required oath or declaration under subsection (a), substitute statement under subsection (d), or recorded assignment meeting the requirements of subsection (e) no later than the date on which the issue fee for the patent is paid.

FEE, OATH OR DECLARATION, AND CLAIMS.—The application shall be accompanied by the fee required by law. The fee, oath or declaration, and 1 or more claims may be submitted after the filing date of the application, within such period and under such conditions, including the payment of a surcharge, as may be prescribed by the Director. Upon failure to submit the fee, oath or declaration, and 1 or more claims within such prescribed period, the application shall be regarded as abandoned.

FILING DATE.—The filing date of an application shall be the date on which a specification, with or without claims, is received in the United States Patent and Trademark Office.

Chapter 4

SUBMITTING THE DOCUMENTS TO THE USPTO PATENT CENTER

CHAPTER 4. SUBMITTING THE DOCUMENTS TO THE USPTO PATENT CENTER

Once you have meticulously prepared all the required documentation for your utility non-provisional patent application, ensuring compliance with the USPTO's guidelines, the next crucial step is to submit your application to the USPTO.

Submitting Non-provisional Utility Patent Application

A nonprovisional utility patent application can be filed with the USPTO through different routes:

- The office's electronic filing system called Patent Center,
- Delivery by U.S. mail,
- Hand delivery to the Office in Alexandria, Virginia.

Documents to submit

A complete nonprovisional utility patent application should contain the elements listed below, arranged in the order shown below:

- Utility Patent Application Transmittal Form or Transmittal Letter

- Appropriate Fees

- Application Data Sheet (see 37 CFR § 1.76)

- Specification (including the description, at least one claim, and an abstract)

- Drawings (when necessary)

- Executed Oath or Declaration

- Nucleotide and Amino Acid Sequence Listing (when necessary)

- Large Tables or Computer Listings (when necessary)

Non-Electronic Filing

New fee structure, Effective as of November 15, 2011, states that any regular nonprovisional utility application filed by mail or hand-delivery will require payment of an additional $400 fee called the "non-electronic filing fee," which is reduced by 50 percent to $200 for applicants that qualify for small entity status under 37 CFR § 1.27(a) or micro entity status under 37 CFR 1.29(a) or (d).

The only way to avoid paying the additional $400 non-electronic filing fee is by filing the non provisional utility application electronically via *Patent Center*.

Electronic Filing - Patent Center

Patent Center is a Web-based patent application and document submission system in which anyone with a Web-enabled computer can file patent applications without downloading special software or changing document preparation tools and processes.

Patent Center is the new web-based patent tool which has replaced the old electronic filing system called EFS-Web.

The Patent Center electronic filing system introduces the ability to electronically file the complete specification including the description, claims and abstract in one DOCX file rather than three separate files, making it easier to file in DOCX.

Format for filing in the Patent Center

Patent Center accepts electronic documents *formatted in DOCX.*

DOCX is a word processing file format based on open standards, including Extensible Markup Language (XML). DOCX is supported by many popular word processing applications, such as Microsoft Word 2007 or higher, Google Docs, Office Online, LibreOffice and Pages for Mac. As an open standard format, DOCX offers a safe and stable basis for authoring and processing intellectual property documents.

DOCX submissions in the Patent Center may be filed in separate documents, one each for specification, claims, abstract and drawings or as a multi-section document. Multi-section DOCX processing is available for utility non-provisional initial filings (specification, claims, abstract and drawings) in one single document.

The complete specification (description, claims, and abstract) can be created using a word processing program such as Microsoft® Word, Google Docs, Office Online, LibreOffice and Pages for Mac, or Corel® WordPerfect.

Beginning January 17, 2024, the description, claims, and abstract for a nonprovisional utility patent application specification must all be filed in DOCX format in order to avoid an additional fee of $400, which is reduced to $160 for small entity applicants and $80 for micro entity applicants.

As set forth at 37 CFR § 1.16(u), this additional fee will be required where the specification's written description, claims, and/or abstract does not conform to the USPTO requirements for submission in DOCX format.

(u) Additional fee for any application filed on or after January 17, 2024, under 35 U.S.C. 111[1] for an original patent, except design,

---

1.   *https://www.govinfo.gov/link/uscode/35/111*

plant, or provisional applications, where the specification, claims, and/ or abstract does not conform to the USPTO requirements for submission in DOCX format:

By a micro entity (§ 1.29) $80.00

By a small entity (§ 1.27(a)) $160.00

By a small entity (§ 1.27(a)) if the application is submitted in compliance with the USPTO patent electronic filing system (§ 1.27(b)(2)) $160.00

By other than a small or micro entity $400.00

Other application documents, such as drawings and hand-signed declarations, may be scanned as a PDF file for filing via Patent Center.

Patent Center Step-by-Step Guide for Submitting an Application for a Non-Provisional Utility Patent

Create a USPTO Account

1. Create your USPTO.gov account: Visit the MyUSPTO page: MyUSPTO and select "Create a USPTO.gov account."

My USPTO Registration Process Fig.
Source: https://patentcenter.uspto.gov/

1. Fill out the required information: Enter your full legal name (first name, middle name, and last name) as it will appear on the Patent Electronic Verification Form, along with your address and contact information. Using your complete legal name helps prevent confusion with others who may share similar names.

Create a USPTO.gov account

Already have your USPTO.gov account? Sign in

Entries are restricted to English characters only.

* indicates required

Email address *

Title

Select

First name *

Middle name

Last name *

Suffix

My USPTO Registration Process Fig.
Source: https://patentcenter.uspto.gov/

My USPTO Registration Process Fig.
Source: https://patentcenter.uspto.gov/

Once you fill out all the info, complete the reCaptcha verification, and accept the USPTO Terms of Use and Privacy Policy. Then, click "Next" at the bottom of the page.

reCaptcha verification *

☑ I understand and agree with USPTO's Terms of Use and Privacy Policy.

1. Verify and activate your USPTO.gov account: An email will be sent to your registered email with a link to activate your account. Click on "Activate Account".

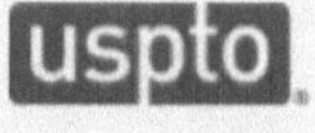

My USPTO Registration Process Fig.
Source: https://patentcenter.uspto.gov/

Once you have completed these three steps, you will have full access to the Patent Center and all its resources available to registered eFilers.

When you are a registered user, you can opt for two-step authentication. Login to MyUSPTO and activate the two-step authentication to verify your account. You can choose to download an Authenticator app on Google Play and the iOS App Store, or use your ID document for ID Verification.

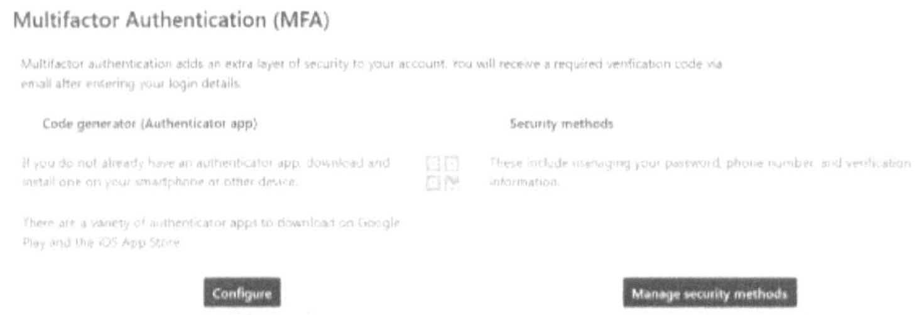

Multifactor Authentication (MFA)

Multifactor authentication adds an extra layer of security to your account. You will receive a required verification code via email after entering your login details.

Code generator (Authenticator app)

If you do not already have an authenticator app, download and install one on your smartphone or other device.

There are a variety of authenticator apps to download on Google Play and the iOS App Store.

Configure

Security methods

These include managing your password, phone number, and verification information.

Manage security methods

My USPTO Registration Process Fig.
Source: https://patentcenter.uspto.gov/

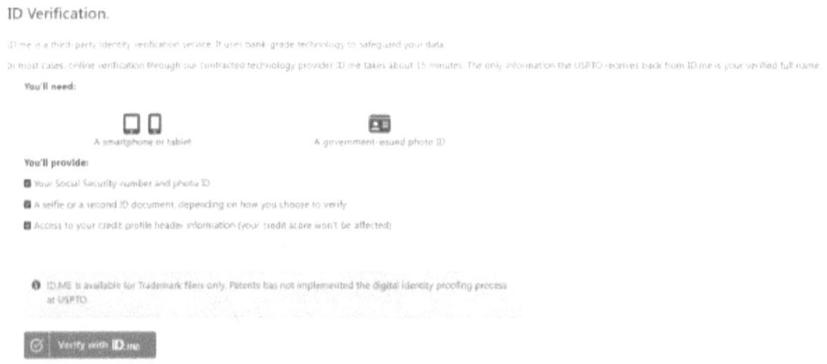

ID Verification.

ID.me is a third-party identity verification service. It uses bank-grade technology to safeguard your data.

In most cases, online verification through our contracted technology provider ID.me takes about 15 minutes. The only information the USPTO receives back from ID.me is your verified full name.

You'll need:

A smartphone or tablet

A government-issued photo ID

You'll provide:

- Your Social Security number and photo ID
- A selfie or a second ID document, depending on how you choose to verify
- Access to your credit profile header information (your credit score won't be affected)

> ID.ME is available for Trademark filers only. Patents has not implemented the digital identity proofing process at USPTO.

Verify with ID.me

My USPTO Registration Process Fig.
Source: https://patentcenter.uspto.gov/

Start a New Submission

1. Access the Patent Center: Go to the Patent Center website:Patent Center[1] and click on "Sign in" to enter your username and password.

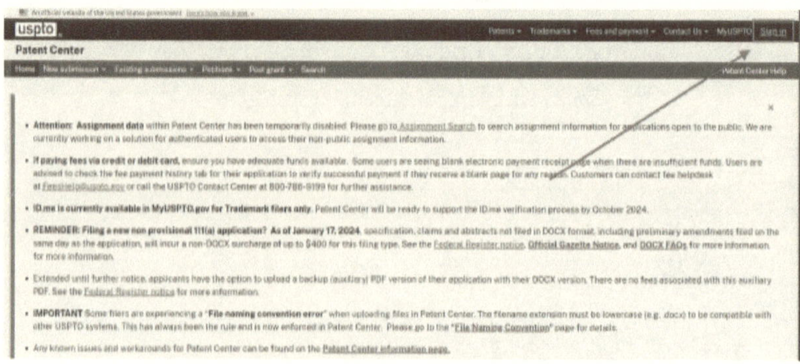

My USPTO Registration Process Fig.
Source: https://patentcenter.uspto.gov/

1. Once logged in, select "New Submission" and then choose "Regular Submission: Utility Nonprovisional."

---

1. https://patentcenter.uspto.gov/

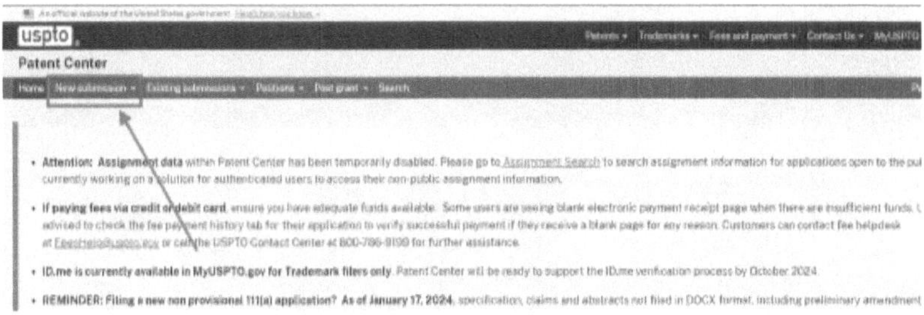

My USPTO Registration Process Fig.
*Source:*https://patentcenter.uspto.gov/

Patent Center

Home | New submission ▾ | Existing submissions ▾ | Petit…

REGULAR SUBMISSIONS

Utility-Nonprovisional

Utility-Provisional

Design

U.S. 371 National stage

Plant Nonprovisional

INTERNATIONAL APPLICATIONS

International application (PCT)

International design application(Hague)

PATENT INITIATIVES

Track One

Accelerated Examination – Utility

Accelerated Examination – Design

NEW INITIATIVES

My USPTO Patent Submission Process Fig.
Source: https://patentcenter.uspto.gov/

1. Application Data Sheet (ADS): You can either fill out the

Application Data Sheet (ADS) online (Web ADS) or upload it as a PDF.

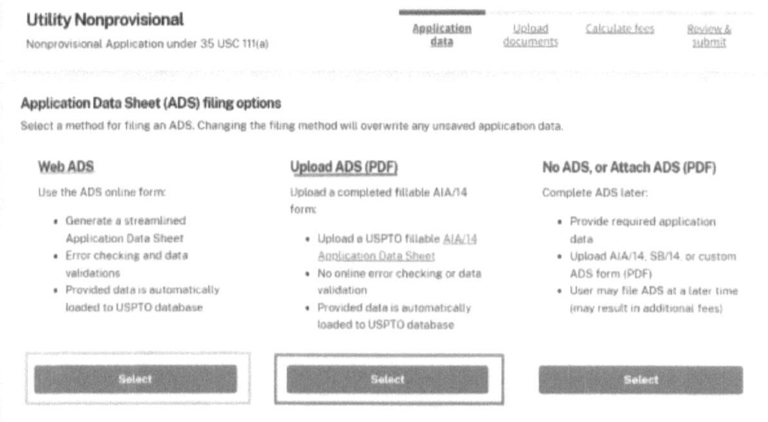

My USPTO Patent Submission Process Fig.
Source: https://patentcenter.uspto.gov/

If using Web ADS:

Complete the required fields, including:

○ Names and addresses of the applicant(s) and inventor(s), along with their citizenship and residency.

○ Details about the application: title of the invention, type of application, and related filings (e.g., provisional or foreign applications).

○ Correspondence information and details about any attorney or agent.

○ If applicable, provide information about related applications (continuation, divisional, or continuation-in-part) and claims of priority.

● After filling out the Web ADS, click "Continue" to proceed to the next section.

For more information on how to fill the Application Data Sheet, please see ADS.

Web ADS   Autofill data

Change filing method

Inventors

Application details

Representatives

Domestic Benefit/National Stage

Foreign priority

First inventor to file

Authorization to permit access

Applicant

Assignee

Summary

Signature

Correspondence information

Customer Number
Enter a customer number

Enter customer number to lookup its associated address or provide a physical address

Application information

Title of invention

Attorney docket # (optional)

Entity status (optional)

Application type — Nonprovisional

Subject matter — Utility

Total number of drawing sheets (optional)

Suggested figure for publication (optional)

Filing by reference

☐ Select this checkbox and complete section ONLY when filing by reference, this section is NOT for making domestic benefit or foreign priority claims. Do NOT complete this section if application papers including a specification and drawings are being filed at the time of filing the application.

Publication Information for Pre-Grant Publication

Publication request

    ⦿ Normal eighteen-month publication

    ○ Request early publication

    ○ Request not to publish under 35 U.S.C. 122(b)

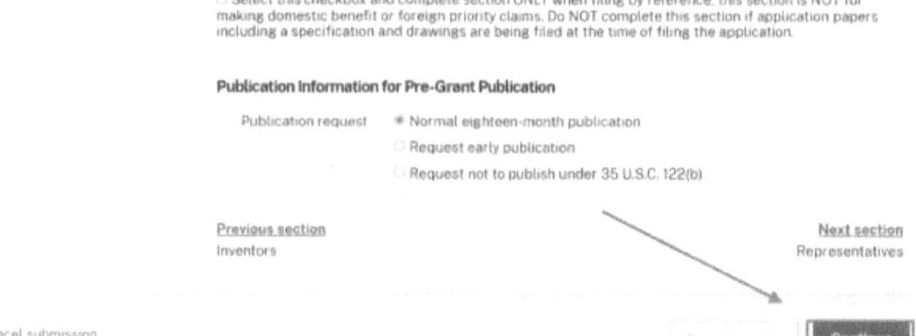

My USPTO Patent Submission Process Fig.
Source: https://patentcenter.uspto.gov/

Upload the documents

1. Upload the necessary documents for a non-provisional utility patent application:

○ Patent Application (Specification)

○ Drawings (if applicable)

○ Oath or Declaration

○ Power of Attorney (if applicable)

○ Information Disclosure Statement (IDS) (if applicable)

○ Fee Transmittal Form

○ Cover Sheet (if applicable)

● After uploading all documents, click "Continue" to move to the next section.

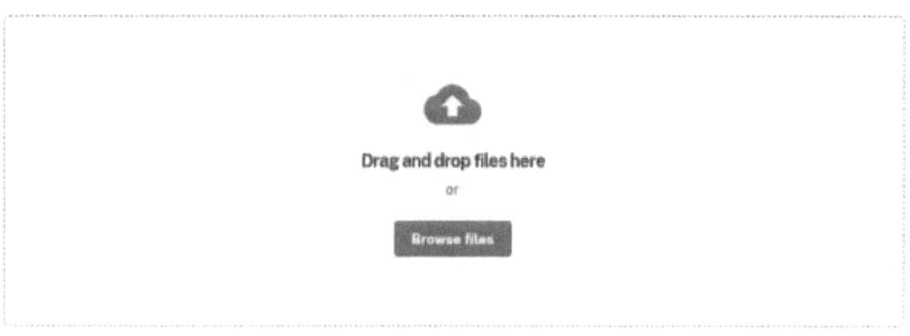

My USPTO Patent Submission Process Fig.
Source: https://patentcenter.uspto.gov/

DOCX Feedback Errors and Warnings

When filing patent applications with the USPTO through the Patent Center, it's important to be aware of some common errors that can occur when submitting documents in DOCX format. These issues often arise due to formatting or structural inconsistencies in the DOCX file, which can lead to rejection or delays.

One of the most frequent mistakes is submitting a single DOCX file that contains the abstract, claims, and specification together, rather than as separate documents. The USPTO requires these sections to be uploaded individually in DOCX format, which allows for smoother processing and handling of the documents.

Additionally, the USPTO Patent Center provides two types of notifications when uploading DOCX files:

Yellow Triangle Warnings: These are automatic corrections made by the system. While they may indicate minor issues, they won't prevent you from submitting the document, but it's still recommended to review and address them where possible.

Red Error Notifications: These are more serious errors that will prevent the submission of your patent application. It is critical to resolve these issues before proceeding.

Following these guidelines will help you avoid many of the common DOCX upload errors, ensuring a smoother and more efficient filing process.

Types of Notifications in the USPTO and Their Meaning

Below, we will outline all the types of notifications that may appear when uploading documents to the USPTO Patent Center, along with their significance.

Errors: System Level

INTERNAL_ERROR: An internal system error occurred.

RENDER_FAILURE: Generation of PDF failed due to a system error.

CHECKER_FAILURE: Checking of DOCX patent application failed due a system error.

SPLITTER_FAILURE: Splitting of DOCX patent application into Spec, Claims, and Abstract failed due to a system error.

CORRECTOR_FAILURE: Correcting of DOCX patent application failed due to a system error.

CORRUPT_OR_NOT_DOC: The provided document is corrupt or not a DOCX file.

DB_MESSAGE_RETRIEVAL_FAILURE: Failed to obtain error/warning message from database.

Errors: Content Level

NO_HEADINGS: This document contains no recognized section headings.

REMOVE_CONTENT_CONTROL: This document contains content controls and cannot be processed.

REMOVE_CUSTOM_XML: This document contains custom XML and cannot be processed.

PAGE_SIZE: The page size of this document exceeds Letter or A4. Please correct the page size before proceeding.

PAGE_ORIENTATION: The orientation of the document is not portrait which may not be rendered correctly by the USPTO. Please correct by changing the orientation to portrait.

INVALID_FONT: The attached document contains fonts that are not recognized by the system. Please correct the fonts in the document before proceeding.

MULTIPLE_SPECS: Only one specification document is allowed.

MULTIPLE_CLAIMS: Only one claims document is allowed.

MULTIPLE_ABSTRACTS: Only one abstract document is allowed.

MULTI_COMPONENT_DOCUMENT: This document contains multiple application parts (specification, claims, and/or abstract). Please upload application parts separately.

INVALID_FIELD_DOC_AUTOMATION: This document contains document automation fields and cannot be processed.

INVALID_FIELD_FORMCHECKBOX: This document contains FORMCHECKBOX fields and cannot be processed.

INVALID_FIELD_FORMDROPDOWN: This document contains

FORMDROPDOWN fields and cannot be processed.

INVALID_FIELD_RD: This document contains RD fields and cannot be processed.

INVALID_FIELD_HYPERLINK_LOCAL: This document contains HYPERLINK fields to local resources and cannot be processed.

INVALID_FIELD_USER_INFORMATION: This document contains user information fields and cannot be processed.

INVALID_FIELD_MAIL_MERGE: This document contains mail merge fields and cannot be processed.

INVALID_FIELD_BOOKMARK_REFERENCE: This document contains fields that reference bookmarks and cannot be processed because bookmarks are not allowed.

INVALID_FIELD_INCLUDEDPICTURE: This document contains INCLUDEDPICTURE fields and cannot be processed. Graphics must be embedded into the document, not linked by filename.

INVALID_FIELD_INCLUDEDTEXT: This document contains INCLUDEDTEXT fields and cannot be processed. Graphics must be embedded into the document, not linked by filename.

INVALID_FIELD_PAGEREF: This document contains PAGEREF fields and cannot be processed.

INVALID_FIELD_STYLEREF: This document contains STYLEREF fields and cannot be processed.

INVALID_FIELD_QUOTE: This document contains QUOTE fields and cannot be processed.

INVALID_FIELD_AUTONUM: This document contains AUTONUM fields and cannot be processed.

INVALID_FIELD_AUTONUMLGL: This document contains AUTONUMLGL fields and cannot be processed.

INVALID_FIELD_AUTONUMOUT: This document contains AUTONUMOUT fields and cannot be processed.

DOCX_FOLLOWONS_DISABLED: DOCX files are not allowed for follow-on or amendment documents.

INVALID_FONT_CHAR: The document references characters that cannot be displayed in the identified font.

PRELIMINARY_AMENTMENT_NOT_ALLOWED_FOR_I A Preliminary Amendment cannot be submitted in an initial filing. Please review and re-submit.

Warnings: Uncorrected

PARAGRAPH_NUMBER: Sequential paragraph numbers were not detected. Please review the document.

LIMIT_WORD_COUNT: Word count in abstract section is over 150 words.

CLAIM_NUMBER_INVALID: The claims are not numbered with positive integers. Please review and revise if necessary.

INVALID_MARGIN: The margins of the attached document do not meet USPTO rules. This may cause processing errors or delays.

COLOR_OR_GRAYSCALE_IMAGE: The document contains color or grayscale images which can cause image distortion problems.

UNKNOWN_CLAIM_STATUS_IDENTIFIER: The claim status identifier is not valid. Please review and revise if necessary.

OLE_WARNING: The document contains OLE objects that are currently not supported. These objects may not be visible in your application documents.

TRACK_CHANGES_DETECTED: Track changes containing insertions/deletions have been detected. These changes will be displayed in the document as underlines/strikethroughs.

LIMIT_ABST_PARA_COUNT: The abstract contains more than one paragraph. Please review and revise if necessary.

CLAIM_NUMBER_MISSING_OR_OUT_OF_ORDER: Missing or out of order claim number detected.

CLAIM_DEPENDS_ON_MISSING_CLAIM: The claims contain an improper dependency (missing or canceled claim). Please review and revise if necessary.

CLAIM_NUMBER_DUPLICATE: The claims contain duplicate claim numbering. Please review the claims and revise if necessary.

CLAIM_NUMBER_DEPENDS_ON_ITSELF The claims contain an improper dependency (with a claim depending on itself). Please review and revise if necessary.

CLAIM_NOT_DEPENDENT_ON_PREVIOUS_CLAIM: The claims contain a claim with an improper dependency as it does not depend on a previous claim. Please review and revise if necessary.

CLAIM_IMPROPER_MULTIPLE_DEPENDENT: The claims contain a claim which references back to another multiple dependent claim. Please review and revise if necessary.

PAGE_NUMBERING_ADDED: No page numbers were detected. Page numbering will be automatically applied after submission.

PARAGRAPH_NUMBERING_DUPLICATE: Duplicate paragraph numbering has been detected. Please review and revise if necessary.

CLAIM_DEPENDS_ON_IMPROPER_CLAIM: The claims contain a claim that depends on an improper claim. Please review and revise if necessary.

INVALID_BACKGROUND_COLOR: The attached document uses a non-white background color. Please review and correct if necessary to avoid processing problems.

CONCURRENT_INSERT_DELETE: Document contains text marked for both insertion and deletion. Please review and revise if necessary.

CLAIM_MISSING_PERIOD_AT_END: A claim does not end with a period. Please review and revise if necessary.

CLAIM_FIRST_LETTER_NOT_CAPITALIZED: A claim does not begin with a capital letter. Please review and revise if necessary.

CLAIM_CONTAINS_MULTIPLE_SENTENCES: A claim contains more than one sentence. Please review and revise if necessary.

CLAIM_NOT_ALTERNATIVE_ONLY_DEPENDENCY: The claims contain a multiple dependent claim that does not use the alternative form. Please review and revise if necessary.

NO_CLAIMS_DETECTED: No claims were detected. Please use preferred claim numbering, such as "1.", instead of including the word "claim" as part of the claim numbering.

CLAIM_REFERENCES_DIFFERENT_FEATURES: The claims contain a claim that references two sets of claims to different features. Please review and revise if necessary

CLAIM_MULTIPLE_PERIODS_AT_END: The claim contains more than one period at the end of the claim. Please review and revise if necessary.

LANGUAGE_NON_ENGLISH: The document submitted has portions not written in English language. Please review and revise.

CLAIM_ENDS_ON_COMMA: A claim number was detected that appears to end with a comma rather than period. Please review and revise if necessary.

PARAGRAPH_NUMBERING_MISSING: Paragraph numbering is missing from the specification. Please review the specifications and revise if necessary.

PARAGRAPH_NUMBERING_NOT4DIGITS: The specification paragraph numbering is not in the proper format. Please review and revise if necessary.

PARAGRAPH_NUMBERING_NOT_CONSECUTIVE: The specification paragraph numbering is not consecutive. Please review and revise if necessary.

FIGURES_IN_SPECIFICATION Figures have been detected in the specification. Please review and revise if necessary.

SPECIFIC_DOCUMENT_CODE_USED The automatic document description has been replaced.

LINE_SPACING_INVALID Line spacing is not valid.

FOUND_ALL_3_SECTION_HEADERS   All   section headers were found.

FOUND_SPEC_SECTION_ONLY   SPECIFICATION section detected.

FOUND_CLM_SECTION_ONLY   CLAIM   section detected.

FOUND_ABST_SECTION_ONLY   ABSTRACT   section detected.

FOUND_DRW_SECTION_ONLY   DRAWING   Section Detected.

FOUND_CLM_AND_ABST_SECTIONS_ONLY   CLAIM/ABST sections detected.

FOUND_SPEC_AND_ABST_SECTIONS_ONLY   SPEC/ABST sections detected.

FOUND_SPEC_AND_CLM_SECTIONS_ONLY   SPEC/CLAIM sections detected.

Warnings: Corrected

ACCEPT_REVISIONS: Tracked revisions were found and have been accepted

REMOVE_COMMENTS: Comments were found and have been removed.

REMOVE_BOOKMARKS: Bookmarks have been detected and will be removed

REMOVE_HIDDEN: Hidden items were found and have been removed.

REPLACED_FONT_UNUSED: Unused invalid fonts set to default.

REMOVE_LINE_NUMBERS: The system removed the continuous line numbering across multiple sections (specification, claims, and/or abstract).

REMOVE_TEXT_DECORATIONS: Text decorations have been removed

REPLACED_AUTO_UPDATE_DATE: Dynamic dates have been converted to static dates.

REPLACED_FORMULA_FIELD FORMULA: fields have been converted to static text.

REPLACED_ADVANCE_FIELD ADVANCE: fields have been converted to static text.

REPLACED_AUTOTEXTLIST_FIELD AUTOTEXTLIST: fields have been converted to static text.

HYPERLINK_CONVERTED_TO_STATIC: Hyperlink detected. Anchor text will be converted to static text and the hyperlink will be removed.

PAGE_NUMBERING_MISSING: The document is missing page numbering. Please review and revise if necessary.

REPLACED_ARTIFACTS_WITH_IMAGES: All artifacts (SmartArt, Drawings, Charts, etc.) have been replaced with images.

Warnings: XML Conversion

XML4IP_CONVERSION_FAILURE: A problem prevented generation of XML4IP.

XML4IP_CONVERSION_WARNING [details of conversion issue provided by XSLT]

XML4IP_TEXT_FRAME_FAILURE This document contains a text frame and cannot be converted to XML4IP.

XML4IP_UNSUPPORTED_GRAPHIC Drawings, SmartArt, charts, and shapes cannot currently be converted to XML4IP.

XML4IP_SVG_FAILURE Conversion of a graphic to SVG failed for [filename]

DOCUMENT_CODE_UNSUPPORTED Unsupported document code used.

DOCUMENT_CODE_INCONSISTENT Provided document code is inconsistent with document contents.

Best Practices to Avoid Common DOCX Warnings and Errors

Unrecognized Fonts

Error Message: "The attached document contains fonts that are not recognized by the system. Please correct the fonts in the document before proceeding."

Solution: Ensure that all fonts in the document are standard fonts recognized by the USPTO system.

Abstract Word Count Exceeds 150 Words

Error Message: "Word count in abstract section is over 150 words. To prevent this warning, use a word count tool if available and ensure the number of words in the abstract is 150 words or less."

Solution: Reduce the abstract to 150 words or less using a word count tool.

Improper Margins

Error Message: "The margins of the attached document do not meet USPTO rules. This may cause processing errors or delays. To prevent this error, make sure your margins meet USPTO requirements. See Patent Rules 1.52."

Solution: Adjust the margins of your document to meet USPTO's specified rules.

Non-Numerical Claim Numbers Detected

Error Message: "Non-numerical claim numbers were detected. This warning is usually caused when claim numbers are included in brackets and/or are not followed by a period. Having steps starting with brackets/parentheses or letters within the claims may also generate this warning."

Solution: Correct the claim numbers so they are numerical, without brackets or parentheses, and followed by a period.

User Information Fields Present

Error Message: "This document contains user information fields and cannot be processed."

Solution: Remove any automated fields or references from the document before filing.

Multiple Specification Documents

Error Message: "Only one specification document is allowed. This error is usually caused when filing a preliminary amendment with your initial filing."

Solution: Submit only the initial specification during the first filing. File amendments or translations as follow-on documents.

Bookmarks Present

Error Message: "This document contains fields that reference bookmarks and cannot be processed because bookmarks are not allowed."

Solution: Remove all bookmark references before submitting.

Document Orientation is Not Portrait

Error Message: "The orientation of the document is not portrait which may not be rendered correctly by the USPTO."

Solution: Change the orientation of your document to portrait before uploading.

Unsupported OLE Objects

Error Message: "The document contains OLE objects that are currently not supported. These objects may not be visible in your application documents."

Solution: Review and remove unsupported OLE objects (e.g., embedded objects or images). Only supported objects like Visio, ChemDraw, and standard equations should be included.

Content Controls Detected

Error Message: "This document contains content controls and cannot be processed."

Solution: Remove all content controls from the document.

Automatic Corrections by the System

Error Message: "Bookmarks were found and have been removed. Text decorations were found and have been removed. Hidden items were found and have been removed. Comments were found and have been removed. Dynamic dates have been converted to static dates."

Explanation: Bookmarks, text decorations, hidden items, comments, and dynamic dates are not allowed in DOCX files. These elements are automatically removed during submission.

Solution: To avoid warnings, ensure these elements are not included in your DOCX documents before uploading.

Calculate the Fees

Select the relevant Entity Status for your application. For more information, see the section on Entity Status.

Enter the number of pages of the specification, including drawings, total claims, and independent claims. For more details, refer to the section on Claims.

Calculate fees

Payment of fees during this stage of the application process is optional, but failure to pay fees in a timely manner may cause delays in the processing of your application.

Skip fees for now

⚠ **Reminder:** As a Guest user, you are strongly advised to pay fees online as part of this submission, or use an alternative method to pay fees on the same day (ET), to avoid a surcharge for late payment. Guest users are unable to access a submitted application to pay fees online after the initial submission session.

Fill in the information below in order to accurately calculate your fees.

Entity status

◉ Regular Undiscounted

◯ Small

◯ Micro

\# of pages in the specification (including any external tables) and drawings

\# of claims

\# of independent claims

Petitions

☐ Check the box if you are filing petition(s) as part of this application

My USPTO Patent Submission Process Fig.
Source: https://patentcenter.uspto.gov/

Fee Calculation:

- Select the three basic Patent Filing Fees: BASIC FILING, SEARCH, and EXAMINATION FEES.

- Additional fees may apply based on application specifics, including Application Size and Claim Fees (e.g., each claim over 20, each independent claim over 3, multiple dependent claims, additional sheets, non-English specifications, non-DOCX filings).

Once you have entered all fee-related information, click "Continue" to review your submission. Ensure all details are correct before proceeding to payment.

For more information on patent fees, refer to the section Patent Fees on this manual.

Calculate fees

Payment of fees during this stage of the application process is optional, but failure to pay fees in a timely manner may cause delays in the processing of your application.

> Skip fees for now

Select fees to pay

	Fee code	Fee description	Item price ($)	Quantity	Item total ($)
⌄	Patent Basic Filing Fees				
☐	4011	BASIC FILING FEE-UTILITY	$64.00	1	$64.00
☐	2111	UTILITY PATENT APPL. SEARCH FEE	$280.00	1	$280.00
☐	2311	EXAMINATION OF ORIGINAL PATENT APPLICATION	$320.00	1	$320.00
⌄	Application Size and Claim Fees				
☐	2203	MULTIPLE DEPENDENT CLAIM	$344.00	1	$344.00
☐	2091	SUBMISSION OF SEQUENCE LISTINGS OF 300MB TO 800MB	$424.00	1	$424.00
☐	2092	SUBMISSION OF SEQUENCE LISTINGS OF MORE THAN 800 MB	$4,200.00	1	$4,200.00
⌄	Miscellaneous Patent Fees				
☐	2054	Non-DOCX Filing Surcharge	$160.00	1	$160.00
☐	2053	NON-ENGLISH TRANSLATION	$56.00	1	$56.00
☐	2051	SURCHARGE-LATE FILING FEE, SEARCH FEE, EXAMINATION FEE, INVENTOR'S OATH OR DECLARATION, OR APPLICATION FILED WITHOUT AT LEAST ONE CLAIM OR BY REFERENCE	$64.00	1	$64.00

Entity status **Small**

\# of pages

\# of claims

\# of independent claims

Petition being filed? **No**

edit information

Total fees selected to pay $0.00

My USPTO Patent Submission Process Fig.
Source: https://patentcenter.uspto.gov/

Review and Submit

1. Choose your payment method (credit card, electronic funds transfer, or deposit account) and complete the payment process. For more information on the payment process, please refer to Payment Methods.
2. Confirm that you have completed all required fields and attached all necessary documents.
3. Submit the application electronically.

Review & submit

Review all the information entered for your patent application. If there are any errors in the data displayed, go back and edit the information before submitting to the USPTO.

Application data

Attorney docket #

.

Entity status

Small

Application type	Subtype
Utility	Nonprovisional Application under 35 USC 111(a)

Title of invention

.

First named inventor

First name	Middle name	Last name
.	.	.

Correspondence address

.

Total documents uploaded: 1

Download all documents

generatedADS668
43005.pdf   (110 KB
/ 5 pages)

Application Data Sheet

Preview

Payment details

⚠ Fee(s) were not calculated for this submission. Please remember to pay any required fee(s) on time to prevent a delay in the application process and to avoid any additional surcharge.   Calculate fees now?

eFiler information

First Name

Last Name

Email

My USPTO Patent Submission Process Fig.

Source: https://patentcenter.uspto.gov/

Review your application to finalize the submission of your application.

If uploading the ADS as a PDF:

● Fill the Application Data Sheet (ADS) and save it as a PDF.

● Upload the ADS either by dragging the files to the Patent Center page or by browsing your computer files.

My USPTO Patent Submission Process Fig.
Source: https://patentcenter.uspto.gov/

Next, follow the instructions as described in step 3 of this Guide: Upload documents, Calculate fees, and Review and Submit.

Receive Confirmation

After you submit your non-provisional utility patent application, the USPTO will provide an electronic confirmation receipt. This receipt includes an Application Number and a Confirmation Number.

The confirmation receipt will be available in the USPTO Patent Center and sent to the email address associated with your USPTO account.

Save and print the confirmation receipt for your records. It serves as proof of submission and includes essential details such as the application number, which you will need for future reference and for monitoring your application/filing status.

USPTO Patent Center Payment Methods

The USPTO Patent Center offers several payment methods for online transactions, including credit cards, debit cards, deposit accounts, and electronic funds transfers (EFT). Here's a breakdown of the available options:

1. Credit Card:

○ Accepted Cards: Visa, MasterCard, American Express, and Discover.

Payments can be made directly through the USPTO's electronic filing system, such as the Patent Center. Ensure that you have sufficient funds available, as insufficient funds may result in a blank electronic payment receipt page. If this occurs, check the fee payment history tab for your application to confirm successful payment.

For assistance, contact the USPTO Fee Helpdesk at FeesHelp@uspto.gov or call the USPTO Contact Center at 800-786-9199.

2. Deposit Account:

○ USPTO Deposit Accounts: This is a pre-paid account maintained with the USPTO that can be used to pay fees.

Deposit funds into your USPTO deposit account in advance. Payments can then be processed through the USPTO's electronic systems by selecting the deposit account as the payment method. You can add the deposit account through the Financial Manager in the Patent Center (explained below).

3. Electronic Payment Systems:

For certain online transactions, you might use the USPTO's integrated payment system, which can include options for ACH and credit card payments.

Patent Center - Financial Manager

Adding a payment method

For registered users in the Patent Center, you can add your preferred method of payment.

1. **Log In:** Access the Patent Center by signing in with your username and password.

2. **Navigate to Financial Manager:** From the Home page, go to "Fees and Payments" and select "Financial Manager."

3. **Add Payment Method:** Click on "Add a payment method" and review the available options and related information.

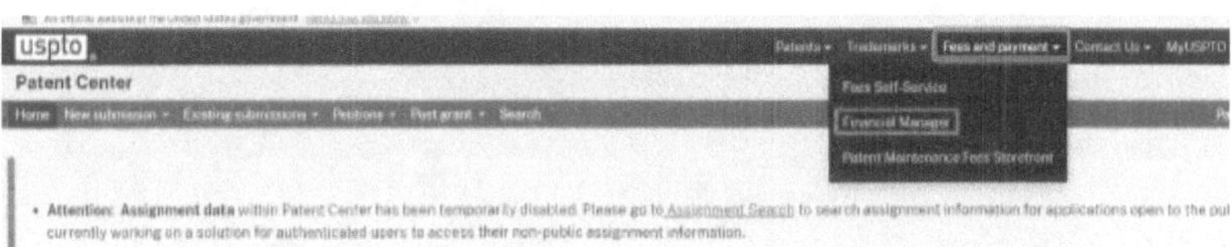

My USPTO Patent Submission Process Fig.

Source: https://patentcenter.uspto.gov/

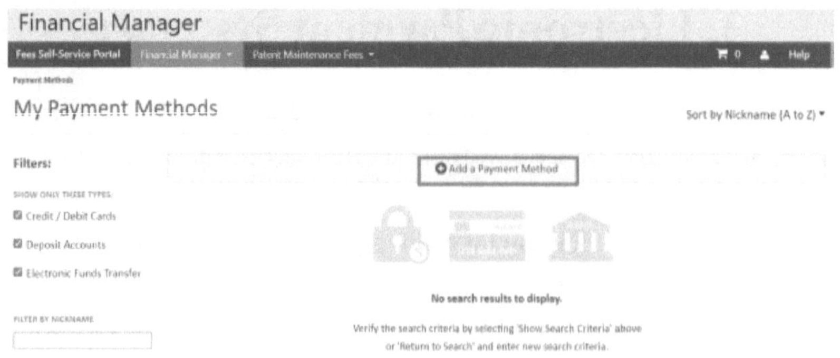

My USPTO Patent Submission Process Fig.
Source: https://patentcenter.uspto.gov/

The page will display the payment methods available to add and the information regarding each one. Choose the method of your preference, click on "Add Now" and fill the information required according to that particular method.

Add a Payment Method

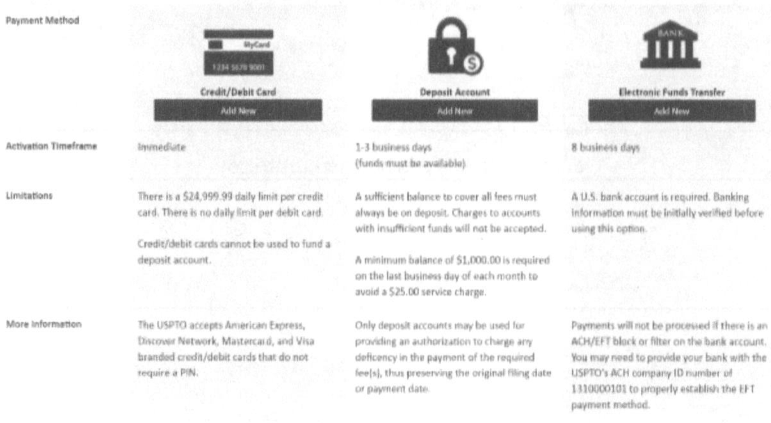

My USPTO Patent Submission Process Fig.
Source: https://patentcenter.uspto.gov/

Monitor Your Application

Once you have submitted the application, you can use your USPTO account to track the status of your application and respond to any Office Actions or requests for additional information from the USPTO.

1. Log In: Use your USPTO account credentials to access the Patent Center (https://patentcenter.uspto.gov).
2. Check Status: Click on Patents - Check filing status.
3. Enter your application number to view the current status and any updates related to your application.

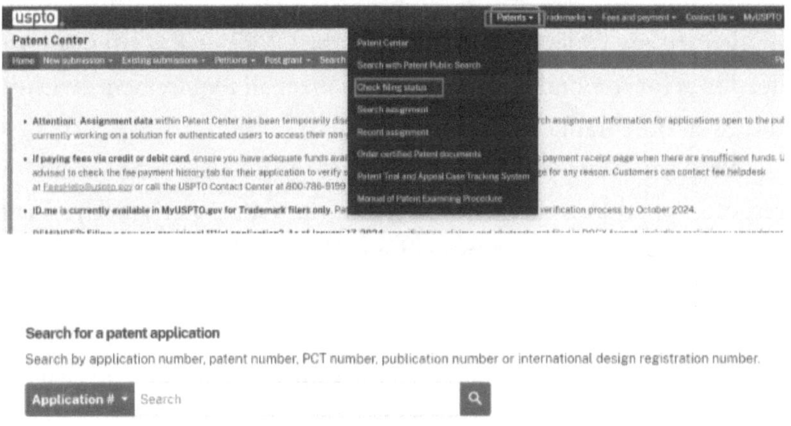

Patent Application filing status Fig.
Source: https://patentcenter.uspto.gov/

Track Key Events

Application Status

Regularly review the status of your application by selecting it from your list of pending applications. The status will be updated as your application progresses through various stages of the review process. The Patent Center will show the status of your application, such as "Filed," "Under Examination," "Rejected," or "Granted."

Office Actions

Office Actions are formal communications from the USPTO that may include requests for additional information, rejections, or other requirements. It is essential to understand the nature of each Office Action to provide an appropriate response.

Through the Patent Center, read the Office Action thoroughly to identify any issues or requests from the USPTO. Pay attention to deadlines for responding to ensure you meet all requirements within the given time frame.

Prepare Your Response: Prepare a detailed and accurate response to address the issues raised in the Office Action. This may involve amending claims, providing additional documentation, or clarifying information.

Submit Your Response: Use the USPTO's electronic filing system to submit your response to the Office Action. Ensure that all required forms and supporting documents are included.

Communication: Review any communications from the USPTO for important deadlines, additional requirements, or clarifications needed.

Respond to Office Actions

- Review: Carefully read any Office Actions or other communications from the USPTO. These may require you to amend your application or provide additional information.

○ Prepare Response: Draft and submit a response to address the examiner's concerns. This often involves making amendments to the claims or providing additional explanations.

○ Submit: File your response through the Patent Center, ensuring all deadlines are met.

Monitor Deadlines

○ Keep Track: Be aware of key deadlines, such as the response period for Office Actions, and maintenance fee due dates.

○ Set Reminders: Use calendar reminders or tracking tools to ensure you don't miss critical dates.

Review Published Documents

● Publication: Your patent application will be published 18 months from the earliest filing date, which is typically when the public can view it.

● Check Publication: Once published, you can access and review the full text of your application through the USPTO Patent Center.

Respond to Requests for Information

● Additional Information: If the USPTO requests further details or clarification, respond promptly to avoid delays.

- Maintain Communication: Keep communication channels open with the USPTO and follow any instructions provided.

Entity status:

Regular Entity Definition: A regular entity is any applicant who does not qualify as a small entity or micro entity.

Requirements: No Specific Restrictions: There are no specific income or size requirements to qualify as a regular entity. This status simply applies to those who do not meet the criteria for being a small or micro entity.

Conditions:

- Standard Fees: Regular entities pay the full amount of USPTO fees for filing, examination, and issuance, without reductions.

Small Entity Definition: A small entity can be an individual, a small business, or a nonprofit organization that meets certain size and ownership requirements. **Requirements:**

Individuals: An individual inventor who files a patent application on their own and has not assigned their rights to a large company.

Small Businesses: A business with fewer than 500 employees in total. This includes all employees of the business and its affiliates. It does not matter if the business is a single entity or a conglomerate, as long as the total number of employees is less than 500.

Nonprofit Organizations: Nonprofit organizations such as universities or research entities that are not operated for commercial purposes and are focused on education, research, or charity.

Not Assigned to Large Companies: The patent application must be in the name of the qualifying small entity and must not be assigned to a large company or an entity that does not qualify as a small entity.

Fee Implications: Small entities receive a 50% reduction in most USPTO fees compared to regular entities.

Micro Entity Definition: A micro entity is an applicant who qualifies for an additional fee reduction based on specific income and size criteria.

Requirements:

- Income: The applicant must meet the income limit for micro entities, which is less than three times the *federal poverty level* for the applicant's family size (this threshold is updated annually).

- Number of Applications: The applicant must not have filed more than four patent applications previously (excluding applications filed for the same invention and international patent applications claiming priority).

- Not Assigned to Large Companies: The patent application must not be assigned to a large company or an entity that does not qualify as a micro entity.

Conditions:

- **Micro Entity Declaration:** You must submit a Micro Entity Status declaration to certify that you meet the requirements. This is typically done when filing the patent application and may involve using a specific USPTO form, such as Form PTO/SB/15[1].

---

1. https://www.uspto.gov/sites/default/files/documents/sb0015b.pdf

Fee Implications: Micro entities receive a 75% reduction in most USPTO fees compared to regular entities.

It is important to check specific criteria and updates on thresholds, as requirements may change. The USPTO provides detailed guidelines and forms for each status on its website, which you can consult for accurate and current information.

What is the Federal Poverty Level?

The federal poverty level is an annual measure established by the U.S. Department of Health and Human Services (HHS) that defines income thresholds considered as poverty in various regions of the country and for different family sizes. These thresholds are updated annually.

How It Applies to Micro Entity Status

To qualify as a micro entity under USPTO rules, the applicant's annual income must be less than 3 times the federal poverty level for their family size.

Example of Application:

1. **Determine the Federal Poverty Level:** First, you need to know the updated federal poverty level for the applicant's family size. For example, in 2024, the poverty level for a single-person family might be $14,580 (this amount varies by year and family size).

2. **Calculate the Micro Entity Threshold:** Multiply the federal poverty level by 3 to obtain the income threshold for micro entity status. Using the poverty level of $14,580, the threshold would be: $14,580 × 3 = $43,740

The applicant must have an annual income of less than $43,740 to qualify as a micro entity in this example.

Steps to Determine Eligibility:

- **Consult Poverty Levels:** Refer to the most recent federal poverty level published by the HHS for the relevant family size.

- **Calculate the Threshold:** Multiply the federal poverty level by 3 to determine the specific micro entity income threshold.

- **Compare Income:** Ensure that the applicant's annual income is below this threshold to qualify as a micro entity.

The "3 times the federal poverty level" threshold is used to determine if an applicant qualifies as a micro entity for patent fee reductions. The federal poverty level is based on family size and is updated annually. To qualify, the applicant's income must be less than three times this level. It is crucial to check the most recent poverty level and calculate the corresponding threshold to ensure eligibility.

Patent Fees

Filing Fees: Filing fees are the charges associated with submitting a patent application to the United States Patent and Trademark Office (USPTO). These fees vary depending on the type of patent (e.g., utility, design, or plant patents) and the size of the entity (large, small, or micro).

Examination Fees: An examination fee is required to initiate the examination of a non-provisional utility patent application. This fee is paid after the application is filed but before the examination process begins. The USPTO uses this fee to cover the costs of reviewing and assessing the patent application, which includes time spent by patent examiners evaluating the claims, drawings, and specifications for compliance with patent laws.

Utility Patent Examination Fee: This fee applies specifically to the examination of utility patents, which cover new and useful inventions or processes. The fee amount may vary depending on the size of the entity and the complexity of the application.

Search Fees: Search fees cover the costs associated with conducting a prior art search. This search is necessary to determine whether the invention is novel and non-obvious in light of existing technologies or patents. The USPTO examiners rely on the search results to assess the patentability of the invention. The fee may differ based on the type of patent application and the entity's status.

Issue Fees: The issue fee is the charge required to finalize and grant a patent after the application has successfully passed examination and met all legal criteria. Payment of the issue fee is necessary before a patent is officially granted by the USPTO.

Utility Patent Issue Fee: This fee is due once the USPTO completes the examination process and determines that the application is allowable. The applicant will receive a Notice of Allowance, which includes instructions for paying the issue fee. The issue fee must typically be paid within three months of receiving the Notice of Allowance. Failure to pay the issue fee within this period can result in additional late fees or abandonment of the application.

Reissue Fees: A reissue fee is required when correcting errors in an already granted patent. A reissue patent is issued to address defects in the original patent, such as errors in the claims, drawings, or specifications that might impact the enforceability of the patent. The reissue fee allows the patent holder to amend the claims or other aspects of the patent to rectify these issues. Like other fees, reissue fees vary based on entity size (large, small, or micro).

Reissue Patent Fee: The fee for reissuing a patent is distinct from the original issue fee and is typically based on the specific error correction sought. Reissue is available when substantive corrections, such as claim amendments, are necessary to maintain the enforceability of the patent.

Maintenance Fees

Maintenance fees are periodic fees required to keep a granted patent in force. These fees are necessary to ensure that the patent remains active and enforceable. Failure to pay these fees can result in the expiration of the patent, meaning that the patent rights are lost and the invention enters the public domain.

Maintenance fees are used to fund the ongoing administrative costs of maintaining patent records and enforcing patents. They help the USPTO manage the large number of patents in force and ensure that only those patents that are actively being utilized remain protected.

After a patent is granted, maintenance fees must be paid at regular intervals (3.5, 7.5, and 11.5 years) to keep the patent in force. These fees must be paid to maintain patent rights. The table below shows the maintenance fees according to the entity status:

Additional Fees

Additional Claims:

When filing a non-provisional utility patent application, the USPTO charges additional fees for each claim beyond the initial set included with the application.

The standard filing fee covers up to 20 claims in a utility patent application. For each claim over 20, there are additional fees.

Additional independent claims

The standard filing fee covers up to three independent claims in a utility patent application. The USPTO imposes additional fees when a utility patent application includes more than three independent claims.

Excess Pages:

For pages beyond a certain number (typically 100 pages for utility patents), additional fees may apply.

The additional fees for each entity status are in the table below:

Late Fees:

Fees may apply if you miss deadlines for responses, maintenance fees, or other required actions.

The fees are constantly being reviewed and updated, which may vary from the above. For updated fees please visit: USPTO fee schedule

Chapter 5

EXAMINERS EVALUATION AND OFFICE ACTION

CHAPTER 5. EXAMINERS EVALUATION AND OFFICE ACTION

Examiner's Duties Divided into Three Specific Sections:

1. Pre-Search Activities

• The examiner is expected to carefully read and understand the invention as described in the applicant's specification. This allows the examiner to grasp what the applicant believes to be novel about their invention.

• The examiner must also assess whether the application sufficiently defines the metes and bounds of the claimed invention. This involves determining whether the applicant has clearly articulated the invention so that someone skilled in the relevant field would understand exactly what is being claimed.

• Before beginning the search stage, the examiner's final pre-search task is to determine the scope of the claim. This involves clarifying exactly what protection will be provided to the applicant if the application is ultimately granted.

2. Search

The examiner conducts a search for existing technology related to the claimed invention. This search is aided by in-house databases as well as external commercial databases to identify "prior art," or previous inventions and publications, that might impact the patentability of the current application.

3. Patentability and Office's Position

- After completing the pre-search and search activities, the examiner drafts an official position in the form of a **Non-Final Office Action**. This document identifies and analyzes all issues relevant to whether the claimed invention is patentable. The examiner will explain to the applicant exactly what is preventing the issuance of a patent.

- If the applicant does not respond to the first Office Action or expressly abandons the application, the examiner may issue a **Notice of Abandonment**. Conversely, if the applicant responds fully and successfully overcomes all rejections and objections, the examiner will issue a **Notice of Allowance**, indicating that the application is allowed and the patent will be granted.

Patent Examination Flowchart:

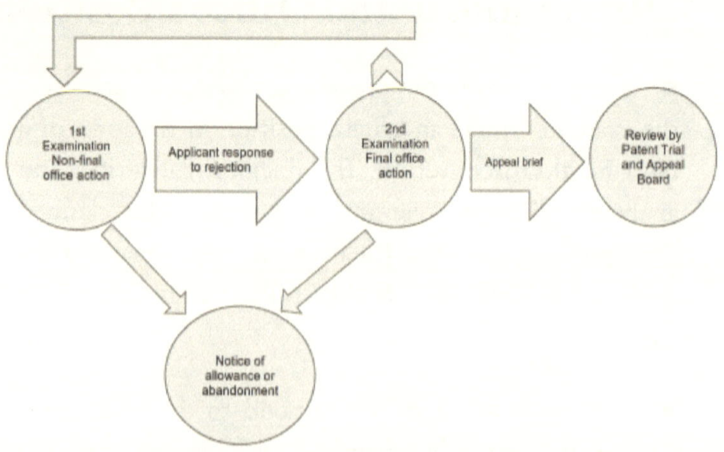

Figure/Graph created by the author

2103-Patent Examination Process (uspto.gov)

Determine what invention is sought to be patented

Patent applicants need a prompt and thorough examination of their applications. During the initial review, each claim must be checked for compliance with all statutory requirements for patentability, even if some claims have deficiencies. Examiners should clearly state all reasons for rejecting claims in the first Office action, especially if deficiencies are present. Whenever possible, they should suggest how to overcome rejections and resolve issues. If a rejection is not based on prior art, such as due to lack of description, enablement, or utility, the reasons should be fully explained, not just concluded. Failing to do so may cause unnecessary delays in the application process.

Identify and Understand Any Utility for the Invention

The claimed invention as a whole must be useful. The purpose of this requirement is to limit patent protection to inventions that possess a certain level of "real world" value, as opposed to subject matter that represents nothing more than an idea or concept, or is simply a starting point for future investigation or research

Examiners must review the application to identify any asserted utility. The applicant or the inventor is best qualified to explain why an invention is useful. Accordingly, a complete disclosure must contain an indication of the practical application of the claimed invention.

Review the Detailed Disclosure and Specific Embodiments of the Invention

The written description provides the clearest explanation of the invention by detailing how it works, its relation to prior art, and the significance of its features. Examiners should:

(A) Determine the function of the invention (e.g., what it does when used as described). (B) Identify the key features needed to achieve at least one practical application.

Claims

The claims define the property rights provided by a patent, and thus require careful scrutiny. The goal of claim analysis is to identify the boundaries of the protection sought by the applicant and to understand how the claims relate to and define what the applicant has indicated is the invention. Examiners must first determine the scope of a claim by thoroughly analyzing the language of the claim before determining if the claim complies with each statutory requirement for patentability.

Examiners should match each claim limitation to the parts of the disclosure that describe that limitation. This must be done in all cases, regardless of whether the claimed invention uses "means-plus-function" or "step-plus-function" language.

In patent law, "means-plus-function" and "step-plus-function" language are specific types of claim language used in drafting patent claims. Here's a breakdown of their meanings:

- **Means-Plus-Function Language**: This is a way to draft a patent claim where the claim defines a component of an invention by its function rather than its structure. For example, instead of describing a "gear mechanism" with specific parts, the claim might describe a "means for transferring rotational motion." The legal significance of this language is that it requires the patent holder to describe the corresponding structure, material, or acts that perform the specified function in the patent's specification. This language is governed by 35 U.S.C. § 112(f) (in the U.S.), which stipulates that the claim must be interpreted in light of the specification, focusing on how the function is achieved rather than the specific name or terminology used.

- **Step-Plus-Function Language**: Similar to means-plus-function, this type of language is used to describe a process or method in terms of the function performed rather than the specific steps. For instance, a claim might describe a "step for achieving a particular result" without detailing the exact process. In the U.S., such claims are governed by the same statutory framework (35 U.S.C. § 112(f)), and the interpretation of these claims depends on the steps described in the patent's specification that correspond to the claimed function.

The key takeaway is that both means-plus-function and step-plus-function claim language require that the claims be interpreted in the context of the detailed description provided in the patent application. This ensures that the claims are not overly broad and that they are supported by a clear and specific disclosure of how the function is achieved or how the process is carried out.

This matching step ensures that examiners correctly interpret each claim limitation in light of the specification.

When evaluating the scope of a claim, all limitations must be considered together, not in isolation. The claim should be analyzed as a whole.

Conduct a thorough search of the prior art

Before evaluating the claimed invention for patentability, examiners must thoroughly search the prior art. This helps them better understand the invention. They should search both the claimed and unclaimed aspects described in the specification if there's a reasonable chance the unclaimed aspects might be claimed later. The search must consider any structure or material described in the specification and its equivalents that relate to the claimed means- (or step-) plus-function limitation, as outlined in 35 U.S.C. 112(f) and MPEP §§ 2181-2186.

Determine whether the claimed invention complies with 35 U.S.C. 101

Consider the Scope of 35 U.S.C. 101 Under Current Law

Section 101 of Title 35, U.S. Code, states:

"Anyone who invents or discovers a new and useful process, machine, manufacture, or composition of matter, or any new and useful improvement thereof, may obtain a patent for it, subject to the conditions and requirements of this title."

35 U.S.C. 101 has four key requirements:

- Only one patent can be obtained for an invention.

- The inventors must be identified in an application filed on or after September 16, 2012, or must be the applicant in applications filed before that date.

- The claimed invention must be eligible for patenting.

- The claimed invention must be useful.

Patent eligibility under 35 U.S.C. 101 is a first step in the examination. Even if an invention is eligible under 35 U.S.C. 101, it still needs to meet other patent requirements like novelty (35 U.S.C. 102), nonobviousness (35 U.S.C. 103), and proper description and clear claims (35 U.S.C. 112).

Eligibility in U.S. patent law refers to the legal framework that determines whether an invention qualifies for patent protection. Under U.S. law, specifically 35 U.S.C. § 101, to be eligible for a patent, an invention must fall into one of the following categories:

- **Process**: A method or series of steps to achieve a certain result (e.g., a manufacturing process or software algorithm).

- **Machine**: A tangible device that performs a function (e.g., engines, computers).

- **Article of Manufacture**: A physical item made by humans (e.g., tools, furniture).

- **Composition of Matter**: Chemical compounds or mixtures, including drugs and synthetic materials (e.g., pharmaceuticals, alloys).

Important Considerations in Eligibility

- **Abstract Ideas, Laws of Nature, and Natural Phenomena**: Even if an invention falls into one of the above categories, it must not be an abstract idea, a law of nature, or a natural phenomenon, as these are considered **ineligible for patenting**. This principle is shaped by U.S. Supreme Court decisions, most notably:

  - *Alice Corp. v. CLS Bank International* (2014) emphasized that abstract ideas implemented through a computer or software are not patentable unless they provide an "inventive concept" that transforms the idea into a patentable application.

  - *Mayo Collaborative Services v. Prometheus Laboratories* (2012) dealt with laws of nature and stated that merely applying a natural law using standard methods is not patentable.

- **The Alice/Mayo Test**: To determine patent eligibility, U.S. courts and the USPTO use the two-step test known as the **Alice/Mayo test**:

  - **Step 1**: Determine whether the claim is directed to a patent-ineligible concept (e.g., abstract ideas, laws of nature).

  - **Step 2**: If so, analyze whether the claim adds something significantly more than the ineligible concept, such as a novel or inventive application of the idea. If so, the claim may still be eligible.

- **Practical Applications**: Ineligible concepts, such as abstract ideas, can still be patented if they are applied in a novel, useful, and specific way. This means that a method or process that involves an abstract idea but applies it to a concrete technical solution may pass the test.

- **Software and Business Methods**: These have been subject to scrutiny under the Alice/Mayo framework. Business methods and software innovations must demonstrate that they do more than merely implement abstract ideas and provide a clear technological improvement or inventive concept to be patentable.

Recent Developments

In recent years, the U.S. Patent and Trademark Office (USPTO) has issued guidelines that provide more clarity about how to apply the eligibility test, especially for emerging technologies like AI, biotech, and financial technologies. These guidelines aim to make the patent process more predictable and transparent for inventors.

Understanding patent eligibility is crucial for ensuring that your invention qualifies for protection before investing significant time and resources into the patenting process.

METHOD OF TREATMENTS

In U.S. patent law, **methods of treatment** are a specific category of inventions that can qualify for patent protection. These patents typically cover ways to treat diseases or medical conditions using drugs, therapies, or specific procedures. They are classified as "process" patents under 35 U.S.C. § 101. However, there are unique aspects and challenges related to patenting methods of treatment due to their interaction with both patent law and public health considerations.

Key Elements of Method of Treatment Patents

Eligible Subject Matter: A method of treatment must meet the basic requirements of patent eligibility under 35 U.S.C. § 101. Specifically, the method must be:

- ○ **Novel**: The treatment method must be new, not previously disclosed in the prior art.

- ○ **Non-obvious**: The method must not be an obvious combination of prior techniques or knowledge.

- ○ **Useful**: The method must have a specific and credible utility, such as treating a particular disease.

Typically, methods of treatment are considered **eligible** for patent protection if they involve a novel process for administering a drug, a new dosage regimen, or a new therapeutic use of a known compound.

Steps of a Method Claim: A method of treatment patent often includes claims that outline specific steps. For instance:

- ○ Administering a specific dosage of a drug.
- ○ Applying a medical device in a particular way.
- ○ Using a particular protocol for therapy.

The **language of the claims** must be clear and define how the method is novel or inventive. The claims might describe administering a drug at a new dosage or in combination with another therapeutic agent in a way that hasn't been done before.

Patentability Challenges

- **Laws of Nature**: One of the biggest challenges in patenting methods of treatment comes from the prohibition against patenting laws of nature. The U.S. Supreme Court case *Mayo Collaborative Services v. Prometheus Laboratories, Inc.* (2012) plays a significant role here.

In *Mayo*, the Court ruled that a patent claim describing a process of determining drug dosage based on measuring natural metabolite levels was not patentable because it essentially covered a law of nature (i.e., the relationship between metabolite levels and health). The decision set the precedent that merely discovering a natural correlation or biological principle is not enough for patentability. Instead, there must be an **inventive concept** beyond the law of nature itself.

For method of treatment patents, this means that:

○ The claim must not merely recite a natural process or phenomenon.

○ The treatment steps must apply the discovery in a novel and non-obvious way.

- **Abstract Ideas**: After the *Alice* decision (2014), concerns arose that some method of treatment patents could be challenged as being directed to abstract ideas, particularly when the methods involved data analysis or diagnosis. However, **treatment methods** that involve concrete steps of administering therapy or performing a medical procedure typically avoid this pitfall, as they are seen as practical applications rather than abstract concepts.

● **Patentability of Dosage Regimens and Combination Therapies**: Patent claims directed to new dosage regimens (such as changing the frequency or amount of a drug administered) and combination therapies (using two or more therapeutic agents together) are often eligible for patenting. However, these claims must demonstrate:

○ That the new regimen or combination is not obvious from prior knowledge (e.g., a skilled professional in the field would not have naturally combined the treatments or adjusted the dosage).

○ That the change results in a new and useful effect, such as reducing side effects or improving efficacy.

Utility and Written Description Requirements

● **Utility**: Under 35 U.S.C. § 101, the method must have a specific and substantial utility, meaning it must actually treat a medical condition or achieve a claimed therapeutic benefit. This is often demonstrated through clinical trials, preclinical studies, or experimental data.

● **Written Description**: The patent application must clearly describe the method and provide enough detail to show that the inventor was in possession of the claimed invention. This includes disclosing sufficient details about the steps of the treatment, dosages, and any novel therapeutic uses.

Enforcement and Infringement Issues

Method of treatment patents face unique enforcement challenges because they often involve actions performed by doctors, hospitals, or patients. In the U.S., 35 U.S.C. § 271 addresses this issue:

- Physicians and medical practitioners are generally exempt from patent infringement liability under 35 U.S.C. § 287(c) for practicing a patented medical or surgical method. This means that doctors cannot be sued for using patented methods of treatment in medical practice.

- However, pharmaceutical companies, drug manufacturers, or distributors may still be held liable for inducing infringement if they market a drug with specific instructions (a "label") that directly correlates to the patented method.

This has led to strategies where patents on methods of treatment focus on the labeling of pharmaceutical products to secure indirect enforcement through the sale and distribution of drugs.

Second Medical Use and the Doctrine of Equivalents

In the U.S., patent law does not explicitly recognize "second medical use" claims (i.e., patents on new uses for known drugs, as is done in Europe), but patent applicants can still seek protection for new methods of using known compounds. The doctrine of equivalents may also allow for broader enforcement, where a treatment method can still be considered infringing if it performs **substantially the same function** in **substantially the same way** as the claimed method, even if not identically worded.

Examples of Method of Treatment Patents

1. **New Uses for Known Drugs**: A patent could cover a new therapeutic application of a known drug, such as using an existing cancer treatment to treat a different disease.
2. **New Dosage Regimens**: A method patent may claim a specific way of administering a drug (e.g., changing the frequency of doses to reduce side effects or improve efficacy).
3. **Combination Therapies**: A patent could claim a method of treating a disease by administering two or more drugs together in a specific way that improves outcomes.

Conclusion

In summary, methods of treatment are generally eligible for patent protection in the U.S. if they involve novel and non-obvious therapeutic approaches. However, inventors must carefully navigate the challenges posed by legal precedents related to laws of nature and abstract ideas. By focusing on specific treatment steps, dosage regimens, or combination therapies, applicants can increase their chances of securing robust patent protection for their medical innovations.

USES AND MEDICAL USES

In patent law, the concept of "uses" and particularly "second medical uses" refers to the protection of new applications or therapeutic indications of known substances or products. This is particularly relevant in the pharmaceutical and biotech fields, where a previously known drug or compound may be discovered to treat a different disease or condition than it was originally intended for.

The legal framework for protecting such innovations varies significantly between different jurisdictions, such as the U.S. and Europe. Here's a deep dive into the nuances of first and second uses in patent law, particularly focusing on second medical uses.

First Medical Use (New Use of a Known Substance)

The first time a new medical use is discovered for a known substance, it is often referred to as the first medical use. Even if the compound itself is already known (e.g., discovered or synthesized previously), if no one has yet patented its therapeutic use, the discovery of its utility in medicine can be eligible for patent protection. This is allowed under the principle that the novelty lies in the application of the substance rather than the substance itself.

Example of a First Medical Use:

Imagine a chemical compound discovered in a laboratory that is known but has no known therapeutic applications. If researchers discover that this compound can be used to treat cancer, they can file for a patent on this first medical use of the compound, even though the compound itself is not new.

Second Medical Use (New Use of a Known Substance)

A second medical use patent refers to the protection of new therapeutic uses of a compound that has already been known and used for other medical purposes. This is especially important in the pharmaceutical industry where drugs are often "repurposed" to treat conditions different from those for which they were initially developed.

Second medical use patents are an extension of this idea, where a drug or compound that already has a known therapeutic application is found to have a new, previously unknown use. Even though the substance itself may not be new, the discovery of this new application can be patented.

Example of a Second Medical Use:

A well-known drug like Aspirin, originally developed to treat pain and inflammation, was later discovered to have anticoagulant properties, making it useful for preventing heart attacks and strokes. Even though Aspirin as a compound was not new, its second medical **use** for cardiovascular disease prevention was patentable.

Legal Framework in Different Jurisdictions

1. Europe and the EPC (European Patent Convention)

Europe is known for having clear provisions regarding second medical use patents. Under the European Patent Convention (EPC), a second medical use can be patented if it involves a new therapeutic application for a known substance.

- **Swiss-type claims**: Prior to 2011, applicants in Europe often used Swiss-type claims to claim second medical uses. These claims were written in the format: "Use of substance X in the manufacture of a medicament for the treatment of condition Y."

Swiss-type claims were used to avoid concerns that direct method-of-treatment claims might conflict with laws preventing patenting of medical procedures. This format was accepted until 2010, after which the EPC formally introduced the option to claim second medical uses directly.

- **EPC 2000**: With the revision of the European Patent Convention in 2000 (EPC 2000), second medical uses could be claimed in a simpler format: "Substance X for use in treating condition Y." This format is now the standard for second medical use claims in Europe.

Key Requirements:

- **Novelty**: The second use must not have been disclosed before. It must be a new therapeutic application for the substance.

- **Inventive Step**: It must not be obvious to a person skilled in the art that the substance would be effective in treating the new condition.

- **Sufficiency of Disclosure**: The patent application must clearly describe how the substance achieves the therapeutic effect in the new use.

2. United States (US)

In the United States, second medical use claims are treated differently. The U.S. does not explicitly allow for "second use" claims in the same way as Europe. Instead, inventors typically seek patent protection for the method of treatment involving the new use of the known substance. This type of claim is allowed under U.S. law, and the patent would cover a process or method that uses the drug in a new way, even if the drug itself is not new.

Key Considerations in the U.S.:

● **Method of Treatment Claims**: Instead of using "for use" language, U.S. patents must claim the **method** or **process** of treating the new condition with the known substance.

○ Example: "A method of treating disease Y by administering a therapeutically effective amount of compound X."

● **Patentability**: The new use must be non-obvious and provide a distinct therapeutic benefit or approach, even if the compound is known.

● **Mayo and Alice Decisions**: The Mayo v. Prometheus (2012) and Alice Corp. v. CLS Bank (2014) decisions emphasize that patent claims involving natural laws or abstract ideas are not eligible unless there is a sufficiently inventive concept. This has led to more scrutiny in method-of-treatment patents, especially where the claims involve dosing regimens or biomarkers related to natural phenomena.

The Doctrine of Equivalents

The doctrine of equivalents can play a role in enforcing second use patents. Under this doctrine, an invention may still infringe a patent even if it does not fall within the literal scope of the claims but performs substantially the same function in substantially the same way to achieve the same result.

This doctrine can sometimes help enforce second medical use patents, especially if competitors try to make small modifications in dosing or administration to bypass the claims.

Patentability Issues and Challenges

1. Obviousness:

One of the major challenges in obtaining second use patents is proving non-obviousness. If the new use is an obvious extension of prior art, it will not be patentable. Courts will examine whether someone skilled in the art could have easily predicted that the known drug would work for the new condition.

2. Sufficiency of Disclosure:

Another common hurdle is meeting the requirement for sufficiency of disclosure. The patent application must provide enough information to demonstrate that the new use is viable and effective, usually through clinical or experimental data. If the application lacks detailed evidence, it may face rejection.

3. Enforcement:

Second use patents, particularly in the pharmaceutical space, can be difficult to enforce because the infringing party is often the patient or healthcare provider, not the manufacturer. As such, these patents are often enforced indirectly by targeting the labeling of the drug. This is done through what's known as "skinny labeling," where generic manufacturers may seek to carve out certain indications from their drug labels to avoid infringement on second use patents.

Pharmaceutical Strategy: Lifecycle Management

Second medical use patents are an important strategy for lifecycle management of pharmaceutical products. Once the initial patent on the active ingredient of a drug expires, pharmaceutical companies can continue to extend market exclusivity by obtaining second medical use patents on:

- New therapeutic indications.
- Novel dosage forms (e.g., controlled-release versions).
- New dosing regimens or combination therapies.

Conclusion

Second medical use patents play a crucial role in incentivizing innovation, especially in the pharmaceutical industry, where drug repurposing can lead to significant advancements in treating diseases. The approach to patenting these uses differs between jurisdictions, with the U.S. focusing on method-of-treatment claims and Europe embracing second medical use claims directly. Successfully navigating the legal landscape of second use patents requires careful attention to novelty, non-obviousness, and sufficiency of disclosure, as well as strategic considerations for enforcement and lifecycle management.

In the United States, patenting new uses for known substances, often referred to as second medical uses, presents a unique challenge due to specific legal frameworks and doctrines that govern how these inventions can be protected. Unlike Europe, where second medical use claims are explicitly allowed, the U.S. relies heavily on method-of-treatment patents. Here's a deep dive into how second uses are handled under U.S. patent law.

Legal Foundation for Method of Treatment Claims

In the U.S., second medical uses are generally claimed as methods of treatment under 35 U.S.C. § 101, which governs patent-eligible subject matter. While a compound or substance may already be known, a new way of using that compound (for example, treating a different disease or using it in a novel therapeutic regimen) can still be patented if it meets the necessary patentability criteria.

To obtain a patent for a second use of a known drug or compound in the U.S., the inventor typically files for a method of treatment patent that claims the specific steps involved in administering the substance to achieve the new therapeutic effect.

Example Claim Format in the U.S.:

"A method of treating [condition Y] in a subject, comprising administering to the subject a therapeutically effective amount of [compound X]."

The focus is on the process of treatment, which involves a step-by-step description of how the drug or compound is used in the new medical context.

Patentability Requirements for Second Medical Uses

1. Novelty (35 U.S.C. § 102):

The new use of a known compound must be novel. In other words, no prior art (previous patents, publications, or public use) should disclose the use of the compound for the specific new condition or method of treatment being claimed. This is relatively straightforward if the new medical use has not been previously known or disclosed.

2. Non-Obviousness (35 U.S.C. § 103):

Even if the new use is novel, it must also be non-obvious. The challenge with second medical use patents often lies in proving that the new use of the drug would not have been obvious to someone skilled in the art. If a drug's new application is too predictable based on its known properties, the USPTO may reject the claim as obvious.

For instance, if a drug is already known to reduce inflammation, and the new claim is its use for a condition characterized by inflammation (e.g., arthritis), the patent examiner might argue that this new use is an obvious application of the drug's known properties.

Factors that Influence Non-Obviousness:

• **Unexpected Results**: If the new use produces unexpected therapeutic benefits, such as treating a condition that is very different from the original use, this can support non-obviousness.

• **Overcoming Long-Felt Need**: If the new use addresses a significant unmet medical need, it can contribute to the non-obviousness argument.

• **Prior Failures**: If prior attempts to use the drug for the new application had failed, this can further support patentability.

3. Utility (35 U.S.C. § 101):

The new use must be useful in a practical, specific, and substantial way. This is often proven through preclinical studies, experimental data, or clinical trials that demonstrate the drug's efficacy in the new therapeutic application. Simply speculating that a known drug could treat another condition without evidence would likely result in a rejection based on a lack of utility.

The Mayo Decision and its Impact

One of the most significant challenges for second medical use patents in the U.S. arises from the Supreme Court decision in Mayo Collaborative Services v. Prometheus Laboratories, Inc. (2012). In this case, the Court ruled that claims based on correlations between drug dosages and natural biological responses were not patentable because they involved a law of nature.

Case Summary:

Prometheus Laboratories had patented a method of determining drug dosage by measuring metabolite levels in the patient's blood and adjusting the dosage accordingly. The Supreme Court ruled that this claim was essentially describing a natural phenomenon—the relationship between metabolite levels and health—and therefore was ineligible for patent protection under 35 U.S.C. § 101. According to the Court, the method merely applied a law of nature using conventional steps that did not add anything "inventive" beyond the natural law itself.

Implications for Second Medical Use Patents:

Following Mayo, method-of-treatment claims involving the discovery of natural correlations (such as biomarkers or physiological responses) are under heavy scrutiny. For a second medical use to be patentable post-Mayo, the claim must include an inventive concept that transforms the natural correlation into a practical application, such as a specific method of treatment that is not simply routine or conventional.

- For instance, a patent claim that simply administers a drug based on a known biological response is likely to be rejected under Mayo. However, if the claim involves a novel therapeutic approach, such as using the drug in combination with another compound to treat a disease in a previously unrecognized way, it might be patentable.

Alice Decision and Abstract Ideas

Following the Mayo decision, the Alice Corp. v. CLS Bank (2014) ruling further tightened the scope of patentable subject matter, particularly concerning abstract ideas. Although Alice primarily deals with software and business methods, its two-part test for determining patent eligibility is often applied in cases involving second medical use patents.

The **Alice/Mayo Test**:

- **Step 1**: Determine if the claim is directed to a patent-ineligible concept, such as a law of nature or an abstract idea.

- **Step 2**: If so, determine whether the claim contains an inventive concept that transforms the nature of the claim into something patent-eligible.

For second medical uses, this means that claims cannot merely recite an abstract idea (e.g., adjusting dosage based on biological data) without adding something inventive, such as a specific treatment protocol or new combination therapy.

Types of Second Use Patents in the U.S.

- **New Use of a Known Drug**: One of the most common types of second use patents involves the discovery of a new disease or condition that a known drug can treat. For example, a cancer drug may later be found to treat an autoimmune disease. The key is to prove that the new use is novel, non-obvious, and provides a clear therapeutic benefit.

Example Claim:

○ "A method of treating [autoimmune disease] in a subject comprising administering an effective amount of [drug X] to the subject."

- **New Dosage Regimens**: Another common approach is patenting a new dosage regimen. Even if the drug is already approved for a specific condition, adjusting the dose (e.g., increasing or decreasing the frequency or amount) in a way that improves efficacy or reduces side effects can be patentable.

Example Claim:

○ "A method of treating [condition Y] in a subject, comprising administering [compound X] at a dosage of [specific amount] once daily."

- **Combination Therapies**: Combination therapies, where a known drug is administered with another drug or treatment modality (e.g., surgery, radiation), can also form the basis of a second use patent. The combination must demonstrate a novel, non-obvious therapeutic effect.

Example Claim:

○ "A method of treating [condition Y] in a subject, comprising administering [drug X] and [drug Y] in combination to the subject."

Enforcement of Method-of-Treatment Patents in the U.S.

One of the unique challenges with method-of-treatment patents, including second medical use patents, is enforcement. In the U.S., the Hatch-Waxman Act governs the interaction between patent law and the approval of generic drugs. Method-of-treatment patents are often enforced through the labeling of pharmaceutical products, especially when a generic manufacturer seeks approval for a version of a patented drug.

Skinny Labeling:

Generic manufacturers may attempt to avoid infringement by using a skinny label—an FDA-approved drug label that excludes the patented use or method of treatment. However, even with a skinny label, a generic manufacturer could be liable for induced infringement if it promotes the drug for the patented use.

Direct vs. Indirect Infringement:

- **Direct Infringement**: Physicians and medical practitioners who administer the drug are typically protected from patent infringement claims under 35 U.S.C. § 287(c), which exempts medical professionals from liability for performing a medical or surgical method.

- **Indirect Infringement**: Enforcement often focuses on pharmaceutical companies, as they can be held liable for inducing infringement if their marketing or labeling encourages doctors or patients to use the drug in the patented way.

Conclusion

In the U.S., patenting second medical uses is primarily achieved through method-of-treatment claims. While this approach allows for protection of new uses for known substances, it must overcome significant hurdles, particularly in light of the Mayo and Alice decisions. These rulings emphasize the importance of adding an inventive step beyond laws of nature or abstract ideas to qualify for patent protection. Despite these challenges, second medical use patents remain a critical tool in pharmaceutical innovation, allowing companies to extend the life cycle of drugs and discover new therapeutic applications.

Use claims and method of treatment claims

Here are several examples of various types of use claims, including use claims, medical claims, second-use claims, and method-of-treatment claims as they are commonly used in the U.S. patent system.

1. Use Claims

These claims describe the use of a product or compound for a specific purpose, not necessarily tied to a medical application.

Example:

- *"Use of Compound X as a corrosion inhibitor in metal pipes."*

  ○ This is a generic "use claim" where the focus is on the use of a compound for a non-medical purpose. The compound X may be known, but the use of it for inhibiting corrosion in pipes might be novel.

2. Medical Use Claims

In U.S. law, medical use claims are typically formulated as method-of-treatment claims. A medical use claim outlines the therapeutic use of a compound or product to treat a specific condition or disease.

Example:

- *"A method for treating hypertension in a patient, comprising administering an effective amount of Compound X to the patient."*

○ In this example, the use of Compound X to treat hypertension is being claimed. The claim focuses on a medical treatment and specifies the therapeutic use.

3. Second-Use Claims

Second-use claims (also known as second medical use claims) protect a new therapeutic use for a known drug or substance. In the U.S., these claims are usually structured as method-of-treatment claims because U.S. law does not permit direct second-use claims (unlike Europe, where second medical use claims are more straightforward).

Example 1: New Therapeutic Use

- *"A method for treating Alzheimer's disease in a patient, comprising administering an effective amount of Compound Y, wherein Compound Y is previously known for treating epilepsy."*

  - In this claim, Compound Y was already known for treating epilepsy, but the patent application is seeking to protect the discovery that it can also treat Alzheimer's disease. This is a classic second-use claim structured as a method of treatment in the U.S.

Example 2: New Dosing Regimen

- *"A method for treating migraine headaches in a patient, comprising administering a daily dose of 50 mg of Compound Z, wherein Compound Z was previously administered at 100 mg every 48 hours for treating pain."*

○ This claim focuses on a new dosing regimen for Compound Z, reducing the dose and altering the frequency of administration for the treatment of migraines, even though Compound Z is already known to treat pain.

Example 3: New Patient Population

- *"A method for treating pediatric patients suffering from asthma, comprising administering a therapeutically effective amount of Drug W, wherein Drug W was previously used only for treating adult asthma patients."*

○ This claim introduces a new patient population (pediatric patients), which is another form of second-use claim. The drug was already known for treating adult asthma but is now being applied to children.

4. Method-of-Treatment Claims

Method-of-treatment claims are the most common way to patent second medical uses, new uses of known compounds, or new treatment protocols in the U.S. These claims describe a specific way of using a drug or medical device to treat a medical condition.

Example 1: Basic Method of Treatment

- *"A method of treating diabetes in a patient in need thereof, comprising administering to the patient an effective amount of Compound A."*

○ This is a simple method-of-treatment claim where Compound A is used to treat diabetes. It describes the steps of administering the drug to a patient.

Example 2: Combination Therapy

- *"A method of treating cancer in a patient, comprising administering Compound B and Compound C in combination, wherein Compound B is a chemotherapeutic agent and Compound C is an immunotherapy agent."*

○ Here, the patent is claiming the combination of two different therapies for treating cancer. While each compound may already be known, the claim protects the novel therapeutic benefit of using them together.

Example 3: Personalized Medicine (Biomarker-Based Treatment)

- *"A method of treating lung cancer in a patient, comprising detecting the presence of biomarker X in a patient sample, and administering Drug D if biomarker X is detected."*

  - This claim involves a personalized treatment method where a patient's biomarker is used to guide the decision to administer a specific drug. This type of claim can be difficult post-*Mayo* due to the association with natural laws, but if there's an inventive step in how the treatment is administered, it may be patentable.

Example 4: Targeted Delivery

- *"A method for delivering an active agent to a targeted tissue in a subject, comprising administering a nanoparticle conjugated with the active agent, wherein the nanoparticle selectively binds to the target tissue."*

○ This method-of-treatment claim focuses on targeted drug delivery using nanotechnology, claiming the specific steps of administering a nanoparticle-bound drug for more precise treatment.

5. New Formulations and Delivery Methods

These types of claims often revolve around reformulating a known drug or finding a novel way to deliver it, which can improve efficacy, reduce side effects, or allow for new routes of administration.

Example 1: Reformulated Drug

- *"A method of treating depression in a patient in need thereof, comprising administering a sustained-release formulation of Drug E."*

○ This claim focuses on a new formulation (sustained-release) of a known drug, Drug E, for treating depression.

Example 2: Novel Delivery Route

- *"A method of treating osteoporosis in a patient, comprising administering Drug F via a transdermal patch, wherein Drug F was previously administered via oral dosage."*

○ This claim is based on the new route of administration for a known drug. It protects the method of treating osteoporosis by using a transdermal patch, even though the drug itself is not new.

Example 3: Extended-Release Dosage Form

- *"A method of reducing blood pressure in a patient, comprising administering an extended-release formulation of Drug G once daily, wherein Drug G was previously administered in an immediate-release form twice daily."*

○ This claim protects a new dosage form (extended-release) and a new dosing regimen (once daily), which provides a therapeutic advantage by improving patient compliance or reducing side effects.

Conclusion

In the U.S., second medical uses, new therapeutic applications, and method-of-treatment claims are primarily protected under the legal framework of method-of-treatment claims. These claims must meet the patentability criteria of novelty, non-obviousness, and utility while avoiding pitfalls related to laws of nature and abstract ideas under the *Mayo* and *Alice* decisions. By focusing on how a drug or treatment is administered, new therapeutic applications, dosing regimens, patient populations, or drug combinations, innovators can secure patents for second uses and improvements to existing therapies.

KIT OF PARTS

In the United States, "kit of parts" claims are a type of patent claim that describe a combination of components or parts that are packaged or provided together for use in performing a specific task or achieving a particular result. These claims are commonly found in a variety of industries, particularly in pharmaceuticals, medical devices, biotechnology, and diagnostics. A kit of parts claim can provide protection for a new way of using, assembling, or administering components, even if the individual components themselves are known.

Key Elements of Kit of Parts Claims

A kit of parts claim typically describes:

- The individual components or parts that make up the kit (e.g., multiple drugs, a drug and a delivery device, or a drug and diagnostic tool).

- How the components are packaged together, often to achieve a specific function, such as administering a treatment or diagnosing a condition.

- Instructions for use or a particular method for assembling or using the parts together.

Kit claims are often used when the components have a synergistic effect or are used together in a novel way that provides a new therapeutic benefit or practical utility.

Common Examples of Kit of Parts Claims in the U.S.

• Pharmaceutical Kits: A kit of parts might consist of two or more drugs packaged together with instructions on how to administer them in combination to treat a disease. This is often seen in combination therapies where two or more drugs are administered at different times or dosages to provide a therapeutic benefit.

• Diagnostic Kits: A diagnostic kit may contain various reagents, tools, or devices used to diagnose a condition. For example, a diagnostic test for detecting a biomarker may include different reagents, a sample collection device, and instructions for performing the test.

• Medical Device Kits: Medical device kits often contain components necessary for performing a surgical procedure or administering a treatment. This could include devices and accompanying reagents or drugs needed for the procedure.

Types of Kit of Parts Claims

Kit of parts claims can take several forms depending on the industry and the nature of the invention. Below are common types of kit claims with examples:

1. Pharmaceutical Kits

Pharmaceutical kits often consist of multiple drugs, biologics, or formulations packaged together to be used in combination, with instructions for their use.

Example 1: Combination Therapy Kit

- *"A kit comprising: (a) a first therapeutic agent for treating cancer, (b) a second therapeutic agent for enhancing the efficacy of the first therapeutic agent, and (c) instructions for administering the first therapeutic agent and the second therapeutic agent in combination."*

- **Explanation**: This kit protects the use of two drugs that are administered together. While each drug may be known, the patent protects the combination therapy and how the drugs are used together according to the instructions provided in the kit.

Example 2: Drug and Delivery Device Kit

- *"A kit for treating diabetes comprising: (a) an insulin formulation, (b) a syringe or an insulin pump for delivering the insulin, and (c) instructions for use."*

- **Explanation**: This type of claim protects the combination of a known drug (insulin) with a delivery device (e.g., syringe or insulin pump). While the individual components may be known, packaging them together with specific instructions on administration can be patentable as a kit.

2. Diagnostic Kits

Diagnostic kits usually involve a set of reagents or tools used to detect a disease, genetic marker, or biomolecule.

Example 1: Biomarker Detection Kit

- *"A kit for detecting biomarker X in a biological sample, comprising: (a) a first reagent that specifically binds to biomarker X, (b) a detection agent that produces a signal upon binding of the first reagent to biomarker X, and (c) instructions for using the first reagent and detection agent to detect biomarker X."*

- **Explanation**: This kit protects the specific components needed to detect a biomarker in a biological sample. It may involve antibodies, enzymes, or other agents that work together to produce a detectable signal, along with instructions for conducting the test.

Example 2: Genetic Testing Kit

- *"A kit for determining the presence of a genetic mutation associated with disease Y, comprising: (a) primers for amplifying a DNA sequence containing the genetic mutation, (b) a reagent for detecting the amplified DNA sequence, and (c) instructions for amplifying and detecting the mutation."*

- **Explanation**: This kit is focused on detecting a specific genetic mutation. It includes the necessary primers and reagents for amplifying and detecting the mutation, as well as instructions for performing the test.

3. Medical Device Kits

Medical device kits often involve a combination of instruments, reagents, or accessories that are packaged together to perform a specific procedure or treatment.

Example 1: Surgical Kit

- *"A kit for performing a laparoscopic surgical procedure, comprising: (a) a laparoscope, (b) a set of surgical tools for use with the laparoscope, and (c) instructions for performing the surgical procedure using the laparoscope and tools."*

- **Explanation**: This kit protects the set of tools necessary to perform a specific laparoscopic surgery. The claim includes the devices and instructions on how to use them together for the procedure.

Example 2: Drug-Device Combination Kit

- *"A kit for delivering a therapeutic agent to a targeted tissue, comprising: (a) a catheter for delivering the therapeutic agent, (b) a therapeutic agent, and (c) instructions for using the catheter to deliver the therapeutic agent to the targeted tissue."*

- **Explanation**: This claim protects a medical device (catheter) combined with a therapeutic agent, along with specific instructions for using the device to deliver the drug to a specific site in the body.

Drafting Kit of Parts Claims in the U.S.

Drafting kit of parts claims in the U.S. requires a careful approach to avoid obviousness rejections and to ensure that the combination of parts is considered novel and non-obvious. Here are key strategies:

1. **Synergistic or Unexpected Results**: If the combination of parts produces a surprising or improved effect that would not have been expected based on the individual components, this can help establish non-obviousness. For example, combining two drugs that together reduce side effects or improve efficacy compared to when they are used separately can support a patentable claim.

2. **Focus on the Instructions**: Instructions for use can be a key aspect of the kit claim. These instructions can provide specificity on how to use the components together and can distinguish the invention from prior art. For instance, the instructions may specify a particular sequence, dosage regimen, or time frame for using the components.

3. **Packaging and Arrangement**: Emphasizing the packaging and arrangement of the components can add novelty to a claim. For example, the parts might be pre-packaged in a way that facilitates ease of use or compliance with a treatment protocol, which could make the kit patentable even if the individual components are known.

4. **Combination with Method Claims**: Often, kit claims are combined with **method claims** to protect the method of using the kit. For instance, a patent might include claims directed to both the kit itself and the method of using the kit to treat a condition or perform a procedure.

5. **Avoiding Double Patenting**: Since kits often involve known components, it is essential to avoid double patenting

issues (i.e., trying to patent the same invention twice). Careful claim drafting can help ensure that the kit claim is distinct from any patents that cover the individual components.

Enforcement of Kit of Parts Patents

Kit of parts patents can sometimes be more challenging to enforce because the components are often sold separately. However, patent holders can pursue induced infringement claims if a third party sells components with instructions on how to assemble them in a way that infringes the patent.

For example, a pharmaceutical company that sells two drugs separately but markets them to be used together according to a patented combination therapy could be liable for inducing infringement if those instructions correspond to the patented kit's use.

Objections

In patent examination, the "Basis for Rejection" typically outlines why a patent examiner has determined that the claims of a patent application do not meet the legal requirements for patentability. Here's what you might expect to find:

1. **Prior Art Rejections**: The examiner may reject claims based on prior art, which includes previously published patents, patent applications, or other literature that shows the claimed invention is not novel or is obvious in light of existing technology.
2. **Lack of Novelty**: If the claims are not sufficiently different from what is already known, they may be rejected for lack of novelty.
3. **Obviousness**: The examiner might reject the claims if they are deemed obvious to someone skilled in the art, given the prior art references.
4. **Insufficient Disclosure**: If the patent application does not fully describe the invention or how it works, the claims might be rejected for failing to meet the requirement for

enabling disclosure.

5. **Inadequate Claims**: Claims might be rejected for not clearly defining the invention or for being too broad or vague. This includes issues with means-plus-function claims where the structure or steps to perform the function are not adequately described.

6. **Formal Issues**: Rejections might also be based on formal issues such as improper claim format, lack of clarity, or failure to comply with specific rules or guidelines.

EVALUATE APPLICATION FOR COMPLIANCE WITH 35 U.S.C. 112

35 U.S.C. 112(b) has two key requirements: (A) the claims must describe what the inventor or joint inventor regards as the invention, and (B) the claims must clearly and specifically define the invention.

An application fails the first requirement if evidence outside the application (like admissions) shows that the inventor considers the invention to be different from what is claimed. The second requirement is not met if the claims do not define the invention with sufficient precision. The clarity of the language must be evaluated in the context of the entire disclosure as understood by someone skilled in the art.

1. Adequate Written Description

For the written description requirement, an applicant's specification must reasonably convey to those skilled in the art that the inventor was in possession of the claimed invention as of the date of invention. See MPEP § 2163[1] for further guidance with respect to the evaluation of a patent application for compliance with the written description requirement.

2. Enabling Disclosure

---

1. https://www.uspto.gov/web/offices/pac/mpep/s2163.html#d0e213583

An applicant's specification must enable a person skilled in the art to make and use the claimed invention without undue experimentation. The fact that experimentation is complex, however, will not make it undue if a person of skill in the art routinely engages in such experimentation.

See MPEP § 2164[2] *et seq.* for detailed guidance with regard to the enablement requirement of 35 U.S.C. 112(a)[3].

3. Best Mode

Determining compliance with the best mode requirement requires a two-prong inquiry:

(1) at the time the application was filed, did the inventor possess a best mode for practicing the invention; and

(2) if the inventor did possess a best mode, does the written description disclose the best mode in such a manner that a person of ordinary skill in the art could practice the best mode.

DETERMINE WHETHER THE CLAIMED INVENTION COMPLIES WITH 35 U.S.C. 102 AND 103

The process of reviewing a claimed invention under 35 U.S.C. 102 and 103 involves comparing the claimed subject matter with prior art. If there are no differences, the invention lacks novelty and is rejected under 35 U.S.C. 102. If differences exist, they must be assessed in light of the knowledge of a person skilled in the art to determine if the invention would have been obvious. If it wouldn't have been obvious, the invention meets the requirements of 35 U.S.C. 103.

CLEARLY COMMUNICATE FINDINGS, CONCLUSIONS AND THEIR BASES

---

2.   https://www.uspto.gov/web/offices/pac/mpep/s2164.html#d0e215224

3.   https://www.uspto.gov/web/offices/pac/mpep/
mpep-9015-appx-l.html#al_d1d85b_2ae60_3d5

Once examiners have completed the analysis of the claimed invention according to all legal provisions, including 35 USC 101, 112, 102, and 103, they must review all proposed rejections to confirm a prima facie case of non-patentability. Only after this confirmation should any rejection be imposed in an Office action. The Office action must clearly communicate the findings, conclusions, and supporting reasons.

2107-Guidelines for Examination of Applications for Compliance with the Utility Requirement

- **Office Actions**

Office actions are written communications from the patent examiner that requires a formal, signed response from the applicant to proceed with the application. The response must address each rejection and objection raised by the examiner.

Office actions include restriction requirements, non-final Office actions, and final Office actions.

1. Restriction Requirement:

A restriction requirement occurs when the examiner determines that an application contains multiple inventions or distinct groups of claims that should be examined separately.

The examiner requests the applicant to choose one invention or group of claims to pursue in the current application, while the other inventions or claims must be pursued in separate applications.

To properly request a restriction between patentably distinct inventions, two main criteria need to be met:

- **Independence or Distinctness:** The inventions must be either independent of each other or distinct as claimed in your application.

The term "independent" (i.e., unrelated) means that there is no disclosed relationship between the two or more inventions claimed, they are unconnected in design, operation, and effect. For example, a process and an apparatus incapable of being used in practicing the process are independent inventions.

- **Search and Examination Burden:** It must be clear that examining all the inventions together would place a significant burden on the examiner, such as making the search or examination process more difficult.

Markush claims:

Markush claims list a set of interchangeable members, known as a Markush group or grouping. These claims allow for various alternatives, all of which are expected to work similarly in the invention. For example, a Markush claim might list several chemical compounds where each could be used in the same way.

Examination Process:

- **Provisional Election:** When a Markush claim includes several distinct inventions, the examiner may ask the applicant to choose one species or a group of similar species for initial examination. This helps manage the search and examination process more efficiently.

- **Proper Markush Grouping:** For a Markush grouping to be valid, all members must share a single structural similarity and a common use. If the members are part of a combination or process, they should be substitutable with similar results. For chemical compounds, the grouping should be assessed as a whole rather than breaking it down into individual elements.

- **Election of Species:** If the claim includes multiple unrelated inventions, the examiner might require the applicant to elect one species for detailed examination. If the grouping is proper and manageable, all members can be examined together. The examiner will not search or examine all members if they are not necessary for the determination of patentability.

- **Final Rejection:** If a Markush claim is rejected, the provisional election is considered final, and only the elected species or group will be examined further. Claims to non-elected species will be withdrawn.

- **Responding to Rejections:** If the applicant amends the Markush claim to exclude the prior art, the claim will be re-examined. If the amendment doesn't overcome the rejection, it may be final unless new grounds are introduced.

- **Election of Species Practice:** When requesting a provisional election, the examiner typically contacts the applicant to choose species. This process ensures that the claim is examined effectively without unnecessary burden.

The applicant must respond by electing one invention or group for examination. If the applicant does not comply, the examiner may require the application to be restricted to a single invention.

2. Non-Final Office Action:

A non-final office action is issued by the examiner during the initial examination of the application. It may include rejections or objections related to various aspects of the application, such as issues with the claims, specification, or drawings.

The non-final Office action provides the applicant with an opportunity to amend the application, address the examiner's concerns, and overcome rejections or objections.

- **Process:** The applicant must submit a response addressing each issue raised in the non-final Office action. The response can include amendments to the claims, arguments against the rejections, or additional information. This action allows for further negotiation and adjustment before a final decision is made.

3. Final Office Action:

A final Office action is issued when the examiner concludes that the application is still not in compliance with patent laws or rules after a non-final Office action has been issued.

The final Office action indicates that the examiner's rejections or objections are maintained, and no further amendments or arguments will be considered unless they address the remaining issues.

- **Process:** The applicant must respond to the final Office action by either making necessary amendments or providing persuasive arguments to convince the examiner to withdraw the rejections. If the applicant is unable to resolve the issues, they may appeal the decision to the Patent Trial and Appeal Board (PTAB).

Response Deadlines

The legally defined timeframe within which specific actions related to a patent application or granted patent must be completed is called the statutory time period.

Most replies to Office actions (official letters) must be received within 6 months from the mailing date of the Office action.

Office actions in almost all instances set a shortened period within which a response can be filed without having to pay extension of time fees. The shortened period is typically either two or three months, depending on the type of Office action.

In certain circumstances, the Office action will specify a different response period. There are no extensions beyond the 6-month statutory time period for reply other than notices that do not have a statutory time period for reply.

If an applicant does not submit an acceptable timely response to an Office action, the application will be held abandoned.

Reply to Non-Final Office Action (37 CFR 1.111):

Applicants must reply to an adverse non-final Office action to request reconsideration or further examination, with or without amendments. Replies must address all objections and rejections, pointing out specific distinctions that make claims patentable.

Supplemental replies may not be entered automatically unless they fall under specific conditions, such as claim cancellation, reply to an Office requirement made after the first reply was filed or correction of informalities. If filed during a period when action is suspended, they will be considered.

When an applicant or patent owner receives an Office action (which typically includes rejections or objections from the patent examiner), they have the opportunity to respond.

The reply must be in writing and should specifically address the alleged errors in the examiner's action. It must also address every ground of objection and rejection mentioned in the prior Office action. Importantly, the reply should genuinely aim to advance the application or reexamination proceeding toward a final decision.

If the claims in an application or a patent under reexamination are rejected, the applicant or patent owner can amend them. In doing so, they must clearly highlight the patentable novelty they believe the claims possess.

This assessment should consider the state of the art as disclosed by the references cited or the objections raised. Additionally, the amendments should demonstrate how they address or avoid those references or objections.

I. First Step: Write a responsive reply to the office action according to patent laws

37 CFR 1.111 Reply by applicant or patent owner to a non-final Office action.

→ In order to be entitled to reconsideration or further examination, the applicant or patent owner must reply to the Office action.

→ The reply by the applicant or patent owner must be reduced to a writing which distinctly and specifically points out the supposed errors in the examiner's action and must reply to every ground of objection and rejection in the prior Office action.

→ The reply must present arguments pointing out the specific distinctions believed to render the claims, including any newly presented claims, patentable over any applied references.

→ The applicant's or patent owner's reply must appear throughout to be a bona fide attempt to advance the application or the reexamination proceeding to final action.

→ In all cases where reply to a requirement is indicated as necessary for further consideration of the claims, or where allowable subject matter has been indicated in an application, a complete reply must either comply with the formal requirements or specifically traverse each one not complied with.

→ Drawing and specification corrections, presentation of a new oath and the like are generally considered as formal matters, although the filing of drawing corrections in reply to an objection to the drawings cannot normally be held in abeyance. However, the line between formal matter and those touching the merits is not sharp, and the determination of the merits of an application may require that such corrections, new oath, etc., be insisted upon prior to any indication of allowable subject matter.

I. Attach supporting documents and evidence

To enhance your response, be sure to include all relevant supporting documents and evidence. Make sure these documents are current, directly relevant, and clearly support your arguments. Reference them explicitly in your response to help the examiner follow and understand your reasoning.

I. Submit the Response

Submit your response electronically through the USPTO's Patent Center to ensure timely submission.

After submitting, confirm receipt of your submission by checking for an acknowledgment receipt from the USPTO.

I. Monitor Application Status

Regularly monitor the status of your application through the USPTO's Patent Center.

Conduct of Ex Parte Reexamination Proceedings (37 CFR 1.550):

In the context of patent law, "ex parte" refers to a type of proceeding where only one party, typically the patent owner, is involved in the interaction with the patent office.

The patent owner in an ex parte reexamination proceeding will be given at least thirty days to respond to any Office action. In response to any rejection, such response may include further statements and/or proposed amendments or new claims to place the patent in a condition where all claims, if amended as proposed, would be patentable.

Extensions of time for responses can be requested under specific conditions. These petitions must specify the requested period of extension and be accompanied by the petition fee.

If a patent owner fails to respond appropriately and timely, the reexamination can be terminated, leading to a certificate concluding the reexamination, or a petition may be filed to revive a reexamination prosecution terminated if the delay in response was unintentional.

Handling Non-Fully Responsive Submissions

When a patent owner's response to a non-final Office action during reexamination is incomplete, the USPTO may consider it "not fully responsive" if it meets the following conditions: the response was a bona fide attempt to address the examiner's non-final action, it was filed before the expiration of the permissible response period (including any extensions), but due to an apparent oversight or inadvertence, a crucial element necessary for a full response was omitted.

If the response meets all the above criteria, the prosecution of reexamination should not be terminated. The examiner has several options: waive minor deficiencies and proceed, accept the amendment while notifying the patent owner of the missing elements with a new deadline, or, in rare cases, require the patent owner to correct the omission within the remaining response period to avoid termination of the reexamination.

If the deficiency is serious and time for response is limited, the notification should include details on what needs to be corrected, and the patent owner should be granted a new time period to respond.

First Action Interview Pilot Program

Under the Full First Action Interview Pilot Program, an applicant is entitled to a first action interview, upon request by filing the *Applicant Initiated Interview Request Form*, prior to the first Office action on the merits. The examiner will conduct a prior art search and provide the applicant with a condensed pre-interview communication citing relevant prior art and identifying proposed rejections or objections.

Within 30 days of receipt, the applicant schedules an interview and submits proposed amendments and/or arguments. At the interview, the relevant prior art, proposed rejections, amendments and arguments will be discussed.

If agreement is not reached, the applicant will receive a first action interview Office action that includes an interview summary that constitutes a first Office action on the merits under 35 USC 132.

35 U.S. Code § 132 - Notice of Rejection; Reexamination:

(a) Whenever, on examination, any claim for a patent is rejected, or any objection or requirement made, the Director shall notify the applicant thereof, stating the reasons for such rejection, or objection or requirement, together with such information and references as may be useful in judging of the propriety of continuing the prosecution of his application; and if after receiving such notice, the applicant persists in his claim for a patent, with or without amendment, the application

shall be reexamined. No amendment shall introduce new matter into the disclosure of the invention.

Applicant Initiated Interview Request Form

This form is used by the applicant or their representative to formally request an interview with the patent examiner. The interview can be used to discuss specific issues related to the application, such as rejections, objections, or claim amendments.

It is typically used when the applicant feels that a direct discussion with the examiner could help clarify issues, potentially leading to a more favorable outcome or a quicker resolution of the application.

Applicant Initiated Interview Request Form

Application No.:   First Named Applicant: ____________
Examiner: ____________   Art Unit: ________   Status of Application: ________

Tentative Participants:
(1)_______________________(2)_______________________

(3)_______________________(4)_______________________

Proposed Date of Interview:_________________   **Proposed Time:**________(○AM○PM)

Type of Interview Requested:
(1) ☐ **Telephonic**   (2) ☐ **Personal**   (3) ☐ **Video Conference**

Exhibit To Be Shown or Demonstrated: ☐ **YES**   ☐ **NO**
If yes, provide brief description: ________________________________

Issues To Be Discussed

Issues (Rej., Obj., etc)	Claims/ Fig. #s	Prior Art	Discussed	Agreed	Not Agreed
(1)________	________	________	☐	☐	☐
(2)________	________	________	☐	☐	☐
(3)________	________	________	☐	☐	☐
(4)________	________	________	☐	☐	☐

☐ Continuation Sheet Attached   ☐ Proposed Amendment or Arguments Attached

Brief Description of Arguments to be Presented: _____________________________________

An interview was conducted on the above-identified application on _______________________

<u>NOTE</u>: This form should be completed and filed by applicant in advance of the interview (see MPEP § 713.01). If this form is signed by a registered practitioner not of record, the Office will accept this as an indication that he or she is authorized to conduct an interview on behalf of the principal (37 CFR 1.32(a)(3)) pursuant to 37 CFR 1.34. This is not a power of attorney to any above named practitioner. See the Instruction Sheet for this form, which is incorporated by reference. By signing this form, applicant or practitioner is certifying that he or she has read the Instruction Sheet. After the interview is conducted, applicant is advised to file a statement of the substance of this interview (37 CFR 1.133(b)) as soon as possible. This application will not be delayed from issue because of applicant's failure to submit a written record of this interview.

_______________________   _______________________
Applicant/Applicant's Representative Signature   Examiner/SPE Signature

____
Typed/Printed Name of Applicant or Representative   _______________________
                Applicant's/Applicant's Representative's Telephone Number

____
Registration Number, if applicable

Applicant Initiated Interview Form Fig.
*Source:*https://www.uspto.gov/web/offices/pac/mpep/
s713.html#:~:text=For%20both%20applicant-initiated%20and[4]

---

4. https://www.uspto.gov/web/offices/pac/mpep/

s713.html#_853ae90f0351324bd73ea615e6487517__4c761f170e016836ff84498202b99827__853ae90f0351

324bd73ea615e6487517_text_43ec3e5dee6e706af7766fffea512721_For_0bcef9c45bd8a48eda1b26eb0c61c8

Normally, granting an interview before first action on the merits of a new application is within the discretion of the examiner and a showing may be required to justify the granting of the interview. For more information on how to file this request

Office Action Summary

The Office Action Summary is a document issued by the patent examiner that summarizes the current status of the patent application after it has been reviewed. It outlines the examiner's findings, including any rejections, objections, and the status of claims.

It is issued by the USPTO after the examiner has reviewed the application and made an initial determination on the patentability of the claims.

1. Mailing Date: This is the date when the communication was sent out. The statutory period for responding to this communication begins from this mailing date.

2. Shortened Statutory Period for Reply: The applicant is given a time period to reply to this communication, which is one month or 30 days. The period can be extended by an additional month under certain regulations (37 CFR 1.136(a)).

3. Request for No First-Action Interview: The document acknowledges the applicant's decision to waive the first-action interview, which is an option provided under the First Action Interview Pilot Program.

4. Status:

- Responsive to Communication(s): Indicates that the office action is in response to previous communications or interviews.

- Condition for Allowance: When an application is nearly ready for approval, with only minor formal issues remaining, the substantive examination is considered complete under the Ex parte Quayle procedure. This indicates that the application has met all

69_20both_0bcef9c45bd8a48eda1b26eb0c61c869_20applicant-initiated_0bcef9c45bd8a48eda1b26eb0c61c8

69_20and

requirements for patentability, and once the remaining formalities are corrected, the patent will be granted.

5. Disposition of Claims:

The document lists the status of the claims in the application. They may be allowed, rejected, objected to, or subject to restrictions.

- Claims Pending: The document states whether claims are still under consideration.

- Claims Withdrawn from Consideration: Indicates if any claims are no longer being considered.

- Claims Allowed: Indicates which claims are accepted as patentable.

- Claims Rejected: Lists claims that have been rejected.

- Claims Objected to: Specifies claims that have issues, usually formal, that need to be addressed.

- Restriction/Election Requirement: Indicates whether claims need to be restricted or if an election of species is required.

6. Application Papers:

- Specification: The examiner may have objections to the description of the invention as filed.

- Drawings: Indicates whether the drawings submitted with the application are accepted or objected to. If objected to, corrections may be required.

- Oath or Declaration: The oath or declaration submitted with the application may have issues that need to be corrected.

7. Priority under 35 U.S.C. § 119: This section acknowledges if the application claims priority to an earlier foreign application. It states whether certified copies of priority documents have been received.

8. Contact Information: Lists the telephone number and work schedule of the examiner handling the case, as well as the name and contact information of the supervisor.

9. Attachments: The document may include several attachments, such as notices of references cited, draftsperson's patent drawing review, information disclosure statements, interview summaries, and more. These attachments provide additional details about the examination process or issues with the application.

This document is a summary of actions taken by the patent office regarding a patent application, providing the applicant with an overview of the status of their application, the disposition of claims, and any objections or rejections that need to be addressed.

Office Action Summary	Application No.	Applicant(s)
(For use in the First Action Interview Pilot Program)		
	Examiner	Art Unit / Page 1 of

-- The MAILING DATE of this communication appears on the cover sheet with the correspondence address --

THE SHORTENED STATUTORY PERIOD FOR REPLY IS SET TO EXPIRE **ONE MONTH OR THIRTY (30) DAYS, WHICHEVER IS LONGER, FROM THE MAILING DATE OF THIS COMMUNICATION.**

This time period for reply is extendable under 37 CFR 1.136(a) for only ONE additional MONTH. This communication constitutes notice under 37 CFR 1.136(a)(1)(i).

☐ Applicant's request to not have a first-action interview is acknowledged.

Status

1)☐ Responsive to communication(s) filed on _____ and interview conducted on _____.

2)☐ Since this application is in condition for allowance except for formal matters, prosecution as to the merits is closed in accordance with the practice under *Ex parte Quayle*, 1935 C.D. 11, 453 O.G. 213.

Disposition of Claims

3)☐ Claim(s) _____ is/are pending in the application.

    3a) Of the above claim(s) _____ is/are withdrawn from consideration.

4)☐ Claim(s) _____ is/are allowed.

5)☐ Claim(s) _____ is/are rejected.

6)☐ Claim(s) _____ is/are objected to.

7)☐ Claim(s) _____ are subject to restriction and/or election requirement.

Application Papers

8)☐ The specification is objected to by the Examiner.

9)☐ The drawing(s) filed on _____ is/are: a)☐ accepted or b)☐ objected to by the Examiner.

    Applicant may not request that any objection to the drawing(s) be held in abeyance. See 37 CFR 1.85(a).

    Replacement drawing sheet(s) including the correction is required if the drawing(s) is objected to. See 37 CFR 1.121(d).

10)☐ The oath or declaration is objected to by the Examiner. Note the attached Office Action or form PTO-152.

Priority under 35 U.S.C. § 119

11)☐ Acknowledgment is made of a claim for foreign priority under 35 U.S.C. § 119(a)-(d) or (f).

    a)☐ All b)☐ Some * c)☐ None of:

      1.☐ Certified copies of the priority documents have been received.

      2.☐ Certified copies of the priority documents have been received in Application No. _____.

      3.☐ Copies of the certified copies of the priority documents have been received in this National Stage application from the International Bureau (PCT Rule 17.2(a)).

    * See the attached detailed Office action for a list of the certified copies not received.

Contact Information

    Examiner's Telephone Number:

    Examiner's Typical Work Schedule:

    Supervisor's Name:

    Supervisor's Telephone Number: (

Attachment(s)

1)☐ Notice of References Cited (PTO-892)

2)☐ Notice of Draftsperson's Patent Drawing Review (PTO-948)

3)☐ Information Disclosure Statement(s) (PTO/SB/08) Paper No(s)/Mail Date _____

4)☐ Interview Summary (PTO-413) Paper No(s)/Mail Date. _____

5)☐ Notice of Informal Patent Application

6)☐ Other: _____

U.S. Patent and Trademark Office
PTOL-413FA (Rev. 09-07)   First Action Interview Office Action Summary   Part of Paper No./Mail Date 20080313

Office Action Summary Form Fig.

Source: https://www.uspto.gov/web/offices/pac/mpep/s707.html

How to amend an office action

When to amend: You can amend your application before or after the first Office action, and after the second one as allowed by specific rules. Amendments are also allowed after a final rejection if they meet certain criteria. If you file an appeal, you can make amendments as long as they comply with specific appeal rules. Additionally, amendments may be required if specifically requested by the examiner. While amendments are not typically made to provisional applications, if they are, they must follow specific rules.

General Rules: It is essential that the content of the application remains consistent, with no new information added that was not in the original application. Amendments should correct any errors and ensure that the claims, specification, and drawings match each other. Furthermore, each section of an amendment, such as claims or drawings, must begin on a new page to keep the document organized. Any amendments that add claims beyond those already paid for must include the required excess claim fees, or the amendment will not be entered.

How to Make Amendments (Post-July 30, 2003): Amendments made after July 30, 2003, must comply with rules revised to support electronic processing of patent applications. Non-compliant amendments will be rejected. Each part of your amendment (such as changes to the specification, claims, drawings, and remarks) must start on a new page to facilitate electronic scanning and processing. It is recommended to use a specific format: start with a cover sheet that includes application information and serves as a table of contents, followed by sections for specification amendments, claims amendments, drawing amendments, remarks, and any updated or new drawings. This structure ensures that each part of the amendment is clearly organized and easy to process electronically.

Amendments to the Specification (Text, Not Claims): To amend the specification of a patent application (other than claims, large tables, or specific listings), you can delete, replace, or add paragraphs in the specification by clearly identifying where and what changes are being made. When making changes, added text must be underlined, and deleted text should be either crossed out or placed within brackets. If you're replacing an entire section, you need to reference the specific section and show the changes using the same markings. If you want to replace the entire specification, you must submit a new version, indicating that it is a replacement. Additionally, once a paragraph or section has been deleted, it cannot be reintroduced without adding it back in a new amendment.

For minor changes to the abstract, a marked-up version showing all changes should be provided. If the abstract is being significantly rewritten, a new clean version can be submitted, along with instructions to cancel the previous version. If amending the entire specification, a substitute specification can be submitted with a clean version, a marked-up version showing changes, and a statement confirming that no new matter has been introduced.

Amendments to Claims: When amending claims in a patent application, the process requires submitting a complete list of all claims ever presented, including those that have been canceled or withdrawn. Each claim must be accompanied by a status identifier, such as "original," "currently amended," "canceled," or "new," to clearly indicate its current status. Any modifications to claims should be visibly marked, using strike-throughs for deletions and underlining for additions, ensuring the changes are easily identifiable. New claims should be marked as "new" without any underlining. The claims must be listed in ascending numerical order, and any canceled claims should not be renumbered. If a claim is canceled, it can only be reinstated as a new claim with a new number. The Office may also accept alternative status identifiers as long as they accurately represent the status of the claims and comply with the amendment guidelines. This table provides a list of status identifiers used in patent applications, along with acceptable alternative terms that can be used to describe the same status. These identifiers are used to indicate the current status of each claim in the application, such as whether it is original, amended, canceled, withdrawn, or new.

Status Identifiers Set Forth in 37 CFR 1.121(c)	Acceptable Alternatives
1. Original	Original Claim; and Originally Filed Claim
2. Currently amended	Presently amended; and Currently amended claim
3. Canceled	Canceled without prejudice; Cancel; Cancelled; Canceled herein; Previously cancelled; Canceled claim; Deleted; and Previously canceled
4. Withdrawn	Withdrawn from consideration; Withdrawn – new; Withdrawn claim; and Withdrawn – currently amended
5. Previously presented	Previously amended; Previously added; Previously submitted; and Previously presented claim
6. New	Newly added; and New claim
7. Not entered	Not entered claim

Status Identifiers Fig.

*Source:*https://www.uspto.gov/web/offices/pac/mpep/
s714.html#:~:text=(E)%20Acceptable%20Alternative%20Status[5]

Amendments to Drawings: Any changes to the drawings must be made on new sheets, and these sheets must be labeled accordingly, such as "Replacement Sheet" for amended drawings or "New Sheet" for additional drawings. When replacing a sheet, all figures from the original sheet must be included on the new sheet, even if only one figure is changed. The amended figures should not be labeled as "amended." Additionally, you may include an annotated version of the drawing, clearly labeled as "Annotated Sheet," which shows and explains the changes. This annotated sheet should be included in the amendment document or in the remarks section that describes the changes to the drawings. If the changes are not approved, the applicant will be notified in the next Office action. Any

---

5. https://www.uspto.gov/web/offices/pac/mpep/
s714.html#_853ae90f0351324bd73ea615e6487517__4c761f170e016836ff84498202b99827__853ae90f0351
324bd73ea615e6487517_text_43ec3e5dee6e706af7766fffea512721__84c40473414caf2ed4a7b1283e48bbf4_
E_9371d7a2e3ae86a00aab4771e39d255d__0bcef9c45bd8a48eda1b26eb0c61c869_20Acceptable_0bcef9c45
bd8a48eda1b26eb0c61c869_20Alternative_0bcef9c45bd8a48eda1b26eb0c61c869_20Status

modifications to the drawing descriptions in the specification must also be updated to ensure consistency with the revised drawings.

Compliant Amendments: Amendments that meet all the requirements and guidelines set by the patent office regulations, including proper formatting, content consistency, and adherence to procedural rules. These amendments are likely to be accepted and entered into the patent application record without issues.

Examiner's Amendments: When the patent office makes changes through an examiner's amendment, they can bypass some of the usual rules to speed up the process. These changes can be made by providing specific instructions rather than replacing entire sections or claims. If an amendment submitted by the applicant is non-compliant but would allow the application to be approved, the examiner can correct the issues and enter the amendment. Minor corrections, like fixing typos, don't require approval from the applicant. However, if the changes are more significant, such as canceling a claim, the examiner must get the applicant's authorization within the response period.

Non-Compliant Amendments: If an amendment does not comply with 37 CFR 1.121, the patent office will issue a Notice of Non-Compliant Amendment. This notice will specify the non-compliant section, the necessary corrections, and the reasons for non-compliance. The response required and the timeline depends on the type of amendment:

Preliminary Amendment: An amendment filed before the first Office action or along with the initial patent application. If filed after the application date, it must be corrected within 2 months without extensions, or it won't be considered. If filed with the application it must be corrected within 2 months, with extensions allowed. If not corrected, the application may be abandoned.

Non-Final Amendments: Non-Final Amendments are made after the initial submission of the patent application but before a final rejection or allowance has been issued by the patent examiner. Non-final amendments allow the applicant to make changes to the application based on the feedback or objections raised by the examiner during the examination process. Must be corrected within 2 months, with extensions allowed. Failure to correct will result in abandonment.

Non final amendments submitted with Request for Continued Examination (RCE): After a final rejection, if the applicant wants to continue prosecuting the application (i.e., making additional amendments or arguments), they can file an RCE. The amendment submitted with an RCE is treated as a non-final amendment because the examination of the application is effectively restarted, allowing the applicant to address any remaining issues.

After-Final Amendments: This type of amendment is submitted after a final rejection has been issued by the examiner. After-final amendments are generally only entered if they put the application in condition for allowance (i.e., if the changes overcome all the examiner's objections or rejections) or comply with specific criteria. Otherwise, the examiner may not consider them. Non-compliant amendments will not be entered. The examiner may identify the issues but will not provide additional time to correct them. The applicant must respond within the original time frame to avoid abandonment.

Supplemental Amendment: An additional amendment submitted after an initial amendment. The entry and acceptance of supplemental amendments depend on the timing and specific conditions, such as whether the application is under suspension.

Supplemental Amendments (No Suspension): This means that the patent application is continuing through the examination process without any pause or delay. If you submit a supplemental amendment while the examination is ongoing (without any suspension of the process), the examiner has the discretion to decide whether to consider or enter this amendment

Supplemental Amendments (With Suspension): This refers to situations where the examination process is temporarily paused or suspended. The suspension could occur for various reasons, such as awaiting a response from the applicant or due to administrative reasons. If a supplemental amendment is submitted while the application is under suspension, any issues or non-compliance with the amendment must be corrected within 2 months. Importantly, no extensions are allowed beyond this period. If the necessary corrections are not made within this timeframe, the supplemental amendment will not be entered into the record.

Amendments in Response to a Quayle Action: A Quayle Action is a type of Office action that requires the applicant to correct minor errors before the patent is allowed. Amendments in response to a Quayle Action must be corrected within 2 months, with extensions allowed, or the application may be abandoned. Must be corrected within 2 months, with extensions allowed. Failure to correct will result in abandonment.

After-Allowance Amendments: These are changes made to a patent application after the examiner has indicated that the application is allowed but before the patent is officially issued. Once an application is allowed, any subsequent amendments are not automatically accepted or incorporated into the application. The examiner has the discretion to decide whether to accept these amendments. If you submit amendments after the allowance, you must make any necessary corrections before paying the issue fee. You do not receive extra time beyond this to make changes.

Entry of Amendments, Directions for, Defective: If directions for entering an amendment are unclear but can be reasonably inferred, the examiner will make the necessary corrections and notify the applicant. If the intent is unclear, the amendment won't be entered, and the applicant will be informed.

Amendment of Amendments: When changing a previously amended paragraph or section, the entire section should be rewritten, with the old insertion canceled. The changes should be clearly marked with underlining for additions and strike-through for deletions. Canceled content can only be reinstated by presenting it as new, and canceled claims can only be reinstated as new claims with new claim numbers.

How to appeal an office action (if needed)

Process for Filing an Appeal to the Patent Trial and Appeal Board: 35 U.S.C. 134 outlines the procedures for appealing a patent examination decision to the Patent Trial and Appeal Board (PTAB). If an applicant's patent claims have been rejected twice by the primary examiner, the applicant can appeal the decision to the PTAB, provided the appeal fee has been paid. Similarly, in the context of a reexamination, a patent owner can appeal the final rejection of any claim made by the primary examiner to the PTAB, also requiring the payment of the appeal fee. When filing a notice of appeal to the Patent Trial and Appeal Board, you don't need to meet the usual signature requirements. The appeal is understood to address all claims that have been rejected, unless you specifically cancel some claims. Additionally, the deadlines for filing an appeal can be extended based on specific rules for patent applications and reexaminations.

"Forwarding an appeal" refers to the process of sending the appeal from the initial stage, typically after an examiner's decision, to the Patent Trial and Appeal Board (PTAB) for further review and decision. This step is necessary to move the appeal into the formal phase where the PTAB will consider the arguments and evidence provided by the appellant.

Associated fees: According to 35 U.S.C. 41, the fees are as follows:

Notice of appeal	840.00	336.00	168.00*
Filing a brief in support of an appeal	0.00	0.00	0.00
Filing a brief in support of an appeal in an inter partes reexamination proceeding	2,100.00	840.00	420.00*
Request for oral hearing	1,360.00	544.00	272.00*
Forwarding an appeal in an application or ex parte reexamination proceeding to the Board	2,360.00	944.00	472.00*

Appeal fees Fig.

Source: https://www.uspto.gov/learning-and-resources/fees-and-payment/uspto-fee-schedule#:~:text=The%20fee%20schedule%20provides%20information

[6]

The appeal processes are tailored to the specific stages and nature of the proceedings involved, whether it's seeking a patent (applicant) or defending one (the owner).

Appeal by Patent Applicant: A patent applicant can appeal to the Board if dissatisfied with the primary examiner's decision after their claims have been rejected at least twice. To initiate an appeal, the applicant must file a notice of appeal and pay the required fee within the period specified under the rules. An appeal can be filed regardless of whether the claims have been finally rejected. However, an appeal cannot be filed in a continuing application or after filing a Request for Continued Examination (RCE) until the application is rejected.

---

6. https://www.uspto.gov/learning-and-resources/fees-and-payment/uspto-fee-schedule#_853ae90f0351324bd73ea615e6487517__4c761f170e016836ff84498202b99827__853ae90f0351324bd73ea615e6487517_text_43ec3e5dee6e706af7766fffea512721_The_0bcef9c45bd8a48eda1b26eb0c61c869_20fee_0bcef9c45bd8a48eda1b26eb0c61c869_20schedule_0bcef9c45bd8a48eda1b26eb0c61c869_20provides_0bcef9c45bd8a48eda1b26eb0c61c869_20information

If an amendment is filed after a final action along with a notice of appeal, the amendment may not be automatically accepted and must meet certain requirements. If a reply to a second non-final rejection is filed before or on the same day as a notice of appeal, the appeal may be considered premature until the Office acts on the reply.

An appeal is assumed to cover all rejected claims unless the applicant cancels specific claims through an amendment. Failure to address all rejected claims in the appeal brief can result in waiving challenges to those claims. While the notice of appeal does not need to be signed, other associated documents might require signatures. The notice of appeal must be filed within the reply period set in the last Office action, generally three months. Extensions are possible if the appropriate petition and fee are filed. It is recommended to use a separate letter for the notice of appeal and Form PTO/SB/31 for filing. The appeal brief must be filed within two months of the notice of appeal.

Appeal by Patent Owner: For patent owners, appeals to the Board in ex parte reexaminations follow different rules based on when the reexamination was filed. For reexaminations filed before November 29, 1999, an appeal can be filed after the second rejection of claims. For reexaminations filed on or after this date, appeals can only be made after a final rejection of claims.

The fee for filing a notice of appeal is outlined in the regulations, and the timing for paying this fee follows the rules for ex parte reexaminations. If an appeal is not filed, the reexamination certificate will be issued as per the regulations.

Inter Partes Review (IPR): In the context of the USPTO, Inter Partes Review (IPR) is a procedure that allows a third party to challenge the validity of a granted patent. It involves a trial before the Patent Trial and Appeal Board (PTAB) and focuses on the patentability of one or more claims in the patent based on prior art, such as patents or printed publications. IPR is a common post-grant process used to contest the novelty or obviousness of a patent.

For IPR, different rules apply, and appeals are governed by specific sections of the regulations. It is recommended to use a separate letter and Form PTO/SB/31 or Form PTO/AIA/31 for filing a notice of appeal.

Acknowledgement: Applicants can check the status of their application and confirm the receipt date of the notice of appeal using the Patent Center. If the notice of appeal is mailed, the USPTO does not send a separate acknowledgment letter. However, if a self-addressed postcard is included with the notice, it will be date stamped and returned to the applicant as confirmation of receipt.

Defective Notice of Appeal: The Patent Appeal Center reviews notices of appeal for defects. If a notice is found to be defective, the Office will notify the applicant. A notice of appeal is considered defective if it is not timely filed, if the associated fee is not paid on time, or if the claims have not been twice rejected. If an appeal brief is filed without first submitting a notice of appeal, the brief is treated as both the notice and the appeal brief. The applicant must ensure the appeal brief is submitted within the time allowed and accompanied by the required fees.

Reinstatement of Appeal: If the USPTO reopens prosecution after a notice of appeal is filed but before a decision by the Patent Trial and Appeal Board (PTAB), the appellant must file a new notice of appeal and a complete new appeal brief to reinstate the appeal. Previously paid appeal fees do not need to be paid again unless the PTAB has issued a final decision on the first appeal. If the fees have increased, the appellant must pay the difference. If a new appeal is filed after a Board decision, all fees must be paid again. If the appellant opts to reopen prosecution after a Board decision, they must pay the appeal fees if they file a new appeal.

Pre-Appeal Brief Review Request and Conference Pilot Program: The Pre-Appeal Brief Review program allows an appellant to request a review before submitting an appeal brief. This must be done simultaneously with the notice of appeal, and the request can't exceed five pages. The review panel, which includes a supervisor and the examiner, will decide whether the appeal should proceed, if prosecution should be reopened, or if the application should be allowed. If the request is dismissed, the appeal process continues. The review doesn't require additional fees and may extend the deadline for submitting an appeal brief.

Interviews After Notice of Appeal: After a final rejection, one interview is typically allowed before an appeal brief is filed. However, no interviews are permitted once a pre-appeal review request is filed until a decision on the request is made. After filing an appeal brief, interviews are generally not allowed unless there are unusual circumstances, such as canceling claims or proceeding to issue with allowable claims. After the case is under the jurisdiction of the PTAB, interviews are only permitted with special approval and in extraordinary situations.

Official Record on Appeal: "Evidence" refers to items that can prove or disprove a fact, such as testimony, documents, and tangible objects, but for appeals, dictionaries are not considered "evidence" and can be cited freely. The "Record" includes all items listed in the official file of the application or reexamination proceeding, like the Image File Wrapper, but excludes amendments, evidence, or documents not officially entered or considered by the examiner. For issued patents being reissued or reexamined, the Record also includes the original patent file. Documents not entered or considered by the examiner are not part of the Record because they are not subject to review by the Board. Some physical items not scanned into the Image File Wrapper are stored elsewhere but are still part of the Record, with the Wrapper pointing to where they are kept. References listed on an Information Disclosure Statement and considered by the examiner are included in the Record, even if not separately listed in the Image File Wrapper. Dictionaries are not treated as evidence, allowing both applicants and examiners to reference them in briefs or decisions without triggering new grounds for rejection. This approach aligns with legal precedents that permit tribunals to consult dictionaries at any time.

Abandonment:

An abandoned application, in accordance with 37 CFR 1.135 and 1.138, is one which is removed from the Office docket of pending applications through:

(A) formal abandonment

(1) by the applicant,

(2) by the attorney or agent of record , or

(3) by a registered attorney or agent acting in a representative capacity under 37 CFR 1.34 when filing a continuing application; or

(B) failure of applicant to take appropriate action within a specified time at some stage in the prosecution of the application.

Express abandonment (37 CFR 1.138)

An applicant or their attorney/agent can sign a letter to expressly abandon a patent application. The attorney must ensure that this action aligns with the applicant's intentions and best interests. The correct application must be clearly identified in the abandonment letter.

A signed letter of abandonment becomes effective when recognized by the appropriate USPTO official. The date of abandonment can be the date of recognition or a later specified date. For example, when filing a continuing application, the prior application may be abandoned as of the filing date of the new application.

The USPTO will acknowledge the receipt of a properly filed abandonment letter and will indicate whether it complies with the regulations (37 CFR 1.138). If it does not comply, a detailed explanation will be provided.

The abandonment letter must be filed within the appropriate reply period. If filed late, it is not valid to expressly abandon the application and will not be formally entered into the record.

If an applicant is seeking to abandon an application to avoid publication of the application, the applicant must submit a declaration of express abandonment through a petition, along with the required fee, well in advance. The petition and declaration must be received by the appropriate officials at least four weeks before the projected publication date. If submitted later, the petition may not be granted, and the application will likely still be published.

Abandonment letters or petitions to avoid publication should be mailed to Mail Stop Express Abandonment, Commissioner for Patents, P.O. Box 1450, Alexandria, VA 22313-1450 or filed electronically via USPTO's Patent Center.

Specific forms are recommended for filing express abandonment or related petitions to avoid publication or obtain refunds.

PTO/AIA/24: This form is used to file a letter of express abandonment for a patent application or to expressly abandon an application in favor of a continuing application. Applicants use this form when they decide to abandon their current application, either completely or in favor of filing a new, related application (a continuing application).

Doc Code: EABN

Document Description: Letter Express Abandonment of the application

PTO/AIA/24 (06-22)
Approved for use through 05/31/2024. OMB 0651-0031
U.S. Patent and Trademark Office; U.S. DEPARTMENT OF COMMERCE
Under the Paperwork Reduction Act of 1995, no persons are required to respond to a collection of information unless it displays a valid OMB control number.

EXPRESS ABANDONMENT UNDER 37 CFR 1.138

File the petition electronically using USPTO's patent electronic filing system (Patent Center or EFS-Web)
Or Mail the petition to:
Mail Stop Express Abandonment Commissioner for Patents
P.O. Box 1450, Alexandria, VA 22313-1450

Application Number	
Filing Date	
First Named Inventor	
Art Unit	
Examiner Name	
Attorney Docket Number	

Please check only one of boxes 1 or 2 below:
(If no box is checked, this paper will be treated as a request for express abandonment as if box 1 is checked.)

1. ☐ **Express Abandonment**
   I request that the above-identified application be expressly abandoned as of the filing date of this paper.

2. ☐ **Express Abandonment in Favor of a Continuing Application**
   I request that the above-identified application be expressly abandoned as of the filing date accorded the continuing application filed previously or herewith.

NOTE: A paper requesting express abandonment of an application is not effective unless and until an appropriate USPTO official recognizes and acts on the paper. See the Manual of Patent Examining Procedure (MPEP), section 711.01.

TO AVOID PUBLICATION, USE FORM PTO/AIA/24A INSTEAD OF THIS FORM.

TO REQUEST A REFUND OF SEARCH FEE AND EXCESS CLAIMS FEE (IF ELIGIBLE), USE FORM PTO/AIA/24B INSTEAD OF THIS FORM.

I am the:

☐ applicant.

☐ attorney or agent of record. Attorney or agent registration number is _____________________

☐ attorney or agent acting under 37 CFR 1.34, who is authorized under 37 CFR 1.138(b) because the application is expressly abandoned in favor of a continuing application (box 2 above must be checked). Attorney or agent registration number is _____________________

| _____________________ | _____________________ |
| Signature | Date |

| _____________________ | _____________________ |
| Typed or printed name | Telephone Number |

Note: This form must be signed in accordance with 37 CFR 1.33. See 37 CFR 1.4(d) for signature requirements and certifications. Submit multiple forms if more than one signature is required, see below.

☐ Total of _____________________ forms are submitted.

A Federal agency may not conduct or sponsor, and a person is not required to respond to, nor shall a person be subject to a penalty for failure to comply with an information collection subject to the requirements of the Paperwork Reduction Act of 1995, unless the information collection has a currently valid OMB Control Number. The OMB Control Number for this information collection is 0651-0031. Public burden for this form is estimated to average 12 minutes per response, including the time for reviewing instructions, searching existing data sources, gathering and maintaining the data needed, and completing and reviewing the information collection. Send comments regarding this burden estimate or any other aspect of this information collection, including suggestions for reducing this burden to the Chief Administrative Officer, United States Patent and Trademark Office, P.O. Box 1450, Alexandria, VA 22313-1450 or email InformationCollection@uspto.gov. **DO NOT SEND FEES OR COMPLETED FORMS TO THIS ADDRESS.** If filing this completed form by mail, send to: Commissioner for Patents, P.O. Box 1450, Alexandria, VA 22313-1450.

If you need assistance in completing the form, call 1-800-PTO-9199 and select option 2.

Form to express abandonment Fig.

*Source:*https://www.uspto.gov/sites/default/files/documents/aia0024.pdf[7]

---

7. https://www.uspto.gov/sites/default/files/documents/

aia0024.pdf#_853ae90f0351324bd73ea615e6487517__4c761f170e016836ff84498202b99827__853ae90f03

51324bd73ea615e6487517_text_43ec3e5dee6e706af7766fffea512721_A_0bcef9c45bd8a48eda1b26eb0c61c

PTO/AIA/24A: This form is specifically for filing a petition for express abandonment to avoid the publication of a patent application before it is published.

PTO/AIA/24A (05-22)
Approved for use through 06/30/2024. OMB 0651-0059
U.S. Patent and Trademark Office, U.S. DEPARTMENT OF COMMERCE
Under the Paperwork Reduction Act of 1995, no persons are required to respond to a collection of information unless it displays a valid OMB control number.

PETITION FOR EXPRESS ABANDONMENT TO AVOID PUBLICATION UNDER 37 CFR 1.138(c)	Application Number	
	Filing Date	
	First Named Inventor	
File the petition electronically using USPTO's patent electronic filing system (Patent Center or EFS-Web) Or **Mail** the petition to: **Mail Stop Express Abandonment** Commissioner for Patents P.O. Box 1450, Alexandria, VA 22313-1450	Art Unit	
	Examiner Name	
	Attorney Docket Number	

Petition for Express Abandonment to Avoid Publication under 37 CFR 1.138(c)

I hereby petition to expressly abandon the above-identified application to avoid publication.

Petition Fee – must be filed with petition to avoid delays in recognizing the petition.

a. ☐ The Director is hereby authorized to charge the petition fee under 37 CFR 1.17(h) to Deposit Account No. _______________.

b. ☐ Check in the amount of $_______________ is enclosed.

c. ☐ Payment by credit card (Form PTO-2038 is enclosed).

d. ☐ Payment by USPTO's patent electronic filing system (Patent Center or EFS-Web).

NOTE: A paper requesting express abandonment of an application is not effective unless and until an appropriate USPTO official recognizes and acts on the paper. See the Manual of Patent Examining Procedure (MPEP), section 711.01. In addition, the paper will not stop publication of the application unless a petition under 37 CFR 1.138(c) is recognized and acted on by the Pre-Grant Publication Division in sufficient time to avoid publication (e.g., more than four (4) weeks prior to the projected publication date).

TO REQUEST A REFUND OF SEARCH FEE AND EXCESS CLAIMS FEE (IF ELIGIBLE), PLEASE ALSO INCLUDE FORM PTO/AIA/24B WITH THIS FORM.

I am the:

☐ applicant.

☐ attorney or agent of record. Attorney or agent registration number is _______________

☐ attorney or agent acting under 37 CFR 1.34, who is authorized under 37 CFR 1.138(b) because the application is expressly abandoned in favor of a continuing application. Attorney or agent registration number is _______________

_______________________________   _______________________________
Signature   Date

_______________________________   _______________________________
Typed or printed name   Telephone Number

Note: This form must be signed in accordance with 37 CFR 1.33. See 37 CFR 1.4(d) for signature requirements and certifications. Submit multiple forms if more than one signature is required, see below.

☐ Total of _______________ forms are submitted.

Petition to express abandonment to avoid publication Fig.

*Source:*https://www.uspto.gov/sites/default/files/documents/aia0024a.pdf[8]

869_20paper_0bcef9c45bd8a48eda1b26eb0c61c869_20requesting_0bcef9c45bd8a48eda1b26eb0c61c869_20express_0bcef9c45bd8a48eda1b26eb0c61c869_20abandonment

8. https://www.uspto.gov/sites/default/files/documents/
aia0024a.pdf#_853ae90f0351324bd73ea615e6487517__4c761f170e016836ff84498202b99827__853ae90f0

PTO/AIA/24B: This form is used to file a petition for express abandonment to obtain a refund of the search fee and excess claims fee. Applicants use this form when they want to abandon their application and seek a refund of the search fee and any excess claims fee they paid. The petition must be filed before the application has been examined to be eligible for a refund.

PTO/AIA/24B (05-22)
Approved for use through 05/31/2024. OMB 0651-0031
U.S. Patent and Trademark Office; U.S. DEPARTMENT OF COMMERCE
Under the Paperwork Reduction Act of 1995, no persons are required to respond to a collection of information unless it displays a valid OMB control number.

PETITION FOR EXPRESS ABANDONMENT TO OBTAIN A REFUND

Application Number	
Filing Date	
First Named Inventor	
Art Unit	
Examiner Name	
Attorney Docket Number	

File the petition electronically using USPTO's patent electronic filing system (Patent Center or EFS-Web)

Or **Mail** the petition to:
Mail Stop Express Abandonment
Commissioner for Patents
P.O. Box 1450, Alexandria, VA 22313-1450

Petition for Express Abandonment Under 37 CFR 1.138(d) to Obtain a Refund

I hereby petition to expressly abandon the above-identified application to obtain a refund of any previously paid search fee and excess claims fee in the application. Please refund any search fee and excess claims fee paid in this application.

☐ The Director is hereby authorized to credit the fee(s) to Deposit Account No. ___________

NOTE: The provisions of 37 CFR 1.138(d) only apply to applications filed under 35 U.S.C. 111(a) on or after December 8, 2004. A paper requesting express abandonment of an application is not effective unless and until an appropriate USPTO official recognizes and acts on the paper. See the Manual of Patent Examining Procedure (MPEP), section 711.01.

TO AVOID PUBLICATION, INCLUDE FORM PTO/AIA/24A AND PETITION FEE WITH THIS FORM.

I am the:

☐ applicant.

☐ attorney or agent of record. Attorney or agent registration number is ___________

☐ attorney or agent acting under 37 CFR 1.34, who is authorized under 37 CFR 1.138(b) because the application is expressly abandoned in favor of a continuing application.

Attorney or agent registration number is ___________

___________________   ___________
Signature   Date

___________________   ___________
Typed or printed name   Telephone Number

Note: This form must be signed in accordance with 37 CFR 1.33. See 37 CFR 1.4(d) for signature requirements and certifications. Submit multiple forms if more than one signature is required, see below.

☐ Total of ___________ forms are submitted

Petition for express abandonment to obtain a refund Fig.

351324bd73ea615e6487517_text_43ec3e5dee6e706af7766fffea512721_Petition_0bcef9c45bd8a48eda1b26e b0c61c869_20for_0bcef9c45bd8a48eda1b26eb0c61c869_20Express_0bcef9c45bd8a48eda1b26eb0c61c869_ 20Abandonment_0bcef9c45bd8a48eda1b26eb0c61c869_20to

Source: https://www.uspto.gov/sites/default/files/documents/aia0024b.pdf[9]

Abandonment for Failure to Reply Within Time Period (37 CFR 1.135)

An Office action will notify the applicant of any non-statutory or shortened statutory time period set for reply to an Office action. Unless the applicant is notified in writing that a reply is required in less than six months, a maximum period of six months is allowed. If an applicant does not reply to a USPTO Office Action within the specified time frame, the patent application will be considered abandoned unless the Office Action states otherwise.

To prevent abandonment, the applicant must provide a complete and appropriate reply that addresses all the issues or conditions raised in the application. Submitting an amendment after a final rejection or a non-responsive amendment will not prevent abandonment unless it fully addresses the required conditions.

If the applicant's reply is a genuine effort to advance the application and is mostly complete, but accidentally omits something, the USPTO may grant an additional time period for the applicant to correct the omission. This is to ensure that the applicant has a fair chance to respond fully.

Date of Abandonment 711.04(a): Applications are usually reviewed for abandonment after the maximum permissible reply period has expired. The abandonment date is after midnight on the last day of this period, and the specific date depends on when the shortened statutory period ends.

Notifying Applicants of Abandonment 711.04(c): The USPTO sends a "Notice of Abandonment" to the applicant's correspondence address for applications abandoned due to failure to prosecute. If an

---

9. https://www.uspto.gov/sites/default/files/documents/

aia0024b.pdf#_853ae90f0351324bd73ea615e6487517__4c761f170e016836ff84498202b99827__853ae90f0

351324bd73ea615e6487517_text_43ec3e5dee6e706af7766fffea512721_Petition_0bcef9c45bd8a48eda1b26e

b0c61c869_20for_0bcef9c45bd8a48eda1b26eb0c61c869_20Express_0bcef9c45bd8a48eda1b26eb0c61c869_

20Abandonment_0bcef9c45bd8a48eda1b26eb0c61c869_20Under

application was abandoned inadvertently, the applicant may petition to revive it. Prompt action is required to obtain relief.

Letters of Abandonment After Application is Allowed 711.05: If a letter of abandonment is received after an application has been allowed, it is acknowledged by the Publishing Division. If the issue fee has already been paid, the letter will only be accepted if it meets specific criteria under 37 CFR 1.313(c) or if a suspension under 37 CFR 1.183 is justified.

37 CFR 1.313 outlines the conditions under which a patent application can be withdrawn from issue. Withdrawal can be initiated by the USPTO or by the applicant through a petition, which must include a fee and valid reasons. After the issue fee is paid, the USPTO will only withdraw the application for specific reasons such as mistakes, unpatentability, or legal issues. Applicants can request withdrawal after the issue fee for reasons like unpatentability, a request for continued examination, or express abandonment. The petition must be received and approved before the official issue date to be effective.

Extensions of time (37 CFR 1.136)

37 CFR 1.136 provides the framework for applicants to request extensions of time to respond to USPTO actions. Applicants can typically extend the time to reply to any maximum period set by statute or up to five months beyond the original deadline by filing a petition and paying the required fee, unless: (i) applicant is notified otherwise in an office action; (ii) the reply is a reply brief; (iii) the reply is a request for an oral hearing; (iv) the reply is to a decision by the patent trial and appeal board; or (v) the application is involved in a contested case.

These extensions are generally available for most Office actions, and the extension period is determined by the amount of the fee paid. The extension becomes effective immediately upon filing the petition and fee, meaning applicants don't need to wait for USPTO acknowledgment to benefit from the additional time.

However, there are important exceptions where extensions are not permitted, such as in the case of certain proceedings like reexaminations, interferences, or after receiving a Notice of Allowability. In such cases, the applicant must meet the original deadlines, and no extensions are available. Additionally, if a request for continued examination (RCE) is filed before paying the issue fee, a petition for an extension is not required.

If the standard process under 37 CFR 1.136(a) is not applicable, applicants may seek an extension for cause under 37 CFR 1.136(b). This requires demonstrating sufficient reason and must be requested before the reply period expires. Importantly, no extension can push the deadline beyond the statutory six-month limit.

PTO/SB/22 (12-22) PETITION FOR EXTENSION OF TIME UNDER 37 CFR 1.136(a)

Form PTO/SB/22 is used by patent applicants to request additional time to respond to an Office action or other USPTO communication related to their patent application.

<table>
<tr><td colspan="2">PETITION FOR EXTENSION OF TIME UNDER 37 CFR 1.136(a)</td><td>Docket Number (Optional)</td></tr>
<tr><td>Application Number</td><td colspan="2">Filed</td></tr>
<tr><td colspan="3">For</td></tr>
<tr><td>Art Unit</td><td colspan="2">Examiner</td></tr>
</table>

This is a request under the provisions of 37 CFR 1.136(a) to extend the period for filing a reply in the above-identified application.

The requested extension and fee are as follows (check time period desired and enter the appropriate fee below):

		Fee	Small Entity Fee	Micro Entity Fee	
☐	One month (37 CFR 1.17(a)(1))	$220	$88	$44	$______
☐	Two months (37 CFR 1.17(a)(2))	$640	$256	$128	$______
☐	Three months (37 CFR 1.17(a)(3))	$1,480	$592	$296	$______
☐	Four months (37 CFR 1.17(a)(4))	$2,320	$928	$464	$______
☐	Five months (37 CFR 1.17(a)(5))	$3,160	$1,264	$632	$______

☐ Applicant asserts small entity status. See 37 CFR 1.27.

☐ Applicant certifies micro entity status. See 37 CFR 1.29.
Form PTO/SB/15A or B or equivalent must either be enclosed or have been submitted previously.

☐ A check in the amount of the fee is enclosed.

☐ Payment by credit card. Form PTO-2038 is attached.

☐ The Director has already been authorized to charge fees in this application to a Deposit Account.

☐ The Director is hereby authorized to charge any fees which may be required, or credit any overpayment, to

Deposit Account Number ___________________________

☐ Payment made via EFS-Web.

WARNING: Information on this form may become public. Credit card information should not be included on this form. Provide credit card information and authorization on PTO-2038.

I am the

☐ applicant/inventor.

☐ assignee of record of the entire interest. See 37 CFR 3.71. 37 CFR 3.73(b) statement is enclosed (Form PTO/SB/96).

☐ attorney or agent of record. Registration number ___________________________

☐ attorney or agent acting under 37 CFR 1.34. Registration number ___________________________

___________________________	___________________________
Signature	Date
___________________________	___________________________
Typed or printed name	Telephone Number

NOTE: This form must be signed in accordance with 37 CFR 1.33. See 37 CFR 1.4 for signature requirements and certifications. Submit multiple forms if more than one signature is required, see below*.

☐ * Total of ______________ forms are submitted.

Petition for extension of time fig.

Source: https://www.uspto.gov/sites/default/files/documents/sb0022.pdf[10]

I. Complete the Application Information

---

10. https://www.uspto.gov/sites/default/files/documents/

sb0022.pdf#_853ae90f0351324bd73ea615e6487517__4c761f170e016836ff84498202b99827__853ae90f035

1324bd73ea615e6487517_text_43ec3e5dee6e706af7766fffea512721_This_0bcef9c45bd8a48eda1b26eb0c61

c869_20is_0bcef9c45bd8a48eda1b26eb0c61c869_20a_0bcef9c45bd8a48eda1b26eb0c61c869_20request_0bc

ef9c45bd8a48eda1b26eb0c61c869_20under_0bcef9c45bd8a48eda1b26eb0c61c869_20the_0bcef9c45bd8a48

eda1b26eb0c61c869_20provisions

○ Docket Number (Optional): You can enter an internal tracking number for your records.

○ Application Number: Enter the unique number assigned to your patent application by the USPTO.

○ Filed: Indicate the filing date of the application.

○ For: Enter the title or subject of the patent application.

○ Art Unit: Provide the USPTO Art Unit number associated with your application.

○ Examiner: Enter the name of the USPTO examiner assigned to your application.

I. *Select the Desired Extension Period:* Choose the time period you wish to extend (1 to 5 months) by checking the appropriate box and indicate the corresponding fee for the extension according to entity status.

I. *Select the Payment Method:*

○ If you're paying by check, ensure the check covers the correct fee amount.

○ If paying by credit card, attach Form PTO-2038[11] (Credit Card Payment Form).

○ If you've authorized charges to a USPTO deposit account, provide the account number.

---

11. https://www.uspto.gov/sites/default/files/documents/PTO-2038.pdf

○ Indicate if payment is being made via EFS-Web (USPTO's online submission system).

I. *Sign the Form:* The form must be signed by the applicant, assignee, or authorized attorney/agent. Indicate your role by checking the appropriate box. Provide your registration number if you are an attorney or agent of record.

II. *Submit the Form:* The most efficient way to submit the form is electronically via the USPTO's Patent Center. If submitting by mail, send the completed form and payment (if applicable) to the following address: *Commissioner for Patents, P.O. Box 1450, Alexandria, VA 22313-1450*

III. *Confirmation:* After submission, whether electronically or by mail, monitor your application status through the USPTO's Patent Center system to confirm the extension has been granted.

Application Status: Pending, Allowance, and Patent Grant

In the patent application process at the United States Patent and Trademark Office (USPTO), there are several terms that may seem similar but refer to distinct stages. Understanding the differences between "pending", "allowance," and "patent grant" is crucial for navigating the patent process effectively.

Patent pending:

This status refers to the "patent pending" period that begins when a patent application is filed with the U.S. Patent Office and continues until the patent is either granted or the application is abandoned. During this time, the application does not confer any enforceable legal rights against third parties.

The "patent pending" period starts on the day the patent application, complete with the necessary forms, fees, and detailed invention description, is submitted. While the patent is pending, the applicant can use the term "patent pending" in reference to the invention, serving as a warning to others that a patent might be granted, which could result in legal consequences for infringement.

Typically, the "patent pending" period lasts between 1 and 3 years, though it can extend to 3 to 5 years in some cases. The application remains in this status with the U.S. Patent Office until it is either granted or formally abandoned by the applicant.

For the patent application to obtain a patent-pending, there are two basic ways to file the application:

-Provisional patent application: allows inventors to get an early filing date without going through the lengthy process of a full patent application. In turn, inventors can use the term "patent pending", however it does not automatically become a granted patent. To move toward grant, a non-provisional application claiming the benefit of the provisional must be filed within 12 months.

-Non-provisional patent application: grants the invention the status of "patent pending". It includes all the elements of the patent application such as description, claims, drawings, oath or declaration and fees. This application initiates the examination process at the patent office, which may result in the granting of the patent.

The transition from "patent pending" to a "granted patent" involves a multi-step process overseen by the patent office. It begins with a preliminary examination of the patent application, where the office verifies basic requirements such as form, content, and the payment of the appropriate fee. The goal of this initial review is to ensure that all essential criteria for the application are met.

Following the preliminary examination, the application is published approximately 18 months after the filing date. This publication makes the details of the patent application publicly accessible and marks the official start of the "patent pending" status.

The final stage is the substantive examination, during which patent examiners thoroughly review the application to ensure the invention is novel, non-obvious, and useful. They assess prior art, which includes all publicly available information before the filing date. If the application meets all patentability criteria and overcomes any objections, a Notice of Allowance is issued. Once the issuance fee is paid, the patent is granted.

It is illegal to use a "patent pending" notice in any form, whether on a product, webpage, or marketing materials, if the invention is not actually in a patent-pending status. Doing so without a filed patent application can result in fines for infringement.

There are some scenarios where patent pending status does not exist and a patent pending notice should not be used:

-If you have hired a patent attorney to prepare the patent application.

-If the patent attorney sends you a draft of the patent application for review.

-If your patent application has been granted as a patent.

-If your patent application has been abandoned.

The patent pending notice is not legally binding. You can use the patent pending notice in some scenarios:

-A provisional, utility or design patent application has been filed with the U.S. Patent Office.

-An office action has been sent from the U.S. Patent Office within the last six months.

-A Notice of Allowance has been sent from the U.S. Patent Office and you have paid the issuance fee (but the U.S. Patent Office has not yet issued the patent).

There is no mandatory format for a patent pending notice, but here are some commonly used examples:

➜ Patent pending.
➜ U.S. Patent Pending.
➜ Patent Applied For
➜ U.S. Patent Applied For

➜ U.S. and Foreign Patent Applied For

The patent-pending notice you use must be clear and concise that appears conspicuously on the product, marketing materials, websites, and any other product-related materials.

Patent Allowance:

Refers to a notice from the Patent Office informing the patent applicant that the claims of his application are patentable. The notice is issued by an examiner after reviewing the application and verifying that it contains one or more allowable claims. The notice closes the patent prosecution and indicates that the claims have been approved for patent grant.

The notice of grant is issued once the objections have been overcome and the patentability requirements of the application have been met, so that the applicant must pay an issuance fee and a publication fee and then the Patent Office will print the patent and deliver a certified copy to the inventor, granting the patent.

Upon payment of the issuance fee and compliance with other requirements (e.g., drawings) for issuance as a patent, the application is electronically exported to the Final Data Capture (FDC) stage. The FDC makes the necessary updates to the electronic file and places the approved patent application into an issue. The average time an approved application is in the FDC process is 5 weeks (2 weeks processing time for issue date assignment). The "Notice of Issuance" is mailed approximately 3 weeks prior to the patent issuance date.

Notice of Allowance

A Notice of Allowance (NOA) is a USPTO document indicating that a patent application has been allowed. This notice specifies that the applicant must pay the required issue fee and any applicable publication fee within three months from the mailing date of the notice.

Upon payment and processing of the issue fee, the USPTO will assign a patent number and an issue date to the application, along with issuing a Notice of Issuance.

This notice will be sent to the correspondence address provided on the application data sheet or any other document submitted with the application. If multiple addresses are listed on a document, the USPTO will select one of the specified addresses as the correspondence address, prioritizing the address associated with a Customer Number.

The correspondence address may be changed under the following circumstances:

Before the Filing of an Oath or Declaration Under § 1.63: If neither inventor has filed an oath or declaration under § 1.63, the party who originally filed the application may change the correspondence address.

After the Filing of an Oath or Declaration Under § 1.63: If any inventor has filed an oath or declaration under § 1.63, the correspondence address may be changed by:

○ A patent practitioner of record who has been appointed.

○ An assignee, could be a single assignee, multiple partial assignees acting together, or in conjunction with the inventor(s).

○ All applicants for the patent, unless the entire interest has been assigned to one party, and that assignee has taken action in the application as required by the regulations.

The submission of any of the following documents after the mailing of a Notice of Allowance will be treated as a request to charge the correct issue fee or any applicable publication fee to the deposit account specified in a previously filed authorization:

- An incorrect issue fee or publication fee payment; or

- A fee transmittal form (or letter) accompanying the payment of the issue fee or publication fee.

Utility and reissue patents typically issue approximately four weeks after the USPTO receives the correct issue fee and any required publication fee.

UNITED STATES PATENT AND TRADEMARK OFFICE

UNITED STATES DEPARTMENT OF COMMERCE
United States Patent and Trademark Office
Address: COMMISSIONER FOR PATENTS
P.O. Box 1450
Alexandria, Virginia 22313-1450
www.uspto.gov

NOTICE OF ALLOWANCE AND FEE(S) DUE

EXAMINER

ART UNIT	PAPER NUMBER

DATE MAILED:

APPLICATION NO.	FILING DATE	FIRST NAMED INVENTOR	ATTORNEY DOCKET NO.	CONFIRMATION NO.

APPLN. TYPE	ENTITY STATUS	ISSUE FEE DUE	PUBLICATION FEE DUE	PREV. PAID ISSUE FEE	TOTAL FEE(S) DUE	DATE DUE

THE APPLICATION IDENTIFIED ABOVE HAS BEEN EXAMINED AND IS ALLOWED FOR ISSUANCE AS A PATENT. PROSECUTION ON THE MERITS IS CLOSED. THIS NOTICE OF ALLOWANCE IS NOT A GRANT OF PATENT RIGHTS. THIS APPLICATION IS SUBJECT TO WITHDRAWAL FROM ISSUE AT THE INITIATIVE OF THE OFFICE OR UPON PETITION BY THE APPLICANT. SEE 37 CFR 1.313 AND MPEP 1308.

THE ISSUE FEE AND PUBLICATION FEE (IF REQUIRED) MUST BE PAID WITHIN THREE MONTHS FROM THE MAILING DATE OF THIS NOTICE OR THIS APPLICATION SHALL BE REGARDED AS ABANDONED. THIS STATUTORY PERIOD CANNOT BE EXTENDED. SEE 35 U.S.C. 151. THE ISSUE FEE DUE INDICATED ABOVE DOES NOT REFLECT A CREDIT FOR ANY PREVIOUSLY PAID ISSUE FEE IN THIS APPLICATION. IF AN ISSUE FEE HAS PREVIOUSLY BEEN PAID IN THIS APPLICATION (AS SHOWN ABOVE), THE RETURN OF PART B OF THIS FORM WILL BE CONSIDERED A REQUEST TO REAPPLY THE PREVIOUSLY PAID ISSUE FEE TOWARD THE ISSUE FEE NOW DUE.

HOW TO REPLY TO THIS NOTICE:

I. Review the ENTITY STATUS shown above. If the ENTITY STATUS is shown as SMALL or MICRO, verify whether entitlement to that entity status still applies.

If the ENTITY STATUS is the same as shown above, pay the TOTAL FEE(S) DUE shown above.

If the ENTITY STATUS is changed from that shown above, on PART B - FEE(S) TRANSMITTAL, complete section number 5 titled "Change in Entity Status (from status indicated above)".

For purposes of this notice, small entity fees are 1/2 the amount of undiscounted fees, and micro entity fees are 1/2 the amount of small entity fees.

II. PART B - FEE(S) TRANSMITTAL, or its equivalent, must be completed and returned to the United States Patent and Trademark Office (USPTO) with your ISSUE FEE and PUBLICATION FEE (if required). If you are charging the fee(s) to your deposit account, section "4b" of Part B - Fee(s) Transmittal should be completed and an extra copy of the form should be submitted. If an equivalent of Part B is filed, a request to reapply a previously paid issue fee must be clearly made, and delays in processing may occur due to the difficulty in recognizing the paper as an equivalent of Part B.

III. All communications regarding this application must give the application number. Please direct all communications prior to issuance to Mail Stop ISSUE FEE unless advised to the contrary.

IMPORTANT REMINDER: Utility patents issuing on applications filed on or after Dec. 12, 1980 may require payment of maintenance fees. It is patentee's responsibility to ensure timely payment of maintenance fees when due.

Page 1 of 3

PTOL-85 (Rev. 02/11)

Notice of Allowance Form Fig.

Source: https://www.uspto.gov/web/offices/pac/mpep/ s1303.html#:~:text=A%20%E2%80%9CNotice%20of%20Allowance%20and%20Fee(s)%[12]

---

12. https://www.uspto.gov/web/offices/pac/mpep/ s1303.html#_853ae90f0351324bd73ea615e6487517__4c761f170e016836ff84498202b99827__853ae90f035 1324bd73ea615e6487517_text_43ec3e5dee6e706af7766fffea512721_A_0bcef9c45bd8a48eda1b26eb0c61c8 69_20_0bcef9c45bd8a48eda1b26eb0c61c869_E2_0bcef9c45bd8a48eda1b26eb0c61c869_80_0bcef9c45bd8a 48eda1b26eb0c61c869_9CNotice_0bcef9c45bd8a48eda1b26eb0c61c869_20of_0bcef9c45bd8a48eda1b26eb 0c61c869_20Allowance_0bcef9c45bd8a48eda1b26eb0c61c869_20and_0bcef9c45bd8a48eda1b26eb0c61c86 9_20Fee_84c40473414caf2ed4a7b1283e48bbf4_s_9371d7a2e3ae86a00aab4771e39d255d__0bcef9c45bd8a4 8eda1b26eb0c61c869_20Due._0bcef9c45bd8a48eda1b26eb0c61c869_E2_0bcef9c45bd8a48eda1b26eb0c61c 869_80_0bcef9c45bd8a48eda1b26eb0c61c869_9D

PART B - FEE(S) TRANSMITTAL

Complete and send this form, together with applicable fee(s), to: __Mail__ Mail Stop ISSUE FEE
Commissioner for Patents
P.O. Box 1450
Alexandria, Virginia 22313-1450
or __Fax__   (571)-273-2885

INSTRUCTIONS: This form should be used for transmitting the ISSUE FEE and PUBLICATION FEE (if required). Blocks 1 through 5 should be completed where appropriate. All further correspondence including the Patent, advance orders and notification of maintenance fees will be mailed to the current correspondence address as indicated unless corrected below or directed otherwise in Block 1, by (a) specifying a new correspondence address; and/or (b) indicating a separate "FEE ADDRESS" for maintenance fee notifications.

CURRENT CORRESPONDENCE ADDRESS (Note: Use Block 1 for any change of address)

Note: A certificate of mailing can only be used for domestic mailings of the Fee(s) Transmittal. This certificate cannot be used for any other accompanying papers. Each additional paper, such as an assignment or formal drawing, must have its own certificate of mailing or transmission.

Certificate of Mailing or Transmission
I hereby certify that this Fee(s) Transmittal is being deposited with the United States Postal Service with sufficient postage for first class mail in an envelope addressed to the Mail Stop ISSUE FEE address above, or being facsimile transmitted to the USPTO (571) 273-2885, on the date indicated below.

	(Depositor's name)
	(Signature)
	(Date)

APPLICATION NO.	FILING DATE	FIRST NAMED INVENTOR	ATTORNEY DOCKET NO.	CONFIRMATION NO.

TITLE OF INVENTION: CAPTURING AND RESTORING SESSION STATE OF A MACHINE WITHOUT USING MEMORY IMAGES

APPLN. TYPE	ENTITY STATUS	ISSUE FEE DUE	PUBLICATION FEE DUE	PREV. PAID ISSUE FEE	TOTAL FEE(S) DUE	DATE DUE

EXAMINER	ART UNIT	CLASS-SUBCLASS

1. Change of correspondence address or indication of "Fee Address" (37 CFR 1.363).

☐ Change of correspondence address (or Change of Correspondence Address form PTO/SB/122) attached.

☐ "Fee Address" indication (or "Fee Address" Indication form PTO/SB/47; Rev 03-02 or more recent) attached. **Use of a Customer Number is required.**

2. For printing on the patent front page, list

(1) The names of up to 3 registered patent attorneys or agents OR, alternatively,

(2) The name of a single firm (having as a member a registered attorney or agent) and the names of up to 2 registered patent attorneys or agents. If no name is listed, no name will be printed.

1 _______________

2 _______________

3 _______________

3. ASSIGNEE NAME AND RESIDENCE DATA TO BE PRINTED ON THE PATENT (print or type)

PLEASE NOTE: Unless an assignee is identified below, no assignee data will appear on the patent. If an assignee is identified below, the document has been filed for recordation as set forth in 37 CFR 3.11. Completion of this form is NOT a substitute for filing an assignment.

(A) NAME OF ASSIGNEE

(B) RESIDENCE: (CITY and STATE OR COUNTRY)

Please check the appropriate assignee category or categories (will not be printed on the patent):   ☐ Individual   ☐ Corporation or other private group entity   ☐ Government

4a. The following fee(s) are submitted:
☐ Issue Fee
☐ Publication Fee (No small entity discount permitted)
☐ Advance Order - # of Copies _______

4b. Payment of Fee(s): **(Please first reapply any previously paid issue fee shown above)**
☐ A check is enclosed.
☐ Payment by credit card. Form PTO-2038 is attached.
☐ The director is hereby authorized to charge the required fee(s), any deficiency, or credits any overpayment, to Deposit Account Number _______ (enclose an extra copy of this form).

5. **Change in Entity Status** (from status indicated above)

☐ Applicant certifying micro entity status. See 37 CFR 1.29

☐ Applicant asserting small entity status. See 37 CFR 1.27

☐ Applicant changing to regular undiscounted fee status.

NOTE: Absent a valid certification of Micro Entity Status (see forms PTO/SB/15A and 15B), issue fee payment in the micro entity amount will not be accepted at the risk of application abandonment.

NOTE: If the application was previously under micro entity status, checking this box will be taken to be a notification of loss of entitlement to micro entity status.

NOTE: Checking this box will be taken to be a notification of loss of entitlement to small or micro entity status, as applicable.

NOTE: This form must be signed in accordance with 37 CFR 1.31 and 1.33. See 37 CFR 1.4 for signature requirements and certifications.

Authorized Signature _______________   Date _______________

Typed or printed name _______________   Registration No. _______________

Page 2 of 3

https://www.uspto.gov/web/offices/pac/mpep/
s1303.html#:~:text=A%20%E2%80%9CNotice%20of%20Allowance%20and%20Fee(s)%

[13]

---

13. https://www.uspto.gov/web/offices/pac/mpep/
s1303.html#_853ae90f0351324bd73ea615e6487517__4c761f170e016836ff84498202b99827__853ae90f035
1324bd73ea615e6487517_text_43ec3e5dee6e706af7766fffea512721_A_0bcef9c45bd8a48eda1b26eb0c61c8
69_20_0bcef9c45bd8a48eda1b26eb0c61c869_E2_0bcef9c45bd8a48eda1b26eb0c61c869_80_0bcef9c45bd8a
48eda1b26eb0c61c869_9CNotice_0bcef9c45bd8a48eda1b26eb0c61c869_20of_0bcef9c45bd8a48eda1b26eb
0c61c869_20Allowance_0bcef9c45bd8a48eda1b26eb0c61c869_20and_0bcef9c45bd8a48eda1b26eb0c61c86
9_20Fee_84c40473414caf2ed4a7b1283e48bbf4_s_9371d7a2e3ae86a00aab4771e39d255d__0bcef9c45bd8a4
8eda1b26eb0c61c869_20Due._0bcef9c45bd8a48eda1b26eb0c61c869_E2_0bcef9c45bd8a48eda1b26eb0c61c
869_80_0bcef9c45bd8a48eda1b26eb0c61c869_9D

UNITED STATES PATENT AND TRADEMARK OFFICE

UNITED STATES DEPARTMENT OF COMMERCE
United States Patent and Trademark Office
Address: COMMISSIONER FOR PATENTS
P.O. Box 1450
Alexandria, Virginia 22313-1450
www.uspto.gov

APPLICATION NO.	FILING DATE	FIRST NAMED INVENTOR	ATTORNEY DOCKET NO.	CONFIRMATION NO.

EXAMINER

ART UNIT	PAPER NUMBER

DATE MAILED:

Determination of Patent Term Adjustment under 35 U.S.C. 154 (b)
(Applications filed on or after May 29, 2000)

The Office has discontinued providing a Patent Term Adjustment (PTA) calculation with the Notice of Allowance.

Section 1(h)(2) of the AIA Technical Corrections Act amended 35 U.S.C. 154(b)(3)(B)(i) to eliminate the requirement that the Office provide a patent term adjustment determination with the notice of allowance. See Revisions to Patent Term Adjustment, 78 Fed. Reg. 19416, 19417 (Apr. 1, 2013). Therefore, the Office is no longer providing an initial patent term adjustment determination with the notice of allowance. The Office will continue to provide a patent term adjustment determination with the Issue Notification Letter that is mailed to applicant approximately three weeks prior to the issue date of the patent, and will include the patent term adjustment on the patent. Any request for reconsideration of the patent term adjustment determination (or reinstatement of patent term adjustment) should follow the process outlined in 37 CFR 1.705.

Any questions regarding the Patent Term Extension or Adjustment determination should be directed to the Office of Patent Legal Administration at (571)-272-7702. Questions relating to issue and publication fee payments should be directed to the Customer Service Center of the Office of Patent Publication at 1-(888)-786-0101 or (571)-272-4200.

PTOL-85 (Rev. 02/11)

https://www.uspto.gov/web/offices/pac/mpep/
s1303.html#:~:text=A%20%E2%80%9CNotice%20of%20Allowance%20and%20Fee(s)%
[14]

Patent Grant/Issue

A patent grant is the act and approval by the United States Patent and Trademark Office (USPTO) confirming that an invention described in a patent application meets the legal requirements for patentability. Once this determination is made, the USPTO allows the patent to proceed.

When the USPTO grants a patent, it does so by issuing a certificate of grant. The issuance of this certificate officially establishes the patent rights, known as the "grant of patent."

As of April 18, 2023, the USPTO began issuing electronic patent grants (eGrants) for all patents. These eGrants are accessible through the Patent Center, the USPTO's electronic system for patent application filing and management, which also allows for viewing patent documents.

After a patent is granted, the patent holder can view and print the complete issued patent from the Patent Center. During the transition period, the USPTO will also send a paper copy of the electronic patent grant as a ceremonial document to the patent holder's registered correspondence address. However, by law, the electronic patent grant is considered the official patent grant.

---

14. https://www.uspto.gov/web/offices/pac/mpep/

s1303.html#_853ae90f0351324bd73ea615e6487517__4c761f170e016836ff84498202b99827__853ae90f035

1324bd73ea615e6487517_text_43ec3e5dee6e706af7766fffea512721_A_0bcef9c45bd8a48eda1b26eb0c61c8

69_20_0bcef9c45bd8a48eda1b26eb0c61c869_E2_0bcef9c45bd8a48eda1b26eb0c61c869_80_0bcef9c45bd8a

48eda1b26eb0c61c869_9CNotice_0bcef9c45bd8a48eda1b26eb0c61c869_20of_0bcef9c45bd8a48eda1b26eb

0c61c869_20Allowance_0bcef9c45bd8a48eda1b26eb0c61c869_20and_0bcef9c45bd8a48eda1b26eb0c61c86

9_20Fee_84c40473414caf2ed4a7b1283e48bbf4_s_9371d7a2e3ae86a00aab4771e39d255d__0bcef9c45bd8a4

8eda1b26eb0c61c869_20Due._0bcef9c45bd8a48eda1b26eb0c61c869_E2_0bcef9c45bd8a48eda1b26eb0c61c

869_80_0bcef9c45bd8a48eda1b26eb0c61c869_9D

Starting January 30, 2024, the USPTO will also issue electronic certificates of correction (eCofCs) for all certificates with an issue date on or after that date. Paper certificates of correction will no longer be issued, and physical copies will no longer be mailed to the correspondence address of record. Instead, eCofCs will be available for viewing and printing from the Patent Center immediately upon issuance. The eCofC, like the eGrant, is the official statutory certificate of correction.

Example of electronic correction certificates (eCofCs):

UNITED STATES PATENT AND TRADEMARK OFFICE
CERTIFICATE OF CORRECTION

PATENT NO.   : 99,345,678 B2
APPLICATION NO.   : 99/345678
DATED   : February 7, 2023
INVENTOR(S)   : Name

Page 1 of 1

It is certified that error appears in the above-identified patent and that said Letters Patent is hereby corrected as shown below:

In the Specification

At Column 1, Lines 7-9 currently reads: TLorem ipsum dolor sit amet, consectetur adipiscing elit, sed do eiusmod tempor incididunt ut labore et dolore magna aliqua.

Should read: Lorem ipsum dolor sit amet, consectetur adipiscing elit, sed do eiusmod tempor incididunt ut labore et dolore magna aliqua.

Signed and Sealed this
Twelfth Day of December, 2023

Katherine Kelly Vidal

Katherine Kelly Vidal
Director of the United States Patent and Trademark Office

Certificate of Correction Fig.
Source: https://www.uspto.gov/sites/default/files/documents/eCofC-Sample.pdf[5]

---

15. *https://www.uspto.gov/sites/default/files/documents/*

eCofC-Sample.pdf#_853ae90f0351324bd73ea615e6487517__4c761f170e016836ff84498202b99827__853ae9

0f0351324bd73ea615e6487517_text_43ec3e5dee6e706af7766fffea512721_Katherine_0bcef9c45bd8a48eda1b2

6eb0c61c869_20Kelly_0bcef9c45bd8a48eda1b26eb0c61c869_20Vidal_0bcef9c45bd8a48eda1b26eb0c61c869_2

0Director_0bcef9c45bd8a48eda1b26eb0c61c869_20of_0bcef9c45bd8a48eda1b26eb0c61c869_20the

The patent issue marks the final administrative step in the patenting process, where the USPTO formally grants the patent to the applicant. This step signifies the official recognition of the invention as a patented invention, providing the inventor with legal protection. The issued patent grants the inventor exclusive rights to prevent others from making, using, selling, or importing the patented invention without permission. These rights offer a competitive advantage and enable the inventor to monetize the invention in the marketplace.

However, there are limitations to these rights. Patents are jurisdiction-specific, meaning the granted rights are enforceable only within the geographical boundaries of the issuing country.

It's important to note that other companies may attempt to find alternative methods to achieve similar results without infringing on the patented invention. Therefore, inventors should be vigilant about their exclusive rights, which typically last for 20 years from the filing date, providing a significant period of market exclusivity

In the context of patents, "grant" and "issue" are often used interchangeably to refer to the final step in the patent process where the patent office formally provides the patent rights to the inventor.

○ *Grant* refers to the act of officially approving and conferring the patent rights to the inventor.

○ *Issue* refers to the publication and delivery of the official patent document, signifying that the patent has been granted.

Basis for rejection

35 USC 101 - inventions patentable

Statutory Subject Matter: The four categories of subject matter that are eligible for patent protection under U.S. law (35 U.S.C. 101) are:

Process: This refers to a method or series of steps taken to achieve a specific result. A process involves actions performed on a material or subject-matter that transforms it into something different. In patent terms, "process" is synonymous with "method."

Machine: A machine is a concrete, physical device made up of parts or a combination of devices that work together to perform a function or produce a result. It includes any mechanical apparatus or system.

Manufacture: This category covers tangible articles that are given a new form, quality, or property through human-made or artificial means. Manufactures are products that result from a manufacturing process, where raw materials are transformed into something new.

Composition of Matter: This involves the combination of two or more substances to create a composite article. It includes chemical compounds, mixtures, and materials, regardless of their physical state (solid, liquid, gas, etc.).

Physical or Tangible Form Requirement: For categories other than processes, the subject matter must exist in a physical or tangible form. This means that inventions in the categories of machines, manufactures, and compositions of matter must be something concrete or physically perceptible.

Even when a product has a physical or tangible form, it may still not fall within a statutory category if it lacks the required concrete structure. For instance, a transitory signal does not qualify as a machine, manufacture, or composition of matter despite being physical and real.

Judicial Interpretation: The courts have provided interpretations and definitions for each category over time, emphasizing the necessity for inventions to fit clearly within these defined boundaries to be eligible for a patent.

Category Flexibility: It is not necessary to identify a single category into which a claim falls, as long as it is clear that the claim falls into at least one of the four statutory categories: process, machine, manufacture, or composition of matter. For example, a microprocessor, which is generally understood to be a manufacturer, would satisfy the requirements even if it could also be considered under another category, such as a machine. Similarly, a bicycle fits both the machine and manufacture categories because it is a tangible product with physical parts (machine) and is made from raw materials given a new form (manufacture). A genetically modified bacterium also falls into both the composition of matter and manufacture categories, as it is a combination of substances and a product altered to have new properties.

Examples of Patent-Eligible Products: Certain claims are not directed to any of the statutory categories and thus are not patentable. Products without a physical or tangible form, such as abstract data or software claimed without any structural elements, do not fall within any statutory category. Transitory forms of signal transmission, like propagating electrical or electromagnetic signals, are also not patentable. Additionally, subject matter expressly prohibited from being patented by statute, such as humans, is excluded.

Double Patenting Prohibited: 35 U.S.C. 101 ensures that an inventor or discoverer can only obtain one patent for a particular invention. This rule prevents the issuance of multiple patents for the same invention to the same inventor, whether individually or as part of a team, or to a common applicant or assignee. The term "same invention" refers to situations where identical subject matter is being claimed in more than one patent application. If an inventor attempts to obtain multiple patents for the same invention, they will face a statutory double patenting rejection. This rejection applies when claims in more than one application are directed to the same invention.

Naming of inventor: The inventor(s) must be the applicant in an application filed before September 16, 2012 (except as otherwise provided in pre-AIA 37 CFR 1.41(b)), and the inventor or each joint inventor must be identified in an application filed on or after September 16, 2012.

In the rare situation where it is clear the application does not name the correct inventorship and the applicant has not filed a request to correct inventorship under 37 CFR 1.48, the examiner should reject the claims under 35 U.S.C. 101 and 115 for applications subject to AIA 35 U.S.C. 102 (see MPEP § 2157) or under pre-AIA 35 U.S.C. 102(f) for applications subject to pre-AIA 35 U.S.C. 102 (see MPEP § 2137).

Subject matter eligibility: A claimed invention must be eligible for patenting. As explained in MPEP § 2106, there are two criteria for determining subject matter eligibility. First, a claimed invention must fall within one of the four statutory categories of invention set forth in 35 U.S.C. 101, namely process, machine, manufacture, or composition of matter. Second, a claimed invention must be directed to patent-eligible subject matter and not a judicial exception, unless the claim as a whole includes additional limitations amounting to significantly more than the exception. The judicial exceptions are subject matter which courts have found to be outside of, or exceptions to, the four statutory categories of invention and are limited to abstract ideas, laws of nature, and natural phenomena (including products of nature).

Eligible subject matter is further limited by the Atomic Energy Act, explained in MPEP § 2104.01, which prohibits patents granted on any invention or discovery that is useful solely in the utilization of special nuclear material or atomic energy in an atomic weapon.

Utility: The invention must be "useful," meaning it must have a specific, substantial, and credible utility. The utility requirement ensures that the invention provides some identifiable benefit and is not merely theoretical. A rejection on the ground of lack of utility is appropriate when it is not apparent why the invention is "useful" because the applicant has failed to identify any specific and substantial utility and there is no well-established utility, or when an assertion of specific and substantial utility for the invention is not credible. Such a rejection can include the more specific grounds of inoperativeness, such as inventions involving perpetual motion. A rejection under 35 U.S.C. 101 for lack of utility should not be based on grounds that the invention is frivolous, fraudulent, or against public policy.

The statutory basis for this rejection is 35 U.S.C. 101. See MPEP § 2107 for guidelines governing rejections for lack of utility, and MPEP §§ 2107.01 - 2107.03 for legal precedent governing the utility requirement. MPEP § 2107.02, subsection IV, provides form paragraphs to be used to reject claims under 35 U.S.C. 101 for failure to satisfy the utility requirement.

Establish Broadest Reasonable Interpretation of Claim: Before evaluating a claim for patent eligibility, it is essential to interpret the claim in its broadest reasonable manner. This broad interpretation helps determine if the claim falls within the statutory categories and avoids being overly influenced by how the claim is drafted.

The broadest reasonable interpretation (BRI) determines what the claim covers, which affects whether it falls within statutory categories or exceptions. For example, if a claim includes both statutory and non-statutory elements (ineligible for patenting), the entire claim might fail to meet eligibility requirements.

The Mayo test, also known as the Alice/Mayo test, is used to determine if a patent claim is eligible for patent protection when it involves abstract ideas, laws of nature, or natural phenomena, areas that are typically considered exceptions to patentability.

○ Identify Judicial Exceptions: Determine if the claim is directed to a judicial exception, which includes abstract ideas, laws of nature, or natural phenomena. These are concepts that are generally not patentable.

○ Inventive Concept: If the claim is directed to a judicial exception, assess whether the claim includes additional elements that amount to significantly more than the exception itself. This means looking for an "inventive concept" that transforms the exception into something patentable.

Summary of analysis and flowchart: To determine if a patent claim meets the subject matter eligibility criteria, examiners use a structured analysis outlined in a flowchart. Here's a simplified summary:

Step 1: Statutory Categories: Confirm that the claim falls within one of the four statutory categories: processes, machines, manufactures, or compositions of matter.

Step 2: Alice/Mayo Test

Step 2A: Determine if the claim is directed to a judicial exception (abstract ideas, laws of nature, or natural phenomena).

Step 2B: If the claim includes a judicial exception, check if additional elements provide an "inventive concept" or amount to "significantly more" than the exception.

Eligibility Pathways:

Pathway A: Claims that meet the statutory category requirement (Step 1) and whose eligibility is self-evident can be found eligible using a streamlined analysis.

Pathway B: Claims that meet the statutory category requirement (Step 1) and are not directed to a judicial exception (Step 2A) and are eligible without needing further analysis (Step 2B).

Pathway C: Claims that meet the statutory category requirement (Step 1), are directed to a judicial exception (Step 2A), and recite additional elements that amount to significantly more than the exception (Step 2B) are eligible.

If a claim is not immediately found eligible under Pathway A, it should be analyzed further under Pathways B or C. If a claim does not fit any of the pathways, it is considered ineligible and should be rejected.

Finally, even if a claim is rejected under 35 U.S.C. 101, it must also be examined for compliance with other patentability requirements (35 U.S.C. 102, 103, 112, and other relevant sections).

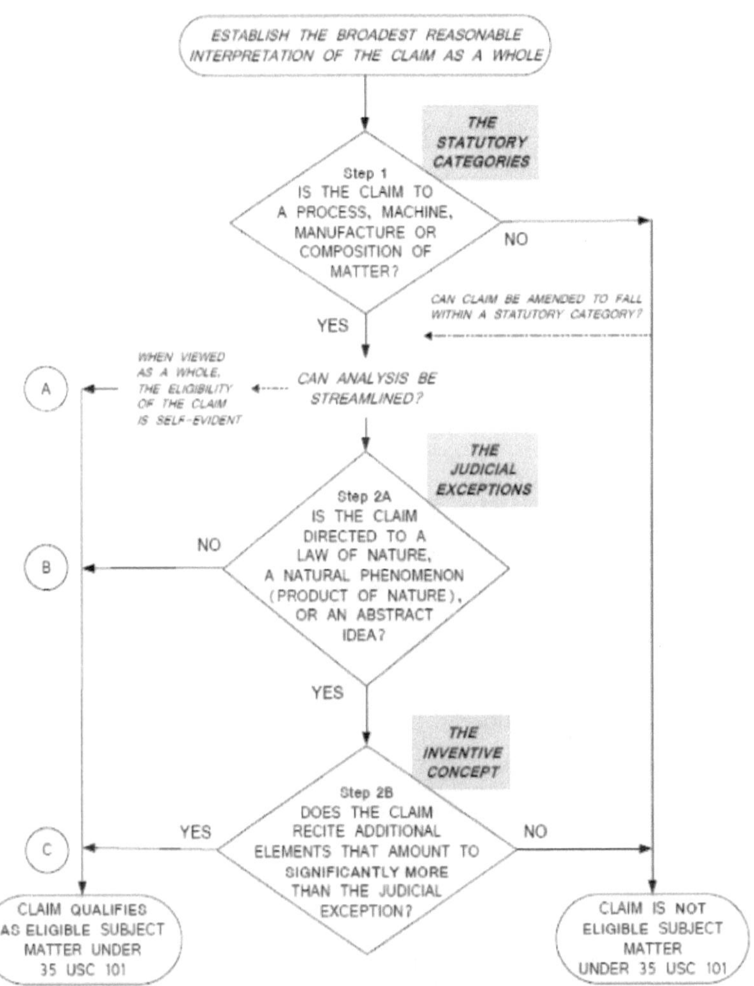

Subject Matter Eligibility Fig.

Source: https://www.uspto.gov/web/offices/pac/mpep/
s2106.html#:~:text=35%20U.S.C.%20101%20enumerates%20four%20cat

35 USC 102 - conditions for patentability: novelty

Under 35 U.S.C. 102 regarding conditions for patentability and novelty, a person is entitled to a patent unless the invention was already known to the public, through a patent, publication, public use, sale, or other means, before the effective filing date of the invention, or if someone else filed a patent application for the same invention earlier.

However, there are exceptions. If the invention was disclosed by the inventor (or someone who learned it from the inventor) within one year before the filing date, that disclosure does not count as prior art. Similarly, if the invention and the previously disclosed subject matter were owned by the same person or entity at the time of filing, it's not considered prior art.

In the context of joint research agreements, if the invention was developed as part of such an agreement and the patent application discloses the names of all parties involved, the invention is treated as being owned by the same entity.

When assessing whether a patent or patent application qualifies as prior art, it is considered filed on the date of the earliest related application, if multiple filings are involved.

A person is entitled to a patent unless one of the following conditions applies:

○ Prior Knowledge or Use: The invention was already known or used by others, or was patented or published before the applicant's invention.

---

16. https://www.uspto.gov/web/offices/pac/mpep/

s2106.html#_853ae90f0351324bd73ea615e6487517__4c761f170e016836ff84498202b998

27__853ae90f0351324bd73ea615e6487517_text_43ec3e5dee6e706af7766fffea512721_35

_0bcef9c45bd8a48eda1b26eb0c61c869_20U.S.C._0bcef9c45bd8a48eda1b26eb0c61c869_

20101_0bcef9c45bd8a48eda1b26eb0c61c869_20enumerates_0bcef9c45bd8a48eda1b26eb

0c61c869_20four_0bcef9c45bd8a48eda1b26eb0c61c869_20categories

○ Prior Public Disclosure: The invention was patented, published, publicly used, or on sale more than a year before the patent application was filed in the U.S.

○ Abandonment: The inventor has abandoned the invention.

○ Foreign Patenting: The invention was patented or subject to an inventor's certificate in a foreign country more than 12 months before the U.S. application.

○ Prior U.S. Patent Application: The invention was described in a previously filed U.S. patent application or a patent granted on such an application, filed before the applicant's invention.

○ Lack of Inventorship: The person did not actually invent the subject matter being patented.

○ Prior Invention by Another: Another inventor made the invention first and did not abandon, suppress, or conceal it.

35 USC 103 - conditions for patentability non obvious subject matter

A patent cannot be obtained if the invention would have been obvious to someone skilled in the relevant field at the time it was made, even if it is not identically disclosed in prior art. This means that if the differences between the invention and existing knowledge (prior art) are minor, the invention may not be patentable. However, the way the invention was made does not affect its patentability.

In the case of biotechnological processes, there is an exception. A biotechnological process, which involves altering organisms or producing specific products through genetic manipulation or cell fusion, can be considered nonobvious (and therefore patentable) if:

○ The process and the related composition of matter are claimed in the same patent application or separate applications with the same filing date.

○ The composition of matter and the process were owned by the same person or were subject to an obligation of assignment to the same person at the time of the invention.

If a patent is granted for such a biotechnological process, it must include claims to the composition of matter involved, or if the composition is claimed in another patent, the process patent must expire at the same time as the other patent.

Moreover, if another person's work qualifies as prior art under specific subsections but was owned by the same person or subject to an assignment obligation at the time of the invention, it does not prevent patentability. This is particularly relevant in the context of joint research agreements, where multiple parties collaborate on a project. If the invention resulted from such a collaboration and the joint research agreement is properly disclosed, the invention can still be patented despite certain prior art.

Chapter 6

INTERVIEW WITH THE EXAMINATOR

CHAPTER 6. INTERVIEW WITH THE EXAMINATOR

What is patent internet usage policy

The "Patent Internet Usage Policy" within the United States Patent and Trademark Office (USPTO) establishes guidelines for how USPTO employees, particularly patent examiners, and other relevant personnel can use the internet in the course of their duties. This policy is particularly concerned with maintaining the confidentiality and security of sensitive information, especially regarding unpublished patent applications.

Confidentiality and Security:

The policy emphasizes that all internet usage must comply with the confidentiality requirements outlined in U.S. law, specifically 35 U.S.C. 122. This means that any communication or search activity that could disclose proprietary information must be handled with extreme care.

If security and confidentiality cannot be ensured for a specific task, such activities are not permitted via the Internet.

Use of the Internet for Communication:

Patent examiners can use email or other internet-based tools to communicate with applicants, but only if the applicant has provided written authorization. This is to ensure that any sensitive information exchanged is properly documented and secured.

The policy provides guidelines for recording these communications in the official patent application file to ensure a clear and traceable record.

Internet Searches:

The policy also covers how patent examiners should conduct internet searches related to patent applications. It advises them to avoid searches that could inadvertently reveal confidential information related to specific applications. This is especially important to prevent unauthorized individuals from capturing search requests or results that could compromise the confidentiality of an application.

How an interview is being handled and how to arrange an interview (requirements)

713-Interviews

An interview should be granted when the nature of the case is such that the interview serves to develop or clarify outstanding issues in an application. Both applicants and examiners should understand that interview time is limited for both, and therefore they should use the interview time efficiently.

All discussions between the applicant/practitioner and the examiner regarding the merits of a pending application <u>will be considered an interview and are to be made of record</u>. This includes any and all records or communications received in connection with the interview via any communication mode.

Where an electronic record is created as part of the interview, e.g., a series of electronic messages, a copy of the electronic record is to be made of record in the application. Where an electronic record is not created, a summary of the interview must be made of record.

USPTO AIR

USPTO AIR is a web-based tool that allows Applicants to request and interview with an Examiner for their pending patent application. AIR is a convenient online form for submitting requests for interviews. After the form is submitted, an examiner will respond to you to confirm your request within two business days.

Main Features:

- **Data Search and Retrieval:** Allows examiners and USPTO staff to quickly access information about applications and patents, facilitating processing and decision-making.

- **Correspondence Management:** Assists in organizing and handling correspondence related to patent applications, including the receipt, classification, and response to documents.

- **Procedure Tracking:** Facilitates the tracking of ongoing procedures, ensuring that all necessary steps are completed in the patent review and adjudication process.

In the USPTO (United States Patent and Trademark Office), it is called "TC Interview Specialist" which refers to a specialist in interviews within a Technology Center (TC). These specialists play an important role in managing and assisting with interviews related to patent applications. The USPTO is organized into several Technology Centers, each focusing on a specific technical area of patents, such as chemistry, engineering, biotechnology, etc. Each TC has a group of examiners who specialize in those technical areas.

Technology Centers and Art Units

A Technology Center (TC) for patent examination is divided among nine examining technology centers (TCs) and the Central Reexamination Unit (CRU). Each TC is led by an Assistant Commissioner (AC), and a group of Directors, (TC Directors) who have jurisdiction over certain assigned fields of technology: They provide leadership over the 10,000 employees of the technology centers, presiding over the implementation of processes, policies and programs created within the Patent Operations organization.

Technology Center 1600 provides examinations for patent applications including Biotechnology and Organic fields.

Technology Center 1700 provides examination for patent applications including Chemical and Materials Engineering fields.

Art Units are more focused groups within a **TC** that handle patent applications related to a specific technical niche within a Technology Center. Each Art Unit focuses on a narrower technical subject matter, allowing examiners within the unit to develop specialized expertise. For example, within a TC dedicated to electrical engineering, there might be separate Art Units for semiconductor devices, digital communications, or computer networks.

Main differences between an Examinator and TC Specialist

At the USPTO, a Patent Examiner is responsible for reviewing patent applications to determine if they meet legal and technical requirements, such as novelty and non-obviousness, and interacting directly with applicants to accept, reject, or request more information, ultimately deciding whether a patent is granted.

In contrast, a Technology Center (TC) Specialist provides specialized technical support within a specific Technology Center, assisting examiners with complex technologies, offering training, and helping develop policies and procedures. While examiners focus on individual patent applications, TC Specialists ensure technical guidance and quality standards across their specific technology area.

713.01 General policy, How Conducted

37 CFR 1.133 Interviews.

An interview for the discussion of the patentability of a pending application will not occur before the first Office action, unless the application is a continuing or substitute application or the examiner determines that such an interview would advance prosecution of the application.

In every instance where reconsideration is requested in view of an interview with an examiner, a complete written statement of the reasons presented at the interview as warranting favorable action must be filed by the applicant. An interview does not remove the necessity for reply to Office actions.

I. WHERE AND WHEN TO CONDUCT INTERVIEWS

- Face-to-face interviews may be accomplished via video conferencing or in-person. Other times, a telephone interview provides an appropriate level of interaction.

NOTE: Video conferencing with a patent examiner gives you the ability to have face-to-face meetings, no matter the location of the examiner or attorney. Video conference interviews will not be recorded. The substance of the interview will be documented by the examiner in an interview summary according to standard practice.

- In-person interviews must be conducted on the Office premises, such as in an examiner's office, a conference room, an interview room or a video conference center, and should be held during normal business hours of 8:30 a.m. – 5:00 p.m. Monday through Friday.

- Interviews other than in-person interviews should be held during normal business hours and may also be held during mutually agreed upon non-traditional business hours, such as Saturday and evening hours.

When an examiner is working remotely from a USPTO campus, there may not be an opportunity to have an in-person interview. The examiner shall accommodate an applicant, attorney, or agent's preference for an interview via telephone or electronic communication using USPTO web-based collaboration tools, consistent with the special requirements of section II. below. Any Examiner may, with the applicant's consent, conduct an interview by video conferencing using the web-based collaboration tools provided by the Office.

II. SPECIAL REQUIREMENTS FOR USING INTERNET COMMUNICATIONS

Internet email, instant message system, or video conferencing shall NOT be used to conduct an exchange or communications similar to those exchanged during telephone or personal interviews unless authorization from the applicants or an attorney/agent of record has been given to use Internet communications.

A. Written Authorization

The following is a sample written authorization which may be used by applicant:

> *"Recognizing that Internet communications are not secure, I hereby authorize the USPTO to communicate with the undersigned and practitioners in accordance with 37 CFR 1.33[1] and 37 CFR 1.34[2] concerning any subject matter of this application by video conferencing, instant messaging, or electronic mail. I understand that a copy of these communications will be recorded in the application file."*

The Internet authorization must be submitted on a separate paper to be entitled to acceptance. The separate paper will facilitate processing and avoid confusion.

B. Oral Authorization

An oral authorization from the applicant/practitioner is sufficient for video conferencing interviews. The oral authorization is limited to the arrangement of video conference interview (including the meeting invitation).

Video Conferencing

---

1. *https://www.uspto.gov/web/offices/pac/mpep/mpep-9020-appx-r.html#aia_d0e317491*

2. *https://www.uspto.gov/web/offices/pac/mpep/mpep-9020-appx-r.html#d0e317605*

- A video conference is an electronic meeting, using USPTO web-based collaboration tools, to visually interact and collaborate with people anywhere in real time.

- Video conferencing should be conducted consistent with the special procedure of subsection II above. Authorization from the applicant, preferably written, should be obtained prior to scheduling and setting up a video conference.

Scheduling and conducting an interview

An interview should be arranged in advance to insure that the primary examiner and/or the examiner in charge of the application will be available. Use of the USPTO's Automated Interview Request (AIR) Form. but in the alternative, the examiner may be contacted by letter, facsimile, electronic mail, telephone or the "Applicant Initiated Interview Request" form (PTOL-413A) to schedule the interview. The AIR form or the PTOL-413A form may be submitted to the examiner prior to the interview in order to permit the examiner to prepare in advance and to focus on the issues to be discussed.

USPTO Automated Interview Request (AIR) Form

USPTO Automated Interview Request (AIR) Form

* This paper requesting to schedule and/or conduct an interview is appropriate because:

○ I have previously submitted an authorization for internet communications in this patent application. See form SB/0439.

○ I am concurrently submitting an authorization to communicate via the internet. See form SB/0439.

○ This submission is requested to be accepted as an authorization for this interview to communicate via the internet. Recognizing that Internet communications are not secure, I hereby authorize the USPTO to communicate with the undersigned concerning scheduling of the interview via video conference, instant messaging, or electronic mail, and to conduct the interview in accordance with office practice including video conferencing.

* ☐ I understand that a copy of this communication will be made of record in the application file.

*Name(s): [____________________]

*S-signature: [____________________] (See 37 CFR 1.4(d)(2)) (/Name/)

Registration Number: [__________] (Five or six characters as format: 12345 / 123456 / L1234 / P12345)

*U.S. Application Number: [__________] (8 digit numeric do not start with 90 or 95: 90###### /95######)
(Note: AIR is intended for regular examination interview requests only and cannot complete interview requests for applications under Re-examination)

*Confirmation Number: [__________] (4 Digit Numeric Only: 1234)

*E-mail Address: [____________________]

*Phone Number: [USA (+1) ▾] [__________] Extension: [____] (Numeric Digit Only)

*E-mail Address: [____________________]

*Phone Number: [USA (+1) ▾] [__________] Extension: [____] (Numeric Digit Only)

*Proposed Date and Time of Requested Interview must be more than five (5) days and less than thirty-five (35) days after today:
(Note: Confirmation of actual interview date and time will be arranged between examiner and requester)

[MM ▾] [DD ▾] [YYYY ▾] [Time ▾] Eastern Time (select date more than 5 days and less than 35 days after today)

*Proposed Type of Interview: [Please select an interview ▾] (Examiners working remotely will offer Video Conference or Telephonic interviews)

Optional Alternative Proposed Date(s) and Time(s) of Requested Interview:
Optional1: [MM ▾] [DD ▾] [YYYY ▾] [Time ▾] Eastern Time (select date more than 5 days and less than 35 days after today)
Optional2: [MM ▾] [DD ▾] [YYYY ▾] [Time ▾] Eastern Time (select date more than 5 days and less than 35 days after today)

Topic for Discussion: [____________________] (Optional: max 500 characters)

* ○ I am the applicant or applicant's representative for this application.

[Submit]

* Indicates fields that are required

Note: To report a problem please email ExaminerInterviewPractice@USPTO.GOV ✉ .

Privacy Act Statement

Interview Form Fig.

*Source:*https://www.uspto.gov/patents/uspto-automated-interview-request-air-form#:~:text=This%20collection%20is%20estimated%20to%20take%2024[1]

Applicant Initiated Interview Request

---

1. https://www.uspto.gov/patents/uspto-automated-interview-request-air-form#_853ae90f0351324bd73ea615e6487517__4c761f170e016836ff84498202b99827__853ae90f0351324bd73ea615e6487517_text_43ec3e5dee6e706af7766fffea512721_This_0bcef9c45bd8a48eda1b26eb0c61c869_20collection_0bcef9c45bd8a48eda1b26eb0c61c869_20is_0bcef9c45bd8a48eda1b26eb0c61c869_20estimated_0bcef9c45bd8a48eda1b26eb0c61c869_20to_0bcef9c45bd8a48eda1b26eb0c61c869_20take_0bcef9c45bd8a48eda1b26eb0c61c869_2024

Under the Paperwork Reduction Act of 1995, no persons are required to respond to a collection of information unless it displays a valid OMB control number.

Applicant Initiated Interview Request Form

Application No.: ___________________ First Named Applicant: ___________________
Examiner: ___________________ Art Unit: _________ Status of Application: ___________

Tentative Participants:
(1)___________________ (2)___________________

(3)___________________ (4)___________________

Proposed Date of Interview:___________________ **Proposed Time:**_________(○AM○PM)

Type of Interview Requested:
(1) ☐ Telephonic   (2) ☐ Personal   (3) ☐ Video Conference

Exhibit To Be Shown or Demonstrated: ☐ YES   ☐ NO
If yes, provide brief description:___________________________________

Issues To Be Discussed

Issues (Rej., Obj., etc)	Claims/ Fig. #s	Prior Art	Discussed	Agreed	Not Agreed
(1)_______	_______	_______	☐	☐	☐
(2)_______	_______	_______	☐	☐	☐
(3)_______	_______	_______	☐	☐	☐
(4)_______	_______	_______	☐	☐	☐

☐ Continuation Sheet Attached   ☐ Proposed Amendment or Arguments Attached
Brief Description of Arguments to be Presented: ___________________________

Applicant Initiated Interview Form Fig.
Source: https://www.uspto.gov/sites/default/files/documents/
PTOL413A.pdf

This form should identify the participants of the interview, the proposed date of the interview, the communication mode (e.g., personal, telephonic, or video conference), and should include a brief description of the issues to be discussed. Upon completion of the interview, a copy of the completed Interview Summary form (PTOL-413/413b) should be given to the applicant (or applicant's attorney or agent) along with any attachments.

When an examiner receives a telephone call and it becomes clear that a lengthy discussion will be required or that the examiner needs time to review the situation again, the call should be terminated with the agreement that the examiner will call back at a specified time.

When it is obvious that the attorney or agent is not so prepared, the interview should be rescheduled. The attorney, agent, or applicant should submit an agenda that indicates in advance what issues they desire to discuss at the interview by submitting, in writing, a proposed amendment or argument. This would permit the examiner to prepare in advance for the interview and to focus on the matters outlined in the proposed amendment.

The examiner should not hesitate to state, when appropriate, that claims presented for discussion at an interview would require further search and consideration. Nor should the examiner hesitate to conclude an interview when it appears that no common ground can be reached or when it becomes apparent that the application requires further amendment or an additional action by the examiner. However, the examiner should attempt to identify issues and resolve differences during the interview as much as possible.

It is the responsibility of all participants to see that the interview is not extended beyond a reasonable period, usually 30 minutes.

During an interview with a pro se applicant (i.e., an applicant who is prosecuting his or her own case and is not familiar with Office procedure), the examiner may make suggestions that will advance the prosecution of this case; this lies wholly within the examiner's discretion. Excessive time, however, should not be allowed for such interviews.

A duplicate copy is unnecessary when the amendment and/or remarks are filed via the USPTO patent electronic filing system as the examiner will be able to quickly access such documents.

The unexpected appearance of an attorney, agent, or applicant requesting an interview without any previous notice may well justify the examiner's refusal of the interview at that time, particularly in an involved case.

The substance of any interview must be made of record in the application. A paper copy of any written communications or transcripts MUST be made and placed in the patent application file as required by the Federal Records Act in the same manner as an Examiner Interview Summary Form is entered.

Viewing of video during interviews

Attorneys or applicants wishing to show a video during an examiner interview must be able to demonstrate that the content of the video has a bearing on an outstanding issue in the application and its viewing will advance the prosecution of the application. The substance of the interview, including a summary of the content of the video, must be made of record in the application.

Examination by an examiner other than the one who conducted the initial interview

Sometimes the examiner who conducted the interview is transferred to another Technology Center or resigns, and the examination is continued by another examiner. If there is an indication that an interview had been held, the second examiner should ascertain if any agreements were reached at the interview. Where conditions permit, as in the absence of a clear error or knowledge of other prior art, the second examiner should take a position consistent with the agreements previously reached.

Collaboration tools

Collaboration tools are the web-based tools provided by the USPTO and include multiple electronic communication tools such as video conferencing equipment and software. Examiners must only use USPTO-supplied equipment and software for interviews. All video conferences for interviews MUST originate or be hosted by USPTO personnel

Substance of the Interview must be made of record

Business to be transacted in writing

37 CFR 1.2 mandates that all business with the United States Patent and Trademark Office (USPTO) must be conducted in writing, as the Office bases its decisions exclusively on the written record. No oral promises, stipulations, or understandings will be considered if there is any disagreement or doubt. Given that the written record must be complete, it is essential to document the substance of any substantial interview with an examiner.

The Interview Summary form provides for recordation of the following information:

(A) application number;
(B) name of applicant;
(C) name of examiner;
(D) date of interview;
(E) type of interview (personal, telephonic, or video conference);
(F) name of participant(s) (applicant, applicant's representative, etc.);
(G) detail all issues discussed;
(H) an identification of any attachment; and
(I) the signature of the examiner who conducted the interview.

Applicant-Initiated Interview Summary	Application No. 99/999,999	Applicant(s) Jones et al.			
	Examiner JOHN A SMITH	Art Unit 9999	AIA (First Inventor to File) Status Yes		Page 1 of 1

All Participants (applicant, applicants representative, PTO personnel)	Title	Type
JOHN A SMITH	Primary Examiner	Telephonic
JANE C DOE	Attorney of Record	

Date of Interview: Insert Date

Issues Discussed:

35 U.S.C. 101
Summary of the discussion of 35 U.S.C. 101.

35 U.S.C. 112
Summary of the discussion of 35 U.S.C. 112.

35 U.S.C. 102
Summary of the discussion of 35 U.S.C. 102.

35 U.S.C. 103
Summary of the discussion of 35 U.S.C. 103.

/JOHN A SMITH/ Primary Examiner, Art Unit 9999	

Applicant is reminded that a complete written statement as to the substance of the interview must be made of record in the application file. It is the applicants responsibility to provide the written statement, unless the interview was initiated by the Examiner and the Examiner has indicated that a written summary will be provided. See MPEP 713.04
Please further see:
MPEP 713.04
Title 37 Code of Federal Regulations (CFR) § 1.133 Interviews, paragraph (b)
37 CFR § 1.2 Business to be transacted in writing

Applicant recordation instructions: The formal written reply to the last Office action must include the substance of the interview. (See MPEP section 713.04). If a reply to the last Office action has already been filed, applicant is given a non-extendable period of the longer of one month or thirty days from this interview date, or the mailing date of this interview summary form, whichever is later, to file a statement of the substance of the interview.

Examiner recordation instructions: Examiners must summarize the substance of any interview of record. A complete and proper recordation of the substance of an interview should include the items listed in MPEP 713.04 for complete and proper recordation including the identification of the general thrust of each argument or issue discussed, a general indication of any other pertinent matters discussed regarding patentability and the general results or outcome of the interview, to include an indication as to whether or not agreement was reached on the issues raised.

U.S. Patent and Trademark Office
PTOL-413/413b (Rev. Oct. 2019) Interview Summary Paper No. 99999999

Applicant Initiated Interview Meeting Summary Fig.
*Source:*https://www.uspto.gov/web/offices/pac/mpep/
s713.html#:~:text=For%20both%20applicant-initiated%20and[1]

---

1. https://www.uspto.gov/web/offices/pac/mpep/
s713.html#_853ae90f0351324bd73ea615e6487517__4c761f170e016836ff84498202b99827__853ae90f0351
324bd73ea615e6487517_text_43ec3e5dee6e706af7766fffea512721_For_0bcef9c45bd8a48eda1b26eb0c61c8
69_20both_0bcef9c45bd8a48eda1b26eb0c61c869_20applicant-initiated_0bcef9c45bd8a48eda1b26eb0c61c8
69_20and

If the interview is initiated by the applicant, they must create a complete written record in the application file, either in response to an outstanding action or within the set period if no action is outstanding. The examiner is responsible for verifying and correcting any material inaccuracies in this record that could affect patentability.

When an applicant requests an interview with the patent examiner, the Interview Summary form will include a reminder that it's the applicant's responsibility to write down what was discussed during the interview. This summary needs to be included in the applicant's next response to the USPTO or submitted within a specific time frame if there isn't an outstanding response due.

It's also recommended that the examiner verbally remind the applicant of this responsibility during the interview, especially when the interview was requested by the applicant (not the examiner).

Examiner-Initiated Interview Summary	Application No. 99/999,998	Applicant(s) Williams et al.		
	Examiner JOHN A SMITH	Art Unit 9999	AIA (First Inventor to File) Status Yes	Page 1 of 1

All Participants (applicant, applicants representative, PTO personnel)	Title	Type
JOHN A SMITH	Primary Examiner	Video Conference
MARY T WILLIAMS	Inventor	

Date of Interview: Insert Date

Issues Discussed:

Objections

Summary of the discussion of the objections.

Proposed Amendment(s)

Summary of the discussion of the proposed amendment(s).

Drawings

Summary of the discussion of the drawings.

☑ Attachment

/JOHN A SMITH/ Primary Examiner, Art Unit 9999	

Applicant is reminded that a complete written statement as to the substance of the interview must be made of record in the application file. It is the applicants responsibility to provide the written statement, unless the interview was initiated by the Examiner and the Examiner has indicated that a written summary will be provided. See MPEP 713.04
Please further see:
MPEP 713.04
Title 37 Code of Federal Regulations (CFR) § 1.133 Interviews, paragraph (b)
37 CFR § 1.2 Business to be transacted in writing

Applicant recordation Instructions: It is not necessary for applicant to provide a separate record of the substance of interview.

Examiner recordation Instructions: Examiners must summarize the substance of any interview of record. A complete and proper recordation of the substance of an interview should include the items listed in MPEP 713.04 for complete and proper recordation including the identification of the general thrust of each argument or issue discussed, a general indication of any other pertinent matters discussed regarding patentability and the general results or outcome of the interview, to include an indication as to whether or not agreement was reached on the issues raised.

U.S. Patent and Trademark Office
PTOL-413/413b (Rev. Oct. 2019)   Interview Summary   Paper No. 99999999

Examiner Initiated Interview Summary Form Fig.

Source: https://www.uspto.gov/web/offices/pac/mpep/
s713.html#:~:text=For%20both%20applicant-initiated%20and[2]

---

2. https://www.uspto.gov/web/offices/pac/mpep/

s713.html#_853ae90f0351324bd73ea615e6487517__4c761f170e016836ff84498202b99827__853ae90f0351
324bd73ea615e6487517_text_43ec3e5dee6e706af7766fffea512721_For_0bcef9c45bd8a48eda1b26eb0c61c8
69_20both_0bcef9c45bd8a48eda1b26eb0c61c869_20applicant-initiated_0bcef9c45bd8a48eda1b26eb0c61c8
69_20and

In the case of an examiner-initiated interview, the examiner must document the substance of the interview using an interview summary form (PTOL-413/413b) or, if the interview results in the allowance of the application, incorporate a complete record in an examiner's amendment. Proper documentation of all communications ensures the transparency and effectiveness of the patent examination process.

For both applicant-initiated and examiner-initiated interviews, it is recommended the examiner begin completing an Interview Summary form in advance of the interview by identifying the rejections, claims and prior art documents to be discussed. The examiner should complete the "Issues Discussed" portion of the Interview Summary form at the conclusion of the interview. Upon completion of the interview, a copy of the Interview Summary form (PTOL-413/413b) should be given to the applicant (or applicant's patent practitioner) along with any attachments.

Examiner to check for accuracy

Examiners are expected to carefully review the applicant's record of the substance of an interview. If the record is not complete or accurate, the examiner may give the applicant a 2-month time period to complete the reply under 37 CFR 1.135(c) where the record of the substance of the interview is in a reply to a non-final Office action.

The completed summary should be given to the applicant at the end of the interview or sent to their correspondence address before the next official communication.

If an applicant-initiated interview results in the allowance of the application, the applicant should promptly file a written record of the interview to avoid delays in the patent issuance.

Recommendations

When documenting the arguments discussed during an interview with the examiner, it's not necessary to provide a detailed or word-for-word account. A brief summary that captures the main points is sufficient, as long as the general nature of the arguments is clear in the context of the application file. However, if the applicant believes that certain arguments were or could be particularly persuasive to the examiner, they may choose to describe those arguments in greater detail.

- A general indication of any other pertinent matters discussed;

- If appropriate, the general results or outcome of the interview; and

- In the case of an interview via electronic mail, a copy of the contents exchanged over the Internet MUST be made and placed in the patent application file as required by the Federal Records Act in the same manner as an Examiner Interview Summary form is entered.

How to submit an internet authorization:

To facilitate processing of the internet communication authorization or withdrawal of authorization, the Office strongly encourages use of Form PTO/SB/439, available at www.uspto.gov/patent/patents-forms[1]. The form may be filed via EFS-Web. Note: After November 15, 2023, EFS-Web and Private PAIR will no longer be available. Patent Center will be the system to electronically file and manage patent applications.

A reply to an Office action or a paper requiring a signature may NOT be communicated by the applicant to the USPTO via Internet email even if written authorization is on record. To ensure security and authorization for replies to Office actions and papers that require a signature, such replies and papers must be filed electronically using the USPTO patent electronic filing system.

Where a written authorization is given by the applicant, communications via Internet email, other than replies to Office Actions under 35 U.S.C. 132[2] or papers that require a signature, may be used. In such case, a printed copy of the Internet email communications MUST be entered into One Patent Service Gateway (via Patent Data Portal) and entered in the patent application file (Doc Code is EMAIL).

Authentication of sender by a patent organization recipient

Email must be initiated by a registered practitioner, or an applicant in a pro se application, and sufficient information must be provided to show representative capacity in compliance with 37 CFR 1.34[3]. Examples of such information include the attorney

---

1. https://www.uspto.gov/patent/patents-forms

2. https://www.uspto.gov/web/offices/pac/mpep/mpep-9015-appx-l.html#d0e303187

3. https://www.uspto.gov/web/offices/pac/mpep/mpep-9020-appx-r.html#d0e317605

registration number, attorney docket number, and patent application number.

502- Communications via internet

No correspondence related to an application should be filed before receiving the assigned application number (i.e., U.S. application number, international application number, or international registration number as appropriate).

Communications via Internet email are at the discretion of the applicant. All Internet communications between USPTO employees and applicants must be made using USPTO tools: AIR system, email USPTO, fax, Priority Mail Express, etc.

Without a written authorization by applicant in place, the USPTO will not respond via Internet email to any Internet correspondence which contains information subject to the confidentiality requirement as set forth in 35 U.S.C. 122[4]. A paper copy of such correspondence and response will be placed in the appropriate patent application by the examiner.

Correspondence submitted to the Office via the Office electronic filing system will receive a receipt date, which is the date on which the correspondence is received at the Office's correspondence address set forth in § 1.1 when it was officially submitted.

A written authorization may be withdrawn by filing a signed paper clearly identifying the original authorization. The following is a sample form which may be used by the applicant to withdraw the authorization.

The returned correspondence will be accompanied by a cover letter informing the sender that if the returned correspondence is resubmitted to the United States Patent and Trademark Office within two weeks of the mail date on the cover letter, the original date of receipt of the correspondence will be considered by the

---

4.   https://www.uspto.gov/web/offices/pac/mpep/mpep-9015-appx-l.html#d0e303054

United States Patent and Trademark Office as the date of receipt of the correspondence.

When the letter concerns a patent other than for the purpose of paying a maintenance fee, it should state the patent number and issue date, the name of the patentee, and the title of the invention. For letters related to the payment of a maintenance fee on a patent, refer to the provisions of § 1.366(c).

"The authorization given on________, to the USPTO to communicate with any practitioner of record or acting in a representative capacity in accordance with 37 CFR 1.33[5] and 37 CFR 1.34[6] concerning any subject matter of this application via video conferencing, instant messaging, or electronic mail is hereby withdrawn."

A letter related to a reexamination or supplemental examination proceeding should identify it as such by the number of the patent undergoing reexamination or supplemental examination, the request control number assigned to the proceeding, and, if known, the group art unit number and the name of the examiner to whom it has been assigned.

Email and instant messaging shall NOT be used to conduct an exchange of communications similar to those exchanged during telephone or personal interviews unless a written authorization has been given under Patent Internet Usage Policy Article 5 to use Internet email. In such cases, a paper copy of the Internet email or instant messaging contents MUST be made and placed in the patent application file, as required by the Federal Records Act, in the same manner as an Examiner Interview Summary Form is entered.

All Internet communications between USPTO employees and applicants must be made using USPTO tools. Video conferencing

---

5.   https://www.uspto.gov/web/offices/pac/mpep/
mpep-9020-appx-r.html#aia_d0e317491

6.   https://www.uspto.gov/web/offices/pac/mpep/mpep-9020-appx-r.html#d0e317605

communications must be hosted by USPTO personnel. All interviews done by video conference must originate from USPTO links provided by the examiner. Links provided by the applicant from non-USPTO video conferencing tools are not acceptable to use for an interview. No personal phones, email, PDAs, etc. may be used by USPTO employees for Official communications.

USPTO video conferencing tools may be used to conduct examiner interviews in both published and unpublished applications under the Patent Internet Usage Policy. Authorization by the practitioner is required and must be obtained prior to sending a meeting invite using an official USPTO communication link or tools. Authorization is required to confirm that the practitioner is able to conduct a video conferencing interview and to confirm the email address to which the invitation must be sent. The practitioner's participation in the interview is considered consent to the use of the video conferencing tool for the interview.

Provide an additional copy of the previously transmitted application under § 1.53(d); and (iii) Include a statement that attests, on a personal knowledge basis or to the satisfaction of the Director, to the previous transmission of the application under § 1.53(d) and is accompanied by a copy of the sending unit's report confirming the transmission of the application under § 1.53(d).

It would be of great assistance to the Office if *all* incoming papers pertaining to a filed application carried the following items:

(A) Application number (checked for accuracy, including series code and serial no.).

(B) Art Unit number (copied from most recent Office communication).

(C) Filing date.

(D) Name of the examiner who prepared the most recent Office action.

(E) Title of invention.

(F) Confirmation number (see MPEP § 503[7]).

Interviews Prior To First Office Action

A request for an interview prior to the first Office action is ordinarily granted in continuing or substitute applications. In all other applications, an interview before the first Office action is encouraged where the examiner determines that such an interview would advance prosecution of the application. Thus, the examiner may require that an applicant requesting an interview before the first Office action provide a paper that includes a general statement of the state of the art at the time of the invention, an identification of no more than three (3) references believed to be the "closest" prior art, and an explanation as to how the broadest claim distinguishes over such references

---

7. https://www.uspto.gov/web/offices/pac/mpep/s503.html#ch500_d1b085_16c20_2f0

CONCLUSION

Filing a patent with the USPTO is a vital step in safeguarding your invention and securing your intellectual property rights. Although the process may appear complex, understanding the key requirements and adopting a structured approach can greatly improve your chances of success. It is essential to thoroughly research the uniqueness of your invention, prepare a well-drafted patent application that adheres to best practices in patent drafting, and seek professional assistance when necessary. By remaining diligent and following the guidelines, you can navigate the patent process successfully, ensuring legal protection for your innovation and setting the stage for future growth.

Thank you for taking the time to review this material.

Chapter 7

GLOSSARY OF TERMS

CHAPTER 7. GLOSSARY OF TERMS:

Abandoned: application which is no longer pending and was not patented. may be expressly requested by the applicant or be as a result of failing to respond within a set period.

Allowed: patent application which has been indicated by an examiner as meeting all statutory (laws) and regulatory (rules) requirements, not patented yet, may or may not have been published

Amendment: A modification made to a patent application to correct errors, clarify claims, or update the specification, drawings, or claims. Amendments can be submitted before or after the first Office action, during the examination process, and sometimes even after a final rejection or allowance of the application. They must adhere to specific rules, including consistency with the original application and proper formatting. Amendments are reviewed by the examiner, who decides whether to accept or reject them based on compliance with patent office regulations. There are two general types of amendments:

Compliant Amendments: Amendments that meet all the requirements and guidelines set by the patent office regulations, including proper formatting, content consistency, and adherence to procedural rules. These amendments are likely to be accepted and entered into the patent application record without issues.

Non-Compliant Amendments: Amendments that do not adhere to the patent office regulations or procedural requirements. This can include issues such as incorrect formatting, failure to follow specific rules for content changes, or submission after deadlines. Non-compliant amendments are typically rejected or returned to the applicant with a notice specifying the deficiencies and required corrections.

Appeal: An appeal is a request made to the Patent Trial and Appeal Board (PTAB) to review and overturn a final rejection issued by a patent examiner during the prosecution of a patent application. The appeal process allows the applicant to argue that the examiner's decision was incorrect based on legal, procedural, or factual grounds.

Application Data Sheet (ADS): is a document used in the patent application process with the USPTO (United States Patent and Trademark Office). This document contains critical bibliographic information about the application, including details about the applicant, inventors, correspondence, priority claims, and other required information.

Art unit: For a patent application, you'll need detailed and precise drawings that illustrate your invention. The ultimate goal is to provide clear and accurate visual representations that fully disclose how your invention works. Consider these elements:

- Technical Drawings: Include views from different angles (e.g., front, side, top).

- Labels and Annotations: Mark parts and components to explain their function.

- Details: Provide enough detail to ensure that someone skilled in the field can understand and replicate the invention.

Assignment: Refers to the transfer of ownership or interest in a patent or patent application from one party (the assignor) to another (the assignee). This legal document essentially allows the assignor to transfer their rights in the invention to the assignee, who then gains control over the patent or application.

Attorney: who is a legal professional specializing in intellectual property law, particularly patents. Here's what a patent attorney does:

- **Patent Application Preparation**: Drafts and files patent applications, including preparing detailed descriptions and claims for inventions.

- **Legal Advice**: Provides advice on patentability, infringement issues, and patent strategy.

- **Patent Prosecution**: Represents clients before the patent office during the examination process, responding to office actions and negotiating with patent examiners.

- **Patent Litigation**: Represents clients in disputes involving patent infringement, including court proceedings and settlement negotiations.

- **Patent Portfolio Management**: Assists with managing and strategizing an organization's patent portfolio, including filing and maintaining patents.

- **Intellectual Property Strategy**: Advises on strategies for protecting intellectual property, including patents, trademarks, and copyrights.

Claim: Formal statement that defines the scope of protection provided by a patent. Each claim describes a specific aspect of the invention and is used to determine whether a particular product or process infringes on the patent. Claims are critical because they specify the boundaries of the patent protection, describe the essential components and their interactions in the invention and demonstrate how the invention differs from prior art. Claims can be either:

Independent Claims: Claims that fully define the invention on their own, including all necessary elements, without relying on any other claims.

Dependent Claims: Claims that reference a previous claim and add additional limitations or details. They include all the elements of the referenced claim and further refine the scope of the invention.

Multiple Dependent Claims: Claims that refer, in the alternative, to more than one previous claim and add further limitations. They include all the elements of the claims they reference but cannot be the basis for another multiple dependent claim.

CRF: often referred to as a "Confirmation Receipt Form" or "Certificate of Receipt Form", is typically used to acknowledge the receipt of a patent application or other documents submitted to a patent office. It serves as proof that the documents were received and processed.

The CRF generally includes:

- Application Details: Application number, filing date, and title.

- Receipt Confirmation: Date and time when the documents were received.

- Submitter Information: Name and contact details of the person or entity submitting the documents.

Entity Status: In the context of patent applications, entity status determines the fee structure and eligibility for various reductions offered by the USPTO. The USPTO classifies applicants into different entity types to apply specific fee schedules and regulations. The primary entity statuses are Regular, Small, and Micro.

Regular Entity: A regular entity is any applicant that does not qualify as either a small entity or a micro entity. Regular entities are subject to the standard USPTO fee schedule without reductions.

Small Entity: A small entity is defined as an individual inventor who files a patent application independently and has not assigned their rights to a large company, a small business with fewer than 500 total employees including affiliates, or a nonprofit organization such as a university or research institution focused on education, research, or charity. Small entities benefit from a 50% reduction in most USPTO fees compared to regular entities.

Micro Entity: A micro entity is defined as an applicant whose income is less than three times the federal poverty level for their family size, who has filed no more than four patent applications previously (excluding applications for the same invention and certain international applications), and whose patent application is not assigned to a large company or an entity that does not qualify as a micro entity. Micro entities receive a 75% reduction in most USPTO fees and must submit a Micro Entity Status declaration, typically using Form PTO/SB/15.

Examiner: a person whose function is to review patent applications to determine whether they meet legal requirements. This includes:

1. Assessing Novelty: Checking if the invention is new and not previously disclosed.
2. Evaluating Non-Obviousness: Determining if the invention is an obvious improvement to someone skilled in the field.
3. Ensuring Utility: Verifying that the invention has a practical application.

Exclusionary rights: Exclusionary rights refer to the legal rights that allow an individual or entity to prevent others from using, accessing, or benefiting from their property or intellectual property. These rights typically encompass the ability to exclude others from:

1. Property: For example, real estate owners have exclusionary rights that allow them to prevent others from entering or using their land without permission.
2. Intellectual Property: Holders of patents, copyrights, and trademarks have exclusionary rights that prevent others from making, using, or distributing their inventions, creative works, or brand identifiers without authorization.

Fee: A fee is a monetary charge required for specific services or actions related to a patent application. Fees are essential for processing and managing patent applications and are categorized based on the type of service provided.

Filing Fees: The cost of submitting a patent application to the USPTO. This fee is paid at the filing time and covers the application's initial processing.

Search Fees: Fees required for the USPTO to search prior art relevant to the invention's patentability. The search helps determine if the invention is novel and non-obvious. The amount varies depending on the entity status.

Examination Fees: Fees are charged for the USPTO to examine the patent application and assess whether it meets all the legal requirements for patentability. This fee also varies based on the entity status.

Additional fees: Including Excess Claim Fees (incurred when the number of claims in a patent application exceeds a predefined limit) and the Application Size Fee (applied based on the size of the application).

Maintenance Fees: Periodic fees required to keep a granted patent active. Failure to pay results in patent expiration and the invention entering the public domain.

Issue Fees: Charges required to finalize and grant a patent after approval by the USPTO, which must be paid before the patent is officially issued.

Fee transmittal form: A Fee Transmittal Form is used to submit payment for various fees related to patent applications, such as filing, search, and examination fees.

Filing date: The filing date of an application shall be the date on which a specification, with or without claims, is received in the United States Patent and Trademark Office.

Final rejections: The examiner will specify the reasons for rejecting the claims, often based on prior art, obviousness, or other issues.

Information Disclosure Statement (IDS): Is a form (PTO/SB/08 or PTO-1449) that allows applicants to disclose prior art or other materials that may affect the patentability of their invention.

Interview Summary Form: is an official document used to record and document the key points discussed during an interview between a patent examiner and an applicant or their legal representative. This interview typically occurs during the evaluation process of a patent application and aims to clarify doubts, discuss objections, and advance the application towards approval.

Markush claims: they are a linguistic tool that permits a concise and precise definition of a group or class of compounds or products sharing a common structural feature, but varying in certain specified portions.

MPEP: (Manual of Patent Examining Procedure) is a comprehensive guide used by patent examiners and practitioners in the United States to understand and apply patent laws and procedures. It provides detailed instructions on the examination process, including:

1. Patent Law: Guidelines for interpreting and applying U.S.

patent statutes and case law.

2. Examination Procedures: Step-by-step instructions for reviewing patent applications, including prior art searches and claim examination.

3. Office Actions: Procedures for issuing and responding to office actions and rejections.

4. Appeals and Amendments: Guidance on handling appeals, amendments, and other procedural aspects.

No further amendments: Usually, it states that further amendments to the claims will not be considered unless they address the rejections.

Non-Provisional Patent Application: A formal application that, if granted, results in an issued patent. It includes a complete set of claims, and a detailed description, and must undergo examination by the USPTO. Unlike a provisional application, it starts the official examination process leading to a patent if approved.

Office action: is a general term for any formal communication issued by an examiner during the examination of a patent.. It includes non-Final and final Office Actions. In an Office Action, the examiner outlines objections, rejections, or requests for additional clarification that the applicant must address. These are the types of office actions:

Non-Final Office Action: It includes rejections or objections regarding aspects like claims, specification, or drawings, and gives the applicant a chance to amend the application and address the examiner's concerns.

Final office action: Is issued by the examiner when the application continues to fail to meet patent laws or regulations after a previous non-final Office Action. This action confirms that the examiner's rejections or objections remain unchanged, and no additional amendments or arguments will be considered unless they address the remaining issues in the application.

Options for response: The applicant can either appeal the decision, request reconsideration, or cancel the claims.

Patented: allowed patent application which has been issued (published) on the patent (issue) date.

Patent Cooperation Treaty (PCT): is an international treaty that allows inventors to apply for a patent in multiple countries through a single application

Patent trial and appeal board: is an administrative body within the United States Patent and Trademark Office (USPTO) that handles disputes related to patents. The PTAB's functions primarily involve reviewing appeals from applicants who have received a final rejection of their patent claims, conducting trials to review the validity of an already issued patent, reviewing the validity of a patent within nine months of its grant, based on a broader range of grounds and resolving disputes regarding whether a patent was derived from an earlier disclosed invention by another inventor.

Pendency: the time from a patent's application filing date until the date a patent is issued or the application is abandoned.

Power of attorney: allows an applicant to authorize a patent attorney or agent to act on their behalf in patent matters, including filing documents and handling communications with the USPTO.

Prior art: refers to any evidence that your invention is not new and, therefore, not eligible for a patent. It encompasses all publicly available information that existed before the filing date of your patent application. If prior art discloses the same invention or a similar invention, it can be used to argue that the invention is not novel. Even if an invention is novel, prior art can be used to show that the invention is an obvious modification of existing technology, which could prevent patentability.

Priority date: is the date that establishes the precedence of an invention in patent law. It is the date used to determine the priority of rights to an invention in the case of multiple patent applications for the same invention. Typically, it is the date on which the first patent application was filed, either in the home country or internationally, and it serves as the reference point for assessing the novelty and originality of the invention.

Proprietary rights: are the legal rights and interests that an individual or entity holds over a particular asset or property. These rights grant the owner control, use, and benefit from the property and may include:

1. Ownership: The right to possess, use, and transfer the property.
2. Control: The ability to decide how the property is used and to prevent others from using it without permission.
3. Exclusion: The right to exclude others from accessing or using the property.
4. Transfer: The ability to sell, lease, or otherwise transfer the property to others.

Proprietary rights can apply to both tangible assets (like real estate and personal property) and intangible assets (such as intellectual property rights, including patents, copyrights, and trademarks). These rights are central to property law and help define the legal relationship between individuals or entities and their assets.

Provisional Patent Application: a preliminary application that establishes an early filing date for an invention but does not itself mature into a patent. It allows the inventor to use the term "patent pending" and gives 12 months to file a non-provisional application with a formal patent claim.

Published patent application: an application published as PGPub.

Request for Continued Examination (RCE): A procedure that allows a patent applicant to continue examination after a final rejection by submitting additional amendments or arguments. This effectively reopens the examination process to address remaining issues and potentially secure a patent.

Specification: A detailed written description of an invention, including the method and process for making and using it, presented clearly and precisely enough for a person skilled in the relevant field to replicate. It must also disclose the best method known by the inventor for carrying out the invention and conclude with claims that define the scope of the invention.

Statutory Time Period: A legally defined timeframe within which specific actions related to a patent application or granted patent must be completed. If the action is not taken within this period, legal rights may be lost or penalties may apply. Extensions are sometimes available, but missing a statutory time period can lead to abandonment or other negative consequences.

Statutory Subject Matter: Refers to the types of inventions eligible for patent protection under U.S. law. Categories include processes (methods of doing something), machines (devices or apparatus), manufactures (articles of manufacture), and compositions of matter (chemical compounds or mixtures). Inventions must fall into these categories to be considered for patenting.

Subject Matter Eligibility: refers to the criteria that determine whether an invention is eligible to be patented under the United States patent laws. According to the USPTO, for an invention to be considered patentable, it must fall into one of four main categories: process, machine, manufacture, or composition of matter. In addition, it must meet certain legal requirements, such as being new, useful, and non-obvious.

Technology center: is a specialized division within a patent office, such as the United States Patent and Trademark Office (USPTO). Each Technology Center focuses on specific areas of technology to streamline the examination process.

Here's how Technology Centers typically operate:

● Specialization: Each TC is staffed by examiners with expertise in particular technological fields, such as electronics, biotechnology, or mechanical engineering. This specialization helps ensure that examiners are knowledgeable about the relevant technical details and industry standards.

● Application Handling: Patent applications are assigned to a TC based on their subject matter. For example, an application related to computer software might be handled by a TC specializing in information technology.

● Examination Process: The TC conducts a thorough examination of patent applications, which includes reviewing prior art, assessing the patent claims for novelty and non-obviousness, and ensuring compliance with patent laws and guidelines.

● Support and Resources: Each TC provides support and resources tailored to its field, including access to specialized databases and technical experts.

Office of Patent Application Processing (OPAP): OPAP is responsible for the initial processing of patent applications when they are first submitted to the USPTO. OPAP conducts a preliminary review to ensure that the application meets basic filing requirements, such as the presence of necessary forms, fees, and formalities (e.g., proper signatures, complete drawings).

- Assigning Application Numbers: They assign a unique application number and filing date to each patent application.

- Communication: If there are deficiencies in the submission, OPAP communicates with the applicant to resolve these issues before the application can proceed to examination.

- Preparation for Examination: Once the application is found to be in order, OPAP forwards it to the appropriate Technology Center for substantive examination.

www.ingramcontent.com/pod-product-compliance
Lightning Source LLC
Chambersburg PA
CBHW021139160726
47994CB00001B/18